The Search for a Common Learning:
General Education, 1800–1960

THE CARNEGIE SERIES IN AMERICAN EDUCATION

The books in this series have resulted from studies supported by grants of the Carnegie Corporation of New York, and are published by McGraw-Hill in recognition of their importance to the future of American education.

The Corporation, a philanthropic foundation established in 1911 by Andrew Carnegie for the advancement and diffusion of knowledge and understanding, has a continuing interest in the improvement of American education. It financed the studies in this series to provide facts and recommendations which would be useful to all those who make or influence the decisions which shape American educational policies and institutions.

The statements made and views expressed in these books are solely the responsibility of the authors.

Books Published

Berelson · Graduate Education in the United States
Clark · The Open Door College: A Case Study
Cleveland · The Overseas American
Conant · The American High School Today
Corson · Governance of Colleges and Universities
Glenny · Autonomy of Public Colleges
Henninger · The Technical Institute in America
McConnell · A General Pattern for American Public Higher Education
Medsker · The Junior College: Progress and Prospect
Perkins and Snell · The Education of Historians in the United States
Pierson · The Education of American Businessmen
Thomas · The Search for a Common Learning: General Education, 1800–1960
Weidner · The World Role of Universities

The Search for a Common Learning: General Education, 1800–1960

Russell Thomas

Professor of Humanities
The University of Chicago

McGraw-Hill Book Company, Inc.   1962

New York   San Francisco   Toronto   London

THE SEARCH FOR A COMMON LEARNING: GENERAL EDUCA-
TION, 1800–1960

Acknowledgments

Doubleday & Company, Inc., from Abraham Flexner, *A Modern College and
a Modern School*, 1923.

The Educational Review, from Robert Morris Ogden, "A Curriculum for the
College of Arts," vol. 65, April, 1923.

Harper & Brothers, from Woodrow Wilson, *College and State: Educational,
Literary, and Political Papers (1875–1913)*, 1925.

Harper & Brothers, from Gail Kennedy (ed.), *Education at Amherst: The New
Program*, 1955.

Harvard University Press, from James Bryant Conant, *Education and Liberty:
The Role of the Schools in a Modern Democracy*, 1953.

Harvard University Press, from A. Lawrence Lowell, *At War with Academic
Traditions in America*, 1934.

Harvard University Press, from *General Education in a Free Society*, The
Report of the Harvard Committee, 1945.

The New Republic, from an unsigned article, "The Survey Course in College," vol. 28, Sept. 28, 1921.

The New Republic, from M. L. Burton, "The Undergraduate Course," vol. 32,
Part 2, Educational Supplement, Oct. 25, 1922.

The New Republic, from Alexander Meiklejohn, "The Unity of the Curriculum," vol. 32, Part 2, Educational Supplement, Oct. 25, 1922.

The New Republic, from H. W. Chase, "The Problem of Higher Education,"
vol. 32, Part 2, Educational Supplement, Oct. 25, 1922.

North American Review, from Roland G. Usher, "The Fundamentals of an
Education," vol. 210, December, 1919.

The Pennsylvania State University Press, from Morris Keeton and Ruth

iv

Churchill, "Antioch Redesigns Its General Education Program," *The Journal of General Education,* vol. 10, July, 1957.

The Pennsylvania State University Press, from Russell Thomas, "General Education in American Colleges, 1870-1914," which appears in this book, slightly revised, as Chapter 3 under the title "The Interest of the Individual and the Common Interest, 1870-1909."

Reed College Bulletin of Reed College, from R. F. Arragon, "The Development of the Reed Curriculum," vol. 24, 1945.

The Bulletin of St. John's College: A Report of Self-study, vol. 7, 1955.

Stanford University Press, from Robert Hoopes and Hubert Marshall, *The Undergraduate and the University,* 1957.

The University of Chicago Press, from William Rainey Harper, *The Trend in Higher Education,* 1905.

The University of Chicago Press, from John Dewey, *The Educational Situation,* 1902.

The University of Chicago Press, from Henry W. Wriston, "Nature, Scope, and Elements in General Education" in *Proceedings of the Institute of Administrative Officers of Higher Education in American Colleges,* vol. 6, 1934.

Yale University Press, from George Wilson Pierson, *Yale College: An Educational History, 1871-1921,* 1952.

Yale University Press, from Archibald MacLeish, "Professional Schools of Liberal Education," *Yale Review,* n.s., vol. 101, 1921.

I am also under deep obligation to:

Alexander Meiklejohn for permission to quote from *The Liberal College,* first published in 1920 by Marshall and Jones, Boston.

The Librarian of Williams College, Wyllis E. Wright, for the Inaugural Address of Paul Ansell Chadbourne as President of Williams College, 1872.

The colleges which have generously permitted me to quote from the reports of their curriculum committees and from self-study reports, unpublished but of great value to the ends of this book.

Capable and Sensible Men

Men are men before they are lawyers, or physicians, or merchants, or manufacturers; and if you make them capable and sensible men, they will make themselves capable and sensible lawyers or physicians. What professional men should carry away with them from a University is not professional knowledge, but that which should direct the use of professional knowledge, and bring the light of general culture to illuminate the technicalities of a special pursuit. Men may be competent lawyers without general education, but it depends on general education to make them philosophic lawyers.

—John Stuart Mill
"Inaugural Address," the University of
St. Andrews, Feb. 1, 1867

Preface

In the autumn of 1951 Columbia University, the University of Chicago, Harvard University, and Yale University engaged in a cooperative enterprise which bore the title "Joint Program for Internships in General Education." The enterprise continued through the academic year 1956–1957, and in the last two years the four universities were joined by Brown University. The project was made possible by funds granted by the Carnegie Corporation of New York. The grant enabled each of the sponsoring universities to award three teaching fellowships each year to three members of the faculties of other American colleges which were interested in the development of their own programs of general studies. Each visiting teacher was asked by his host institution to teach in one of the courses in the general education program which was within the area of his particular competence and interest. Ample time was available to each visitor to study the organization and content of the entire general program and its relationship to the total undergraduate curriculum. In the spring term of each year the interns, together with a few administrative officers and faculty members of the host institutions, gathered for a three-day conference at Arden House to discuss the problems of general education which were the common concern of all the institutions represented by the group.

As the joint program entered upon its fifth year, the Carnegie Corporation asked Prof. Lawrence Chamberlain, then Dean of Columbia College, to direct some studies of contemporary views of the general education "movement"—views about present practices and the movement's promise for the future. When Dean Chamberlain invited me to participate in some of the work, I expressed an interest in placing contemporary practices within the area of general education with their complex and often conflicting points of view

ix

in their historical context. Out of a long experience in the College of the University of Chicago I had learned something of the excitement which had developed in many colleges after 1930 and which had produced extensive curricular reforms several years before the publication in 1945 of the Harvard report *General Education in a Free Society*. What I did not know were the particulars which were antecedent to this wave of educational reform. Histories of higher education had dealt with the changing conception of liberal education throughout the nineteenth and early twentieth centuries, but they had had little to say about the phenomenon called "general education." It seemed to me that it would be well to ascertain when and under what circumstances college and university men began to talk about general education, how they understood it to be related to liberal education, and what problems in the administration of a college program they sought to solve through increased attention to general education. I hoped that an inquiry of this nature would be useful in understanding the obvious differences in concept and practice which have characterized the recent history of the phenomenon.

Dean Chamberlain gave his approval to my proposal and gave me complete freedom to develop it as I saw fit; for his support and continued encouragement I am greatly indebted. I am also grateful to Robert E. Streeter, Dean of the College of the University of Chicago when I began my studies and professor of American Literature. Not only did he arrange for a needed release of time for my work, but he also gave me valuable suggestions during the period when I was working on the historical background of the study. Two other colleagues in the University of Chicago, Profs. Knox C. Hill and Richard Storr, read portions of the manuscript and gave me much useful advice; to them also I express my gratitude. None, however, is more deserving than the administrative officers and faculty members of the colleges whose programs of general education are described herein. Without exception they gave freely of their time, made available much material that I could not have secured except by their courtesy, and read sections of manuscript to correct such errors of fact as there might have been in the accounts of their respective institutions. I cannot name all those who assisted me in these ways, but I can do no less than express my deepest gratitude to them. I can only hope that I have done them and the colleges they represent no grave injustice in the final revision of these pages.

Russell Thomas

Contents

Introduction

For more than a quarter of a century *general education* has been a major concern of higher education in America. In its name curriculums have been reorganized, administrative structures of colleges have been altered, and countless workshops, conferences, and self-study projects have been undertaken to the end that higher education might be improved. A forbidding volume of literature has been published on the subject. This literature reflects not only the immense amount of energy and thought which has been devoted to the idea and practice of general education; it reveals an almost staggering diversity of opinion about both the ends and means of general education and no inconsiderable misunderstanding about many of the experiments which the idea has generated.

To some educators this diversity of opinion about the meaning and purpose of general education is a sign of the strength of an idea which is now sometimes called a "movement." To others it is a sign of hopeless confusion. Certainly there is much confusion about the meaning of the term "general education." It is frequently used as a synonym for "liberal education." In the Introduction to *General Education in a Free Society*, President Conant of Harvard so used it: "The heart of the problem of a general education is the continuance of the liberal and humane tradition." He adds: "... today, we are concerned with a general education—a liberal education—not for the relatively few, but for a multitude." [1] In an explanation of the reasons why the term "general" rather than "liberal" is used in the title of the volume, he attributes the choice to the character of the anticipated audience rather than to any substantive difference in meaning. For

[1] *General Education in a Free Society: Report of the Harvard Committee*, Harvard University Press, Cambridge, Mass., 1945, pp. viii–ix.

1

an audience restricted to the Harvard faculty, he said, either term might have sufficed, but for many people in a wider audience the term "liberal education" has connotations which might affect adversely their reception of the work. In a later essay President Conant wrote:

> By experimenting with various types of college courses, we in the United States are attempting to find the modern equivalent of the kind of liberal education which was once the product of "the collegiate way of life"—the ideal of the founders of the first colleges in colonial days. When literacy could be defined in terms of language, literature, and history, the task of a college was relatively easy.... Today, however, I doubt if anywhere in the world the mere device of collegiate living (excellent though such a way of life may still be for young men with intellectual ambitions) suffices to provide the beginnings of a general education. The cultural background of the students is too diverse, the impact of modern science and scholarship has been far too great. These two factors have made necessary a reexamination of the older idea of a liberal education.[2]

But this conception of general education as the modern equivalent of an older idea of liberal education is not universally acceptable either to those who reject general education or to many of its advocates.

The *Report of the Self-study Committee of Lawrence College* (1954) states that:

> Though general education may at times be a satisfactory corrective for the ills of over-specialization in the larger universities, it is not relevant to our problems. What we have been doing for the last generation or two under the name of liberal education is aimed at substantially the same purposes and utilizes similar and often identical methods. For us to adopt general education then, would simply be to give our old program a new name, a procedure at best muddle-headed and at worst dishonest.

Subtle and elusive the differences between general and liberal education must be if the purposes are substantially the same and the methods often identical yet the substitution of one name for the

[2] James Bryant Conant, "The American College," in *Education and Liberty: the Role of the Schools in a Modern Democracy*, Harvard University Press, Cambridge, Mass., 1953, p. 52.

other dishonest. Other observations in the Report indicate that the committee applies the term "general education" to curriculums which are largely or wholly prescribed or to curriculums which place a major emphasis on introductory courses which depart from the conventional departmental organizations of subject matters.[3] If these practices are the bases of the committee's conception of the meaning of general education and their rejection of it, it may be observed, in response, that there are colleges which have long proclaimed their devotion to the purposes of general education yet allow their students more freedom of election than does Lawrence College. On the other hand, St. John's College, which is perhaps without rival in the unorthodoxy of its curriculum and in its absolute rejection of the elective principle, makes no reference to the term "general education" in describing its program, but offers it as "at least the beginnings of a sound liberal education." [4]

The identification of general education with wholly prescribed programs or with general or so-called "interdepartmental courses" is, however, a relatively recent development in the history of the idea. Lawrence College does require its students to distribute some portion of their studies extensively enough to include all major fields of knowledge. As the historical account to follow will show, the distributional principle was introduced in American colleges early in this century explicitly as an experiment in general education. Honesty, therefore, is hardly the issue which the committee faced. This does not mean that there may not be muddle-headed programs, whether called "general" or "liberal" education.

There are many colleges, however, which use the term "general education" freely in referring to certain elements of their program, yet which would agree with the authors of the Lawrence College report that there are important differences between a general education and a liberal education. General education, they say, consists of that part of the undergraduate curriculum which constitutes a common requirement though not necessarily common courses for all

[3] The *Report of the Self-study Committee of Lawrence College* and similar reports prepared by many colleges may be obtained on loan from the Association of American Colleges, 726 Jackson Place, Washington, D.C.

[4] *Bulletin of St. John's College in Annapolis: a Report on a Project of Self-study*, vol. 7, no. 2, April, 1955, p. 3. This report was aided by a grant from the Fund for the Advancement of Education.

students. It is an essential part but not the whole of a liberal education; for a liberal education must include an exploration, in some depth, of at least one area of knowledge which may be determined by the student's own personal interests or by his vocational needs. Such an exploration, they add, a general education cannot provide, since at best it can only give an introduction to the broad areas of knowledge from which further exploration must follow.

The present status of general education might be less confusing, though not necessarily better, if these same colleges were in agreement concerning the nature of this common requirement, both substantively and quantitatively. But they are not, and herein lies a principal area of dispute, misunderstanding, and doubt with respect to the great body of educational experiment now called "the general education movement."

Disagreement can be a stimulus to creative thought or it can compound confusion. Undoubtedly the disagreements about the ends and means of a general education have produced both of these results. But confusion is not a good and can only impede inquiries which may lead to goods. There is sufficient confusion about the meaning of general education—its goals and its methods—to warrant an inquiry into its present state and into those circumstances which have contributed to the acknowledged diversity in theory and practice. Such an inquiry cannot, of course, remove all differences of thought and practice; but if it helps us to understand the grounds upon which the differences rest, it will be useful. It may assist us in determining to what extent the differences are inevitable and whether some of them arise from conflicting educational philosophies or from the absence of any philosophy.

There are two parts to this inquiry. The first is a historical study of the idea of general education in America. This is not to be confused with a history of higher education, though it is of course related to the history of all educational thought and practice in the nation. Like all ideas, general education has affected and has been affected by the intellectual and social climate of which it is a part. But like any other idea, its history must also be understood independently of its social context at any given point in time, since its continuity depends upon its antecedents and consequences in the realm of ideas. Ideas often flourish most at times when the cultural and intellectual climate seems to offer the least nourishment, just as they lose their vigor when they are most taken for granted. The current interest in the idea of general education is a resurgence of an interest that is as old as formal education. Traces of this resurgence were evident before the end of the nineteenth century, and by 1930 the idea had reached such proportions that somthing akin to a "movement" was discernible. Yet these manifestations appeared at a time when the dominant educational practices seemed most hostile to the idea.

This account will be limited to conceptions and applications of the idea of general education in America from the beginning of the nineteenth century. The account is inextricably related to the revolutionary advances in learning in this period, to the political and social character of America, and to the development of the administrative structure of its educational system. It does not pretend to be an exhaustive account but rather an introduction to an important but neglected part of the story of liberal education in America. Much has been written about theories of general education, but there has been only limited reference to their historical context. Much more has been written which is chiefly descriptive of countless experiments. But a history of general education which, for at least twenty-five years, has been a continuous subject for debate among college teachers and which has been a source of hope to some and of annoyance to others, has not been undertaken.

The historical phase of this inquiry is, however, only preparatory for the second, for it is the meanings currently attached to the term "general education" and the translation of these meanings into action with which we are most concerned. The second phase of the inquiry will therefore be analytical. Admittedly, the study will not be exhaustive. The analysis will be based upon a study of a small number of undergraduate liberal arts college programs. It is intended, however, to be representative.

It is representative in that the institutions selected for study constitute a fair cross section of the types of colleges and universities of America committed to offering a liberal education. The list includes both privately and publicly supported institutions. Among the publicly supported institutions, state universities, land-grant colleges, one state liberal arts college, and two municipal universities are represented. Among the privately supported institutions, both independent and church-related colleges have been chosen, and among the latter, there are colleges with both Protestant and Catholic affiliations. Men's colleges, women's colleges, and coeducational colleges are included. There are also privately endowed universities which maintain strong graduate and professional schools. The size of the student bodies ranges from about two hundred to more than twenty thousand. The cultural backgrounds of the students are extremely diversified; some of the institutions draw their students from the entire nation and from all social and economic levels, and others draw almost entirely from a limited region, geographically close to the institutions. The economic backgrounds of the students are equally varied. In one college no student is admitted who does not need to work in order to support himself, and the college operates an elaborate program of student industries to provide the needed work. In a few the majority of the students are financially independent.

In so far as the specific educational objectives of an institution, its traditions, and its student body are determinants of its curriculum, I hope that this selection fairly represents the diversity as well as the common practices of American colleges. It must not be supposed that these institutions have been selected for either the merits or the defects of their programs. Nor was it essential that any one of them should be selected. Other equally large though entirely different groups might have been selected which would reflect the same degree of diversity.

The institutions chosen are representative in another way. Each of them, with perhaps the exception of St. John's College, has accepted the *term* "general education" in its accounts of its program and has undertaken, in some degree, to give meaning to the term. St. John's recognizes no difference between a truly general education and a liberal education and prefers the older term. In some of the institutions, the present program of general education has existed for many years; in others it has been developed within recent years. In some there has been relatively little change over a period of several years; in others there has been frequent change. In one institution there are two entirely different programs of general education, specifically planned for two groups of students, which reflect different educational theories. The list therefore represents different stages of experience with the means of general education.

If, then, these institutions may be accepted as a just microcosm of American colleges and universities, we may hope that the analysis of their efforts to offer a general education will enable us to understand better the divergent roads by which American colleges are traveling in their search for a sound general education. One thing is certain. Whatever the score of successes and failures may be among the experiments which have been undertaken in the name of general education, most of the experiments have been honest efforts to correct weaknesses in our educational system. The problems which provoked the experiments still exist, and in one way or another, educators will continue their search for solutions.

Part I

*The Historical Background
of General Education
1800-1930*

Chapter 1

A Century of Expanding Knowledge and Social Evolution

1800-1900

The historical account begins with a simple and easily documented statement of fact. The term "general education" has been in continual use since the early years of the nineteenth century to denote a basic concept which still characterizes its contemporary usage. This fact refutes the widely held belief that the idea of general education is a product of the twentieth century which germinated in the decade after World War I and attained its present maturity in the years following World War II. The term came into use early and quite naturally in the process of distinguishing between the functions of a broad liberal education and the more specialized functions of professional and vocational education.

The spirit of this passage from an article by Prof. A. S. Packard of Bowdoin College in the *North American Review* in 1829 has been echoed in many contemporary statements:

> Our colleges are designed to give youth a general education, classical, literary, and scientific, as comprehensive as an education can well be, which is professedly preparatory alike for all the professions. They afford the means of instruction in all the branches, with which it is desirable for a youth to have a general acquaintance before directing his attention to a particular course of study, while professional studies are pursued at separate institutions, the law, divinity, and medical schools dispersed over the land.[1]

[1] A. S. Packard, "The Substance of Two Reports of the Faculty of Amherst College to the Board of Trustees, with the Doings of the Board thereon," *North American Review*, vol. 28, 1829, p. 300.

The conditions in the early nineteenth century which led to the use of the term "general education" were exactly the reverse of those which have invoked its more extensive use today. At the beginning of the century, the curriculum of the colleges was limited in scope, prescribed, and heavily weighted with classical studies. The majority of college students were preparing for the major professions—law, medicine, or divinity. The range of disciplines studied was general even though it was lacking in depth in most areas except classical languages and mathematics. College education did not claim to be either professional or vocational. The colleges were nevertheless under great pressure to extend the scope of their services in the interests of students not intending to enter these professions, to introduce new subject matters in consequence of the tremendous expansion of knowledge, and to modify the single fixed standard of requirements for graduation. As the pressure increased and various modifications were introduced, there was a tendency to differentiate the basic disciplinary and cultural functions of higher education from numerous vocational functions. No one doubted that the more general functions were an essential responsibility of the colleges. Yet despite this agreement, there was considerable disagreement about the precise means of fulfilling it.

The idea developed of a curriculum which consisted of a common core of disciplines considered essential to all liberally educated students and other studies from which students might choose according to their vocational interests or individual preferences. Educators often referred to the common element by such terms as "general education," "general studies," and "general training," although many regarded the whole curriculum as a liberal education and, indeed, as more liberal than the classical curriculum because of its greater flexibility. This flexible conception of liberal education was extended with the development of the idea of the free elective principle. As the principle grew in favor, however, the time devoted to general studies gradually diminished. Meanwhile professional and vocational schools began to establish fixed prerequisites for graduation. By the end of the century a new tendency was clearly perceptible. The required element in a student's course of study was more likely to consist of vocational specifications than of courses serving a common cultural need. Thus in a century the principles by which specific degree requirements were determined had been reversed.

By the close of World War I many educators believed that the trend threatened the survival of the cultural objectives of the colleges. They were asking whether the colleges, in becoming more liberal in the service of individual interests, had not become less liberal in serving the common cultural needs of students—whether, in fact, the meaning of liberal education had not undergone a profound change. The problem as they saw it was to restore some essential common requirements and to reorganize the curriculums in order to secure a more satisfactory achievement of the cultural objectives of education. They continued to use the terms "general education" and "general studies" in referring to these objectives, and they applied the terms to many experiments in curricular reconstruction by which they hoped to achieve them.

Quite clearly, Professor Packard thought that the classical curriculum of American colleges provided both a liberal and a general education—liberal because of its emphasis on the liberal arts and classical languages, and general because of the scope of its subjects. His article was provoked by recent reforms at Amherst College, which expressed a different view of liberal education—a view which was already beginning to have formidable effects upon education in several American colleges. In 1826 the faculty of Amherst College submitted proposals to its Board of Trustees for important revisions of the curriculum. The proposals show that the Amherst faculty regarded the classical curriculum as neither sufficiently liberal nor general.

The principal proposal, which was approved by the board and became effective in the autumn of 1827, was for the establishment of two courses of study. One was the traditional Classical Course and the other, designated the Scientific Course, was planned for students who wished to enter careers other than law, medicine, or divinity. Several subjects were common to both courses. The Scientific Course, however, substituted studies in French and Spanish, the history of English literature, the history of philosophy, and others of a technical character for the study of classical languages and literature.[2] All students were to be admitted to the college by the same standards; they might elect either course of study and upon its completion receive the degree of Bachelor of Arts.[3]

---

[2] The two courses of study as offered in the 1827 catalogue of Amherst College are reproduced in William T. Foster, *Administration of the College Curriculum*, Houghton Mifflin Company, Boston, 1911, appendix I, pp. 353–356.

[3] Professor Packard's criticism was directed almost exclusively to the last of

There is no doubt that the Amherst faculty regarded the new course as the equivalent, in its liberal and general character, of the Classical Course. The first Report to the Board of Trustees stated: "The American public is not satisfied with the present course of education in our higher seminaries. And the great objection is, that it is not sufficiently modern and *comprehensive,* to meet the exigencies of the age and country in which we live." Conceding that there were differences among enlightened men about the expediency of modernizing our colleges, it continued: "... in one thing they are entirely agreed. These Institutions do not at present, afford all the facilities which they want, for the *liberal education* of their sons." [4]

In the second Report, the faculty declared:

> Our decided and unanimous judgment is, that if a new course is introduced, it ought to proceed on a most *liberal* scale. By whatever name it may be called, it should be fully equivalent to the course which we now pursue. It should fill up as many years— should be carried on by as able instructors—*should take as wide and elevated a range*—should require as great an amount of hard study, or *mental discipline,* and should be rewarded by the same academic honors.[5]

I have italicized the words and phrases which suggest the attitude of the faculty regarding the general and liberal character of the proposed course.

By establishing two courses of study, each of which shared some subjects in common and each of which provided others regarded as appropriate to the vocational interests of the students, Amherst de-

---

these provisions. A traditionalist, he would not acknowledge the propriety of awarding the degree which was the established insignia of a liberal education for the completion of any course of study which did not include the classical languages. He did, however, give full approbation to the plan of the two courses and to enlarging the scope of collegiate education, asserting that it was the duty of our colleges not to be fettered by past usages, that the interests of the youth of the nation, whether directed to mechanical arts, agriculture, or commerce, ought to be served by the colleges with courses appropriate to their needs. Furthermore, he proposed that those who completed their studies should receive some degree or certificate of recognition other than the Bachelor of Arts degree.

[4] Foster, *op. cit.,* pp. 99–101. Abstracts of considerable length from the two reports are quoted by Foster. Italics mine.

[5] *Ibid.,* p. 103. Italics mine.

veloped in 1827 a curricular structure which sought to preserve a general or common content while enlarging the vocational appeal of college education. It employed a principle which was ultimately to prove acceptable to the majority of colleges in the nation.

Stated in terms of the broad divisions of knowledge commonly used today in describing what is often called a "common core" in college programs, both courses of study contained the following quantitative distribution:

Mathematics	2⅓ years
Language arts (grammar, logic, and rhetoric)	1⅔ year
Physical sciences (including geography)	2⅔ years
Biological science (including natural history)	1 year
Philosophy and religion	1⅓ year
History	1 term

Literature, in the broad sense, was a common requirement, although it was studied primarily through the foreign languages. Students in the Classical Course studied Greek and Latin works throughout the first three years, and in the second term of the senior year might continue Greek or begin Hebrew. Students in the Scientific Course studied French and Spanish throughout the first two years, although they were permitted to substitute Latin for Spanish if they wished. In the second term of the senior year, they might resume the study of a modern language or mathematics. All candidates for admission were assumed to have received a foundation of Greek and Latin in preparatory schools.

The precise content of these courses and the competence and the methods of instruction are irrelevant here, since our concern is with the principles which were employed in determining the *common elements* of a liberal education. Granting that most high schools now offer much of the mathematics and science which Amherst offered in 1827, it is not universally accepted today that so much as was included in that curriculum, even with improvements in content and in methods of instruction, is indispensable to a general education. As we shall see at a later point in this study, it is possible, for example, to obtain a Bachelor of Arts degree in reputable colleges with no mathematics beyond elementary algebra as taught in high school and with no course in a laboratory science. Except for the social sciences which were still in their infancy, the distribution of basic disciplines and the quantitative requirements of the Amherst curriculum had a range and depth which surpass the common core of studies required by many colleges today.

The Amherst experiment was one of several undertaken during the early years of the century to free the colleges from the limitations of the single classical curriculum. Most of them adopted the principle of alternate courses of study, though some reserved the baccalaureate degree only for those who completed the classical course. The experiments were generally short-lived. That the Amherst curriculum failed to survive more than three years does not diminish its historical significance. It was an early and important undertaking to solve some of the problems arising from the advances of knowledge and the demands for a wider scope of vocational education without seriously diminishing—it was hoped—the breadth and depth of intellectual experiences which most educators considered essential to a liberal education.

Before we continue the account of the early interest in ideas which influenced conceptions of general education, however, we shall review the circumstances which, at the beginning of the nineteenth century, were to be the chief determinants of the whole course of college education in America.

It is a paradox that education begets new knowledge more rapidly than educational institutions can assimilate this knowledge into their formal systems of instruction. Implicit in every educational system are theories about the organization of knowledge, the nature of the learning process, the ends of formal instruction, and the methods appropriate to them. The theories are generally determined by the extent of learning at some critical point in history and the prevailing conditions of society. The systems which are erected upon these theories are complex, evolve slowly, and do not yield readily to change. Yet they are under constant stress as new learning demands its place in the educational structure which has, more often than not, given it birth.

In democratic societies, a second paradox derives from the application of democratic principles to educational practices. The principles of equal rights and equal opportunities for all citizens command the expansion of the content of education to serve the needs of every citizen. Yet in a society in which the governed are ultimately the governors, responsibility for the welfare of the state is the obligation of all just as surely as equality of right and opportunity is the privilege of all. Since the preservation of a democracy depends upon the competence of each citizen to fulfill the duties implied in this responsibility, the application to education of the principle of common responsibility leads to the formulation of the content of education in terms of that knowledge which all must share for the intelligent understanding of their culture and for the intelligent direction of its growth.

In each of these paradoxes the opposing tendencies are clear. On the one hand, there is the demand to expand the services of educational institutions almost without limit as knowledge increases and as each citizen demands services appropriate to his personal needs or interests. On the other hand, there is the imperative need for a controlled expansion to the end that the educational system shall be directed by what John Dewey called "a philosophy of unity." The consequence of undirected expansion is intellectual chaos; the consequence of intransigence in the face of growing knowledge and changing social conditions is academic stagnation.

In the history of education during the past two hundred years, the tensions which derive from these paradoxes have become increasingly acute. In America they have had a significance not paralleled in the history of any other nation. At the moment in history when the advance of learning, particularly in the sciences, gained everywhere in the Western world a momentum of revolutionary force, a new nation in a land of unsurpassed natural resources created its own educational system in the first strength of the democratic ideal. This coincidence, unique in history, has unmistakably shaped the course of American education in all its parts.

Before the colonial era had passed, dissatisfaction with the aristocratic traditions of the preparatory schools and colleges, inherited from England, was openly expressed, and demands for schools better suited to the needs of all classes of society were common. Whatever political course the new nation might have followed, the growth of knowledge must inevitably have compelled the colleges to enlarge the scope and modify the requirements of their curriculums. But the particular course which the nation did follow has been a vital force in determining the administrative and curricular organization of the American educational system and in formulating answers to the problems created by the organization of the educational system and by the steadily mounting increase of knowledge.

The great growth during the nineteenth century in the number of colleges, both privately and publicly supported, was a manifestation of our democracy. Most of the private colleges were sectarian. Their existence was a sign of the equality of privilege in the area of religion. The public institutions, both universities and land-grant colleges, were affirmations of the states' responsibility to provide equal opportunities for higher education in all fields. The increase in the number of colleges, while in part the result of a growing and highly mobile population, was stimulated by a competitive spirit among the many religious denominations and to some extent between private and state interests. Despite the good that came from these ambitious enterprises, there is no doubt that the resulting differences in aims, scope of studies, and competence of instruction contributed to a growing confusion about the meaning of liberal education.

Even more phenomenal than the increase in the number of colleges was the growth of the public school system. This growth, particularly of the secondary schools, was, like that of colleges, accompanied by great differences in the scope of studies and the competence of instruction. Moreover, the schools were directly under the supervision of local officers of the states, and the colleges were predominantly under private administration. As a consequence, articulation of the work of the schools and that of the colleges was difficult, and the lack of articulation proved to be one of the greatest obstacles to the orderly development and application of new concepts of liberal education.

It was inevitable that the advance of learning, stimulated by the maturing of the nation, should lead to the founding of universities. Despite frequent urging that the functions of the university and the college be clearly distinguished, the lines between them were from the beginning ambiguous. The democratic temper of American society was in large measure responsible for the conditions which produced this ambiguity; the ambiguity has in turn materially affected conceptions of liberal education in America.

Finally it should be observed that the decline of the classical tradition signified only that the majority of educators had agreed that certain subjects were *not* the *sine qua non* of a liberal education. They were not agreed about what *was* essential. It was easy to argue that, since almost any subject was valuable to someone, all subjects were of equal value. Thus, while everyone was firmly committed in principle to some idea of both liberal and general education, the content of either came less and less to depend upon any commonly acceptable "hard core" of disciplines.

The short life of the Amherst experiment was attributed to a lack of financial resources adequate to the ambitious program and to its failure to attract the anticipated number of students. But these explanations merely reflected the prevailing division of opinion about the purposes of a college education.[6] The demand for enlarging the scope of instruction would not, however, be denied; and the expedient to which most colleges resorted was one of simple addition. During the first fifty or sixty years of the century a few colleges introduced optional courses, but these electives did not, in general, dislodge the basic courses of the classical curriculum. As a rule, new courses were added to the curriculum but none was dropped; only the time allotted for the numerous subjects was reduced.

[6] There were many advocates of the aristocratic traditions. Arthur E. Bestor, *Educational Wastelands*, University of Illinois Press, Urbana, 1953, p. 29, cites a newspaper editorial in 1830 which insisted upon natural distinctions of capacity and declared that "the mechanic cannot abandon the operations of his trade, for *general* studies; if he should, most of the conveniences of life and objects of exchange would be wanting." Italics mine. There was still a strong conviction that the classical curriculum was superior with respect to the knowledge it imparted and the discipline it afforded. For an excellent account of the basic issues upon which schoolmen were divided, see Richard Hofstadter and C. DeWitt Hardy, "The Age of the College," in *The Development and Scope of Higher Education in the United States*, Columbia University Press, New York, 1952, pp. 3-28.

Chapter 2

Mid-century: Four Views
about College Education
1842-1869

The paradox of the situation was plain to discerning minds by mid-century. A few extracts from four documents by four distinguished college presidents, published between 1842 and 1869, will serve as a useful index to the very considerable range of theories for educational reform. Each of these documents deals explicitly with the function of the college, its place in the educational system, and its relation to liberal and general education. By any reckoning, Francis Wayland of Brown University, Henry P. Tappan of the University of Michigan, Charles Eliot of Harvard University, and Paul Ansell Chadbourne of the University of Wisconsin must be regarded as among the most progressive educators of their day. They shared many common views. They were all aware of the necessity of drastic reforms. The differences in their ideas about the function of the colleges and the practical measures which might clarify their role and strengthen their influence, however, are as important as the grounds of agreement. These differences reveal clearly some of the choices about educational policy which had to be made in the middle years of the century—choices which were of immense consequence to the subsequent history of general education.

Wayland's treatise, *Thoughts on the Present Collegiate System in the United States,* was published in 1842. Nine years later Tappan's work, *University Education,* appeared. The points of agreement between the two may be briefly summarized:

1. Education under the old curriculum, though its scope is too restricted for today, was more thorough than it is at present.

20

2. Learning has advanced so far that the traditional college term of four years is inadequate for the tasks the colleges are now undertaking.

3. The educational functions which the colleges are now assuming must be distributed over a longer span of years and must be extended to other branches of the educational system.

4. The goals of liberal education (as distinct from purely professional or vocational education) are a legitimate part of the work of the colleges and must be preserved.

Their specific proposals for reform were only superficially alike. Wayland asked for changes which he believed to be within the realm of practical achievement. Tappan proposed a reconstruction of the entire educational system.

As a premise to all reforms, Wayland asserted that he would "have [the] standard as high as possible, to which the candidate for the certificate of a liberal education shall conform"; that he "would elevate rather than depress it"; and that he opposed "the efforts made in various forms to render the requirements for a degree *less exact or comprehensive or scholarlike.*" [1] The first step in reform, he said, should be the elevation of requirements for admission to college. Some of the instructional duties performed by the colleges would thus be transferred to the academies, thereby freeing the colleges for more advanced work and incidentally improving the academies by raising the level of their work. Supposing that this change could be effected, Wayland offered three proposals for the internal reform of the colleges: (1) a reduction in the number of subjects studied and more intensive work in those that remained, *or* (2) an increase in the length of the college program to five or six years if a reduction in the number of subjects required should not prove feasible, and (3) an extension of the services of the colleges "more nearly to resemble a real University" so that they "might properly include instruction in all professional, as well as ante-professional science." [2] In a college thus enlarged, he added, one course of study might lead to the degree of Bachelor of Arts and another to a degree of Bachelor of Science, and "in order to bring the whole course of study within the scope of University stimulants, the degree of Master of Arts . . . might be conferred only on those who have pursued successfully the whole circle

[1] Francis Wayland, *Thoughts on the Present Collegiate System in the United States*, Gould, Kendall and Lincoln, Boston, 1842, p. 102. Italics mine.

[2] *Ibid.*, p. 110.

of study marked out for the candidates for both degrees. The degree of Master of Arts would then designate a degree of positive attainment." [3] In this final proposal there is the implication that the fulfillment of a truly liberal education lies beyond the traditional years of undergraduate education.

The goal which determined all of Wayland's proposals, however, was to make the colleges, in the widest possible sense, institutions devoted to the service of the public.

> Let the College be the grand centre of intelligence to all classes and conditions of men, diffusing among all the light of every kind of knowledge, and approving itself to the best feelings of every class of the community. Let it, besides being a preparatory school to the professions, be a Lowell Institute to the region in which it is placed.... Nothing would so surely annihilate that division of the community into classes, which, already, in spite of our democratic institutions, threatens the direst evils to our republic.[4]

Tappan's principal interest was the founding of universities; but he was convinced that a true university depended upon the coordination of the entire educational structure from the common schools to the top. His theme therefore was *a university system*. His conception of liberal education had meaning only within the context of the entire system, because he regarded liberal education as a function of the whole system in which each division had its special tasks.

Tappan took his model for an American university system from Germany. The function of the American college should be analogous

---

[3] *Ibid.*, p. 111.

[4] *Ibid.*, p. 156. Wayland's treatise prepared the way for the *Report to the Corporation of Brown University on Changes in the System of Collegiate Education*, G. H. Whitney, Providence, R. I., 1850, submitted by the faculty and approved by the corporation in 1850. The plan was more flexible than the Amherst program, offering a limited range of electives and making provision for students who might not wish to become candidates for a degree. Like the Amherst program, it survived only a few years, and was abandoned for similar reasons. In a critique of the Report, Noah Porter, then professor of moral philosophy at Yale, agreed that the colleges had admitted more studies than could properly be taught, but charged that the defect arose from a "false assumption that pervades this report from beginning to end, that the college is bound to qualify a man fully to discharge the duties of any profession, which he may choose to follow; that it is a school of *special* as well as of *general* training." "Reforms in Collegiate Education," New Englander, vol. 9, 1851, pp. 110–144. Italics mine.

to the *Gymnasium*. Instruction for all students would thus consist of a rigorous introduction to the basic arts and sciences under the close supervision of tutors competent to develop sound habits of study and investigation. In the university the student would exercise freedom of choice in his studies, and the successful prosecution of his work should be marked by "habits of independent thought and study, an acquaintance with method, and a general survey of the field of knowledge." [5] A university is not formed, he said, "by collecting together schools under the different faculties. These may be merely collegial schools." [6]

Though Tappan was no less concerned than Wayland with the practical services that educational institutions should render to society, he was convinced that their greatest service lay in the cultivation in the highest possible degree of all the faculties of each individual. Other forms of education—in the common utilities of life, the practical arts, and the professions—were subordinate to this, which he called the "ideal" or "philosophical" form of education. Moreover, this form should permeate the entire educational system from the elementary years through the university. [7]

In modern discussions of general education no term has been more abused than "integration"; but Tappan's belief that the "true idea of education is the development of the soul in all its faculties" was a genuine expression of the ultimate integrative function of education. "We ought to aim," he said,

> ... to make apparent the difference between a mere professional and technical education, and that large and generous culture which brings out the whole man, and which commits him to active life with *the capacity of estimating from the highest points of view all the knowledges and agencies which enter into the well-being and progress of society. That is not really the most practical education which leads men soonest and most directly to practice, but that which fits them best for practice.* [8]

General education, therefore, in Tappan's view was not simply a broad preparation for a vocation or a superficial antecedent to the more serious business of professional study. It was the result of an

[5] Henry P. Tappan, *University Education*, G. P. Putnam's Sons, New York, 1851, p. 85. Tappan became President of the University of Michigan in 1852.

[6] *Ibid.*, p. 46.

[7] *Ibid.*, pp. 10–13.

[8] *Ibid.*, pp. 15–16. Italics mine.

educational philosophy which adhered at all levels to this integrative purpose. The colleges alone could not bear the whole burden of so large a goal. He believed that the youth of the nation would willingly spend more time in achieving such an education and asserted that *"the very pressure which the Colleges are under to enlarge their courses of study, shows plainly enough the demand for higher and more general education."* [9]

Within the decade after 1850 the conflict between the defenders of the old classical conception of liberal education and the protagonists of reform was, for all practical purposes, dead. The arguments continued but defenders of the old order were fighting for a lost cause. [10] But the calm assurance with which the classical curriculum had once been accepted as the certain standard of both a liberal and a general education was not matched with an equal certitude by the new generation of educators. The situation was described in the opening paragraphs of President Eliot's Inaugural Address at Harvard in 1869. Because the elective system which he vigorously defended in this address has so frequently been called one source of the major educational ills of the present century, they deserve special attention. Eliot began his address with these remarkable words:

> The endless controversies whether language, philosophy, mathematics, or science supplies the best mental training, whether *general education* should be chiefly literary or chiefly scientific, have no practical lesson for us today. This University recognizes no

[9] *Ibid.*, p. 85. The reforms adopted by the University of Michigan during Tappan's administration were similar to those adopted at Brown. For a statement by Tappan on the practical problems of education in the state of Michigan, see Henry P. Tappan, *Public Education: an Address Delivered in the Hall of the House of Representatives, in the Capitol at Lansing, on the Evening of January 28, 1857*, H. Barns, Tribune Office, Detroit, 1857. Italics mine.

[10] Expressions of complacent satisfaction with past traditions were often heard, as in an address to the alumni of Harvard by Cornelius Conway Felton on the occasion of his inauguration as President in 1860, in which he declared that "every record of the proceedings of our ancestors...shows that they had large and liberal purposes. They aimed to educate a learned clergy but not that alone. The general education of the people was embraced in the scope of their enlightened plans, and *they included in their idea of a scheme of general education the general principles of the highest possible education."* Thereafter he proceeded to defend the classical tradition. Cornelius Conway Felton, "Characteristics of the American College," *American Journal of Education*, vol. 9, 1860, pp. 112–128. Italics mine.

real antagonism between literature and science, and consents to no such narrow alternatives as mathematics or classics, science or metaphysics. We would have them all, and at their best. To observe keenly, to reason soundly, and to imagine vividly are operations as essential as that of clear and forcible expression; and to develop one of these faculties, it is not necessary to repress and dwarf the others. *A university is not closely concerned with the applications of knowledge, until its general education branches into professional.*[11]

Considerable time could be gained for so large a course of study, Eliot claimed, in the improvement of teaching methods. Each broad division of knowledge, he said, is attended by its own method of thought.

There is a method of thought in language, and a method in mathematics, and another of natural and physical science, and another of faith.... The actual problem to be solved is not what to teach, but how to teach.... With good methods, we may confidently hope to give young men of twenty to twenty-five *an accurate general knowledge* of all the main subjects of human interest, besides a minute and thorough knowledge of the one subject which each may select as his principal occupation in life. To think this impossible is to despair of mankind; *for unless a general acquaintance with many branches of knowledge, good so far as it goes, be attainable by great numbers of men, there can be no such thing as an intelligent public opinion; and in the modern world the intelligence of public opinion is the one indispensable condition of social progress.*[12]

He argued that the colleges should raise admission standards and that the schools must improve their instruction and enlarge their curriculum to bear their proper share of general education. These, then,

[11] Charles William Eliot, "Inaugural Address as President of Harvard College," in *Educational Reform: Essays and Addresses,* Century Company, New York, 1898, p. 1. President Eliot's phrasing indicates that the term "general education" was already widely used. Italics mine.

[12] *Ibid.,* pp. 3–4. Eliot's exposition of the kinds of methodological revisions needed is interesting. Teachers of history involved in discussions of "the block-and-gap" method may be interested in his observation that "for the young especially, it is better to enter with intense sympathy into the great moments of history, than to stretch a thin attention through its weary centuries" (p. 7). Italics mine.

were the assumptions upon which Eliot established his argument for the principle of free election.

> In education, the individual traits of different minds have not been sufficiently attended to. Through all the period of boyhood the school studies should be representative; all the main fields of knowledge should be entered upon. But the young man of nineteen or twenty ought to know what he likes best and is most fit for. If his previous training has been sufficiently wide, he will know by that time whether he is most apt at language or philosophy or natural science or mathematics.[13]

There is no reason to doubt the sincerity of Eliot's belief at this time in the need for a thorough general education. But there are good reasons, in the light of subsequent events, for questioning the soundness of his faith in the ability of the schools and the colleges to hold firm to so high a purpose, and good reasons, too, for questioning the soundness of his judgment. The public high school system was still in its infancy. It was naïve to suppose that many schools could successfully improve their methods of teaching and offer thorough instruction in the wide range of subjects essential to produce an "informed public opinion." Perhaps no one could have foreseen the extent of the social revolution which was to be produced by the industrial era and its effects upon the entire public school system, but the time was not far off when the high schools would use Eliot's arguments to justify the elective principle in their own curriculum. There was nothing in the administrative structure of the American educational system which guaranteed that students seeking admission to a liberal arts college would have received the training in the basic disciplines that Eliot expected. Only the firm and united determination of the colleges themselves to insist upon high standards of admission covering both the quality and the breadth of previous training could give this assurance. The social pressures and the industrial demands of the nation were so strong that even this protection did not long survive. Undoubtedly, too, Eliot overestimated the capacities of the average youth to make wise choices or to find within himself the motivation which could make the best use of the privileges which the elective system accorded him.

The principles upon which Eliot justified the elective system, how-

[13] *Ibid.*, p. 12.

ever, did as much as anything else to undermine the force of his plea for a general education. The civilization of a people may be inferred, he said, from the variety of its tools.

> There are thousands of years between the stone hatchet and the machine-shop. As tools multiply, each is more ingeniously adapted to its own exclusive purpose. So with the men that make the State. *For the individual, concentration, and the highest development of his own peculiar faculty, is the only prudence.* But for the State, it is variety, not uniformity of intellectual product, which is needful. These principles are the justification of the system of elective studies which has been gradually developed in this College during the past forty years.[14]

This materialistic yardstick for the progress of civilization had great appeal to a society feverishly bent upon exploiting its natural resources and expanding its industries. The danger to education of such a yardstick lay in the fact that it strengthened the position of everyone, inside and outside the academic world, who would emphasize specialization at the expense of general knowledge. By defining the interest of the individual and the interest of the state emphatically in terms of the principle of a division of labor, Eliot's theory excluded the possibility that the state has more than one kind of interest in the individual and that in certain spheres of action uniformity in the intellectual experiences of the students may be as valuable as variety in other spheres. It tended to ignore the fact that man is a creature of many faculties, not all of which are immediately productive, but all of which are equally important to the nourishment, in Tappan's words, of "the whole man." The principle, when applied literally and fully, contradicts the very grounds upon which Eliot defended general education. Its literal application became the object of many colleges, with support from both the schools and the universities, for at least another forty years.

Eliot regarded *general education* as a part of a *liberal education,* the whole of which each student would complete with those studies which he freely elected. On this he was explicit. "The choice offered to the student does not lie between liberal studies and professional or utilitarian studies. All the studies which are open to him are liberal and disciplinary, not narrow or special." [15] This is an assertion which

---

[14] *Ibid.,* p. 13. Italics mine.
[15] *Ibid.,* p. 13.

has grown commonplace with repetition. Its significance lies in the fact that attitudes toward it have led to material differences in current conceptions of both general education and liberal education. The assertion left unexamined the question what precisely distinguishes liberal studies from professional or utilitarian. This question had been begged by some of the defenders of the old classical curriculum. Many advocates of reform, arguing that all subjects taught in the colleges were equally useful as disciplines, concluded that any combination of courses must afford a liberal education. In defining liberal education exclusively in terms of subjects, both groups failed to consider the possibility that it is only within the total context of the educational experience of each student that any subject can be defined as either liberal or professional or that in the proper context a subject may have both liberal and professional values. If the critics of the classical curriculum were right in claiming that the modern languages were as liberal in their disciplinary value as the classical, they only compounded the error of some of the classicists by supposing that either the classical or the modern languages would necessarily contribute to liberal education under any condition.

A month before Eliot gave his Inaugural Address, President Chadbourne published an article which attacked the idea that vocational education was a principal concern of the colleges. Professional and technical schools, he said, exist for that purpose. In a society built on a caste system, vocational training may hold a primary position. "But," he declared, "the very theory of our government demands a broad culture for all our young people. The time comes when they must choose their special pursuits, but all that is needful to fit them for the duties of citizenship they should enjoy in common. Liberal culture on this principle may not secure so many good machines for certain kinds of work, but it will increase the number of able men, which is far more important." [16]

The purpose of education, he stated, is to make men happy. In a democratic society, men must be educated not only to produce goods but to use the products of their labor for their enjoyment and mental culture. The highest education develops the powers which raise men

---

[16] P. A. Chadbourne, "Colleges and College Education," *Putnam's Magazine*, n.s. 4, 1869, p. 335. Chadbourne was, like Eliot, a scientist. In 1872 he succeeded Mark Hopkins as President of Williams College and later became President of Massachusetts Agricultural College.

above other animals—the intellect, the taste, and the social and moral faculties. It is accomplished through the study of the abstract sciences, the arts, history, and "the study of man himself, and his relations to the universe and to God." This, he added, "is the true field of college education in distinction from all professional or technical training." [17]

A vigorous champion of the very best technical and scientific education, Chadbourne was only concerned that both the technical institutions and the colleges understand and perform well their respective duties. Each, he claimed, was injuring itself by extending its activities beyond its resources and by invading fields that belonged to the other. With admirable foresight he recognized that the states would in time ably support business and technological education. Grants from the Federal government and state legislatures and the popular attraction of the practical ends of vocational education would secure the necessary resources for state-supported institutions. On the other hand, he feared that the states would be less likely to support the cultural goals of the colleges because of political conflicts, rivalries among the various educational branches, and a general distrust of the cultural purposes for which the colleges should stand.

For these reasons he suggested that the states should accept responsibility for the common schools and for the higher branches of technical and professional education, leaving the support of the colleges primarily to private capital. He approved of the idea of a true university in which all branches of higher education would be offered, but only upon the condition that economic means adequate to the needs of every branch should be available. He argued also that the colleges, whether independent or part of a university, should be small. "The

---

[17] *Ibid.*, pp. 335–336. The theme developed in this article was expanded in Chadbourne's Inaugural Address as President of Williams College in 1872. Again he argued for a clear distinction between the functions of the college and the technical and professional schools. "The influences that have been at work to make every college a semi-technical school cannot easily be checked. The difference between general and special education is not yet so manifest before the community, nor in the college, as it ought to be.

"The college seeks to educate, not the lawyer, the minister, the farmer, the artisan, the merchant or the teacher as such, but the man, so that he may engraft professional knowledge upon his education to the best advantage, that all professions may have the same basis, as they ought to have, since the man is of more importance and has a more important work to do in the world than mere professional labor." Quoted from the Program of the Inauguration by permission of the Williams College Library.

more the student comes in contact with a real educator the better. He will gain more strength by coming into real intellectual conflict with a great man, than he will to be shot at from the ablest lecturers for months." [18]

Colleges should not be limited to an intellectual elite. "An education is at the present day called for which shall put the business man and the working man on the road to acquire something, at least, of this culture, for the sake of enjoyment and improvement and usefulness in the latter part of life, after its hard-working days are over." [19]

Chadbourne insisted upon the improvement of the public schools, the technical schools, and the colleges, and he understood that the improvement of each was related to that of the others. Yet without prejudice to the importance of any other branch, he maintained that it was the business of the colleges "to give the best conditions for mental culture to the best minds in the world, who choose to seek culture for its own sake, or for that higher good to the race than material wealth alone can give." [20] Needless to say, the colleges did not commit themselves to this single objective. The demands of specialization were already too strong to be denied.

To each of these authors it was transparently clear that the growth of learning and the prevailing conditions of American society demanded radical changes in the pattern of education. In the course of the changes the American college of the future would not bear much resemblance to the college of the past. Whatever the changes might produce, there was not the slightest suggestion by any one of them that they anticipated anything except an increase in the intellectual rigor of education at all levels. They were wholeheartedly committed to making the college of the future more serviceable to the whole of society. They understood that the college could not bear the burdens of higher education as it had formerly done, and for this reason they demanded the improvement of the schools and the development of universities and improved professional and technical schools. They acknowledged a distinction between the purely professional or vocational goals of education and a knowledge which constitutes the foundation of an understanding of our common culture. Yet upon one crucial issue there were important differences in the ideas which

[18] *Ibid.*, p. 341.
[19] *Ibid.*, p. 337.
[20] *Ibid.*, p. 341.

they put forth, namely, the role which the college should assume as a consequence of the changes. The institutional structure of the college of the future could not be divorced from ideas about the relative importance of educational objectives, the processes of learning, and the relationship between the general and liberal functions of education and the specialized functions.

High in importance among the ideas for reform advanced by President Wayland was the conception of the college as an institution devoted to public service. His conception of the college as "the grand centre of intelligence to all classes and conditions of men" and as "a Lowell Institute to the region in which it is placed" would, when realized, produce a college infinitely more complex than any college America had hitherto known. The critical question posed by this conception was whether so complex a collegiate structure could be devised—a structure which could diffuse "*among all the light of every kind of knowledge,*" serve the practical interests of every class of society, and still maintain a respect for the differences in the intellectual rigor and values essential to each of the many kinds of activities to which the institution would be committed. American colleges and universities have achieved no greater distinction in any area during the past seventy-five years than in their many public services. They have perhaps gone far beyond the realization of Wayland's conception, responding to and often anticipating the manifold demands of the public which they serve. But by the beginning of the present century it was far from certain that the energy which they devoted to serving the immediate practical interests of society had been matched by an equal determination to diffuse among all the light of every kind of knowledge.

President Tappan's conception of a college modeled upon the German *Gymnasium* was based upon his belief in the importance of an institution intermediate between the common schools and the university. Different educational functions, in his total conception, required appropriately different administrative units. In his conception, the primary function of the university was to offer specialized education, but the success of the university's operations would depend upon the foundations in the general disciplines of the arts and sciences, because specialized education is not an end in itself. Rather, it is a stage in the development in the individual student of "the capacity of estimating from the highest points of view *all* of the knowledges and agencies which enter into the well-being of society." A college curriculum which provided vigorous instruction in all the basic disciplines was a necessary antecedent of and complement to the university in achieving the ultimate goal of education, for without such a college curriculum, the students would be unable to place their specialized studies within a proper perspective. Tappan's view implied that the public welfare is best served when the educational system is so organized that the entire system contributes, each part in its way and by its proper methods, to the development of the "whole man." Tappan's conception of the college could not have been fully realized apart from a change in the structure of the entire educational system of the nation.

President Eliot's conception of the structure of the college derived from a concern for the needs of the individual student no less intense than Tappan's. Yet the differences in their conceptions of the ultimate interest of the student and the proper means of satisfying it were very great and of the highest importance. Eliot's view that the ultimate goal of formal education for each student was "the highest possible development of his own peculiar faculty" was so strong that it was the determining principle in his ideas about the functions of the college. The most obvious aspect of his conception is that it proposed an ambiguous institution, responsible for the *completion* of general studies and the *beginning* of specialized studies. The college would thus merge with the university, and the chief difference between the two branches would be that the university carried specialization to higher and more professional levels than the college.

In this view specialization becomes the final cause of higher education, and general studies have their chief value as instruments for locating one's special aptitude. The public interest is best served by the development of each individual talent with assistance from general studies, which are expected to develop an informed public opinion. Without imputing to Eliot the sole responsibility for the genesis of this conception of the college, we can be certain that it became a primary determinant of the structure and functions of the modern American college.

President Chadbourne's conception of the college, whether independent or a part of a university, was of an autonomous unit, having as its specific task the broad cultural education of the students. Such an education, general in its scope and common to all students, is a liberal education and is a proper end in itself. It differs from specialized education in content and in methods and in the service it renders to society, for it is the education of men as citizens whereas specialized education trains men directly or indirectly for the production of wealth. Liberal education must be general, not because it prepares one for specialized study, but because each department of knowledge which it surveys is essential to an understanding of our common culture. President Chadbourne's ideas might well be regarded as a modern conception of the older liberal arts college, adapted to the changing character of society and the enlarged realm of learning, but one that avoided compromise with vocational objectives.

Each of these conceptions of the functions and structure of the American college has recurred in the expressions of educational thought and practice during the past three-quarters of a century. Those of Wayland and Eliot were most immediately and vigorously expressed in practices; ideas closely related to those of Tappan and Chadbourne have gained currency in more recent years. All of them are directly related to the history of general education throughout the period.

Chapter 3

The Interest of the Individual and the Common Interest

1870-1909

Concern for general education, even to the degree that Eliot had shown in his Inaugural Address, declined after 1870. There were, to be sure, conservative voices which protested the course that college education was taking under Eliot's direction; but it was not until the closing decade of the century that a rising generation of young men began to express a vigorous dissent to the dominant theories and practices of the times—a dissent unmarked by any appeal to the virtues of a dead tradition. From A. Lawrence Lowell, Woodrow Wilson, William Rainey Harper, John Dewey, and a few other courageous and responsible leaders in educational thought there came a series of firm declarations that the American college had not yet clearly perceived its proper function or the best means of fulfilling that function. Not until two decades after Lowell had first openly expressed his distrust of the elective principle was he, as President of Harvard, able to take bold action to effect important changes in policy.

The causes of the declining interest in general education are clear enough. The administrative structure of the American educational system had begun to assume in its general outlines the principal characteristics which it retains today. This structure was less a first cause than an instrumental cause of the decline; for the structure itself was in large part a product of educational policies which placed a much higher priority upon the interests of the individual than upon the common needs of a democratic society. In fact the prevailing view was that the common good was best served by serving the individual interest. The quarter of a century after 1870 was a period which gave preeminent support to all forms of specialization. Tremendous growth in population and industrial and economic expansion combined to make heavy technological demands upon an educational system poorly equipped to meet the demands made upon it. But the issue was not solely a conflict between vocational interests and general education. Even among those who accepted the view that the proper and immediate task of all educational institutions was the education of the individual student, there remained the question, what were the best means of serving the needs of the individual, regardless of whether the ends were liberal or vocational. The science of psychology and with it the sister science of education attained maturity in this same quarter of a century, and these developments had quite as significant a place in determining educational policies in some parts of the system as did external economic and social pressures.

If we are to understand the position of general education in the history of this period properly, we shall have to place it in the context of the following developments in American education after 1870: (1) the growth of the secondary school system and the relations between the schools and the colleges, (2) the rise of the American university, (3) the growth of "collegial" schools and departmentalism, (4) the expansion of the "elective system," and (5) the growth of psychology and other social sciences and their application to educational theory and practice. The first three of these topics are immediately concerned with the organizational structure of American education, and the last two with theories and methods of education. Since administrative structure and educational theory always interact, it is impossible to consider any one of these topics in complete isolation from others.

1

There was practically unanimous agreement among the leaders of the colleges that the standards of admission must be raised and that the secondary schools must accept responsibility for elementary instruction in several areas hitherto undertaken by the colleges. This opinion meant that the general education of students was a shared responsibility. The standards were raised but the gains were uneven and illusory. The gain in time for more advanced study was offset by the continuous addition of courses to college curriculums. The public high schools were at the beginning of their phenomenal growth; it was too much to expect that the breadth and quality of instruction in all the areas added to their course of study could achieve a uniform standard throughout the nation. It was at first generally assumed that the mastery of the subjects transferred to the schools would be a condition of admission to college. The assumption gradually came under attack from both the schools and the colleges.[1]

Within the colleges a division of interests about admission requirements gradually developed as the various "schools" and departments allowed professional prerequisites to become their first and sometimes their only concern. As pressure from the colleges abated, the schools found little reason to press for a balanced distribution of subject matters by prospective college students. The interests which prompted an expanding college curriculum were also felt by the schools, and the arguments which justified the elective principle in the colleges were equally persuasive to school authorities. The administrative authority of the public school system and the higher branches of state-supported education was divided, communication about their common problems was increasingly difficult, and most state institutions eventually were obliged by law or custom to admit nearly all the graduates of high schools within their respective states, a policy which practically eliminated control over qualitative standards of admission. The private colleges were free to establish whatever admission standards they wished with respect to both subject-matter prerequisites and scholarly aptitude; but their wishes were often conditioned by social pressures and, in many instances, by economic necessities. The highest ideals of many small colleges were frequently forced to yield to the need for students.

The spectacular advances in the field of psychology had a peculiar effect upon the relations of the schools and the colleges.[2] The backbone of the new science of education, its effects were felt more im-

[1] Statements by Wayland, Tappan, Eliot, and Chadbourne in the articles referred to in Chap. 2 warrant the inference that they all would have been shocked by such minimal requirements in the areas of the sciences, language, the arts, and history as will today satisfy some colleges not only for admission but also for a baccalaureate degree.

[2] In 1841 Harvard offered only one course in psychology (elective) in the junior year. As late as 1871 Bowdoin College offered one course, optional in the senior year.

mediately and more profoundly in the elementary and secondary schools than in the colleges. New theories about learning processes, instructional methods, and the content of the curriculum of elementary and secondary schools were widely applied experimentally, while instruction in the first years of college often deteriorated, almost insensibly, under the influence of methods employed by and adapted to the graduate and professional schools.

The relations of the schools and the colleges became a subject for frequent study by national committees of educators, but in the long run little was done to check the widening gap between the two branches.[3] Some educators recognized the danger and declared that the content and methods of the college course, in its early years, were properly a continuation of the general educational function of the secondary school. Eliot had said as much in his Inaugural Address. It was emphatically stated by William Rainey Harper in 1899. After commenting on the waste resulting from a sharp line between the eighth grade and the first year of high school, he added:

> But a still greater waste is involved in the division between the fourth year of the high school or academy and the freshman year of college.... The work of the freshman and sophomore years in the colleges in this country ... is but a continuation of the academy or high school work. It is a continuation, not only of the subject matter studied, but of the methods employed. It is not until the end of the sophomore year that university methods of instruction may be employed to advantage.... As it is now arranged, however, this consecutive period of preparation, covering five or six years, is broken into; and what follows? The student finds himself adrift. He has not reached the point where work in any of his preparatory subjects is finished. This work is continued now under new and strange conditions, with new and strange instructors.[4]

In 1902 John Dewey pointed to the need for a close affiliation of the first two years of college with the work of the high school. Asserting that "what is termed *general training* and *general culture* is

[3] For an account of the growth of the secondary schools, the problems of articulation between the schools and the colleges, and the work of several national committees concerned with these problems see Edgar W. Knight, *Fifty Years of American Education,* The Ronald Press Company, New York, 1952, chap. 3, pp. 85–126.

[4] William Rainey Harper, "Waste in Higher Education," in *The Trend in Higher Education,* University of Chicago Press, Chicago, 1905, p. 83.

the function of the secondary school," he continued to say that "formally, the first two years of college work probably belong to the secondary period," and that this is a period in which the student should acquire an orientation with the larger world through "a survey, at least, of the universe in its manifold phases." This task could be completed, he thought, for the average student by the time he was eighteen or twenty "with proper economy of instruction, and harmonious organization instead of blind confusion in the curriculum." [5] Dewey considered it inevitable that there would be some "encroachment" of the high school and the professional school on the college; he declared that the efforts of the colleges to avoid the encroachment would perpetuate their amorphous and artificial character.

The views of Harper and Dewey recall the distinction which Tappan had drawn between the college and the university. A closer union of the first two years of college with the high school would have created essentially the kind of college Tappan hoped for. The last two years might then have been incorporated into the university. Any hopes that such an organization might be realized failed in part because of the absolute division of administrative authority between the high schools and the colleges and in part because the conditions under which the universities were founded united the officers of the colleges intellectually and spiritually closely with the universities.

By the middle twenties of this century it was impossible to assume that students who entered college would possess a common background of comparable breadth and thoroughness in the basic disciplines of language, mathematics, science, literature, and history; nor were there many colleges prepared to demand that deficiencies in all these areas be removed (but without credit) as a condition of graduation. A century before, the preparatory school or academy was the principal means of gaining admission to college, and its curriculum was usually adapted to the requirements of the colleges. By the end of the nineteenth century the free public high school had supplanted the preparatory school as the principal source from which

---

[5] John Dewey, *The Educational Situation*, University of Chicago Press, Chicago, 1902, pp. 101–102. This passage is practically a recapitulation of Eliot's observations in 1869. It shows how much more receptive both educators and the public had been to Eliot's defense of the elective principle than to his plea for a thorough general education which embraced the secondary school and the early years of college. Italics mine.

the colleges drew their students. But the services of the high schools had grown more diversified as their student bodies became more heterogeneous. Only a fraction of high school graduates continued in college. There was more than a little confusion about the best ways of serving the needs of those who did plan to enter college, and it cannot be said that the colleges did much to dispel the confusion.

2

Prof. Richard Hofstadter has called the era after 1870 "the age of the university." [6] We may accept the dominance of the university after that date as a fact and recognize that the addition of the university to the American educational system was an imperative, yet question whether the institutional form which the American university took has been an unmixed blessing to the cause of general education.

Though the name "university" had been applied to several institutions early in the nineteenth century, everyone understood that these were not universities in the European sense of the term and that at best the designation represented a hope rather than an achievement. The ideal which had occupied many minds for the first half of the century was an institution devoted to the advancement of learning through research and to the training of young scholars in the disciplines necessary to carry on research in all fields of knowledge. Such an institution would not merely consist of professional schools of medicine, law, divinity, or science, though it would be concerned with the advancement of knowledge in these fields as well as in all others. The salient fact about the translation of the dream into a reality is that the university was grafted onto the American college. At first a few colleges began, as President Wayland had proposed, "more nearly to resemble a real University" through the addition of lecture courses of a graduate character. Then came the development of a graduate department, and the awarding of the degree of Doctor of Philosophy, and finally in a limited number of institutions a graduate division of true university scope and caliber. Faculties which

[6] Richard Hofstadter and C. DeWitt Hardy, *The Development and Scope of Higher Education in the United States,* Columbia University Press, New York, 1952, chap. 2, pp. 29–56.

had hitherto been college faculties became both undergraduate and graduate faculties. Even when new institutions, such as The Johns Hopkins University, Stanford University, and the University of Chicago, were founded as true universities, they included undergraduate students. At Stanford and Chicago the number of students enrolled as undergraduates was larger than the total of those in the graduate divisions and professional schools.

Tappan's treatise of 1851 had recognized, in principle at least, the advantages of separating administratively the collegiate and university functions; but the idea of such a separation was not original with him. It had occurred in discussions concerning reforms at Harvard in the 1820s and in the preliminary plans and proposals for an educational system in the state of Virginia which culminated in the founding of the University of Virginia. The beginnings of compromise, however, on the question of the administrative and curricular relations of the American college to the university can be located in policies such as those adopted at Harvard and Virginia about 1825.[7]

Thus while the administrative structure of the American educational system created a sharp division between the secondary school and the college, the conditions under which the universities developed bound the college and the university in an intimacy which has never been broken. The force of that intimacy has been so great that it has affected institutions which were determined to remain colleges, strictly devoted to what they believed to be the goals of a liberal education. A university by its very nature was concerned with specialization of the highest order in all fields of learning. Its physical presence in an institution which was also a college could scarcely avoid giving added impetus to specialization at the collegiate level, particularly since a very considerable part of the faculty was engaged in both university teaching and college teaching. Inevitably the faculty regarded the specialized studies which the students pursued in their college years as falling within the scope of university work. William Rainey Harper commented upon this view in an address in 1902 in which he attacked proposals to reduce the term of the college course to three years. "To cut off a full year means either the crowding of this higher preparatory or college work of the freshman and sophomore years, or the shortening of the real univer-

[7] Richard J. Storr, *The Beginnings of Graduate Education in America*, University of Chicago Press, Chicago, 1953, chaps. II and III, pp. 7–28.

sity work done in the junior and senior years of the college course." [8]
Observe the distinction between *college work* and *real university
work.*

There was a natural affinity between the specialization begun in
college and the more highly specialized work of the postgraduate
years. The specialized study begun in college was, in fact, the necessary first stage of university work, and even if it consisted, as it did
for the majority of college students, only in receiving the fruits of
research in one's chosen field, the experience was necessary for all
who planned to continue into advanced fields of research.

The troublesome consequences of the institutional structure of the
universities arose from the combination of three circumstances: the
dualism of *functional commitments* within the college, *the institutional affiliation* of the entire college with the university, and *the
institutional separation* of the college from the secondary school.
That part of college studies which was regarded as the culmination
of general education fell under the control of an administration more
and more committed to the purposes of a university. The secondary
school years were under the control of an administration committed
to the elementary education of all citizens, the vast majority of whom
would never enter a college. Whatever portion of college work was
concerned with a general education was therefore in the position of
an orphan, and the traditional neglect of the orphan was its all too
common fate.

The psychological effect of the university upon not only the institutions which united college and university work but also those
which remained liberal arts colleges can scarcely be overestimated.
Within the large colleges and universities the level of instruction in
the upper years undoubtedly improved. It had often been observed,
however, that the methods of instruction appropriate to university
work differed from those proper to the general work of the college.
By the end of the century there was considerable complaint that the
instructional methods of university courses were not always suitable
to the lower college years. There was also criticism of the practice
of assigning instruction in these years to less experienced and less
competent teachers. In an address previously cited (p. 37), President
Harper called attention to this unhappy condition and remarked that

[8] William Rainey Harper, "The Length of the College Course," in *The Trend
in Higher Education,* University of Chicago Press, Chicago, 1905, p. 339.

in the large institutions instruction in the freshman year was often worse than in the academies. William DeWitt Hyde, President of Bowdoin College, writing in the *Educational Review* in 1891, was keenly aware of the power which the universities were exerting on the small liberal arts colleges. He protested against the inclination to multiply highly specialized electives because "the expense is too great and the profit to students at this stage too small," and maintained that the task of the college was still a liberal education for students

> whose knowledge of ancient and modern languages and literatures, higher mathematics, experimental science, political and economic history, psychology, ethics, and sociology, enables them to grasp the principles of medicine, or law, or politics, or theology; to guide social progress and form public opinion; to enjoy the companionship of wise and good men of all lands and ages; and to appreciate the results in some department of scientific investigation or historical research.[9]

Thirteen years later he was still outspoken against the plight of the independent colleges. Some of these had been forced by lack of means to do little more than the work of the schools; others, fashioning their curriculums and methods after the universities, had lost the humane and broadly cultural purpose of the college. He reasserted that "the function of the college is liberal education; the opening of the mind to the great departments of human interest; the opening of the heart to the great spiritual motives of unselfishness and social service; the opening of the will to opportunity for wise and righteous self-control." [10] His suggestions for a curricular revision were a bold departure from prevailing practice and a very early hint of possible new ways of organizing subject matters. "Each of the leading subjects should be presented in at least three consecutive courses extending over a year each: one elementary; one or more broad, general, interesting, practical; at least one specific, intensive, involving research, initiative, and a chance for originality. These broad middle courses are the distinctive feature of the college, and they are the hardest to get well taught." [11]

[9] William DeWitt Hyde, "The Policy of the Small College," *Educational Review*, vol. 2, 1891, pp. 313–315.

[10] William DeWitt Hyde, "The College," *Educational Review*, vol. 28, 1904, p. 476.

[11] *Ibid.*, p. 467.

In a little more than a quarter of a century America witnessed the beginnings of perhaps a dozen universities which were acceptable rivals of the best in Europe. They changed the pattern of higher education throughout the nation and raised the standards of scholarship immeasurably. But they had been erected without due consideration of the educational structure upon which they rested. In the eagerness to get on with the necessary task of advancing learning, few were willing and able to attack the basic problems of the institutional organization, a necessary task if the goals of a sound general education were to be achieved.

3

The organization of the typical American college in 1800 was very simple. There were no departments; instead, the curriculum was distributed among a number of professorships. It was unnecessary for a college to proclaim itself a liberal arts college. The business of a college was liberal education, based upon the traditional principles of the liberal arts curriculum. By 1900 it was not uncommon to find within the complex structure of one institution an administrative unit which was called the "college of liberal arts" or the "college of arts and sciences," or some other equally revealing title, which distinguished it functionally from other undergraduate units such as the colleges of engineering, commerce, agriculture, or education. This administrative division implied that the task of liberal education belonged to one branch of the institution which would not intrude or would intrude only minimally upon the task of educating engineers, businessmen, farmers, and teachers. The degree of intrusion was often inversely proportional to the amount of autonomy granted the several branches to fix their own admissions standards and curricular requirements. Colleges which chose not to divide into multiple administrative units found it necessary to describe themselves as "liberal arts colleges" and to affirm their dedication to the goals of liberal education annually in their announcements.

Parallel with the organization of undergraduate education into administratively and functionally separate schools or colleges within an institution was the growth of a departmental organization of the curriculum. The subdivision of a college or university into various schools was largely a response to the democratic demand for the adaptation of education to the practical needs of all classes of citizens and to the competition of independent vocational institutions. Departmental organization followed the expansion of knowledge in all subject-matter fields and was undoubtedly stimulated greatly by the rise of the graduate schools and the subdivisions of the sciences. The record of changes in administrative organization during the century is bewildering in its variety and complexity, but the complexity does not conceal the fact that the changes, almost without exception, were the result of efforts to extend the opportunities for specialization in a steadily increasing number of fields. The founding of the land-grant colleges was, for example, a major victory for specialization at the undergraduate level.

The creation of each new school and department within an institution meant some degree of decentralization in administrative control of the curriculum; consequently, achieving a common opinion about the meaning of general education and its place in an undergraduate program became more difficult. The problem for general education, however, was not whether the growth of separate vocational colleges and departments within the structure of a college or university was good or bad but how the newly created units—both vocational colleges and departments—would use the powers which accrued to them as they grew in strength. The first business of a college of engineering was to train engineers and of a department of history to train historians. How important would the concept of a general education seem to be to the faculties charged with securing specific vocational ends?

The motive of the colleges and universities in establishing vocational schools was not wholly opportunistic. There was clearly a desire to build better schools and no doubt a conviction that the liberal atmosphere of a college or university would elevate the quality of the education. There seems to have been little concern whether the proximity of vocational colleges might not lower the standards of a liberal education. Independent professional and technical schools had existed before the colleges added their own branches to their regular academic courses in any considerable numbers. Although the professional standards of the independent schools varied widely, few of them demanded much in the way of a general education either prior to admission or afterward. Their standards seem to have influenced the earliest schools incorporated into the colleges and universities. The Lawrence Scientific School was established at Harvard in 1847. The Catalog of Harvard for 1849 states that a candidate for admission to Lawrence must be eighteen years old and have a common school education. The number and choice of courses was optional; courses were offered in chemistry, zoology, geology, and engineering, with others to be added upon sufficient demand. According to the Catalog of the University of Virginia in 1876 a student might qualify for the degree of Bachelor of Science by completing courses in three departments ("schools," in the traditional terminology of that institution). These were mathematics, natural philosophy, and general chemistry. A student might elect courses in other areas but was not required to do so. The catalog affirms the dedication of the university to the elective principle but also states that the curriculum provides for "systematic prosecution of a complete plan of *general education*" and that the students in the *academic department* are "required, as a rule, to attend at least three schools." Since a school amounted to a single subject-matter field, the requirement does not seem excessive. There is no indication, however, that a general education was a matter of concern to the medical, law, or agricultural departments.

In 1893 the general indifference of the professional schools to a liberal education was attacked by Woodrow Wilson (then a professor at Princeton) in an address entitled "Should an Antecedent Liberal Education Be Required of Students in Law, Medicine and Theology?" Although the principal objects of his criticism were the independent schools, he attacked all specialization which was not founded upon a liberal education. Conceding that a liberal education "does not necessarily disclose general principles [because it] is too often so *il*liberal in its survey of subjects as to leave upon the mind no trace of the generalizing habit," he defended it as essential to the preparation for all professions precisely because it is general. "Without a survey of the field of knowledge . . . it is hard to see how a man is to discern *the relations of things,* upon the perception of which all just thought must rest." [12] Concerning the dangers of the current drift toward specialization, which he claimed was producing a "new ig-

[12] Woodrow Wilson, "Should an Antecedent Liberal Education Be Required of Students in Law, Medicine and Theology?" in *College and State: Educational, Literary and Political Papers 1875–1913)*, Harper & Brothers, New York, 1925, vol. 1, p. 224. Italics mine.

norance," he asserted that "there is no common mastery, but everywhere separate baronies of knowledge, where a few strong men rule and many ignorant men are held vassals—men ignorant of the freedom of more perfect, more liberal knowledge." He hoped that the universities, by creating better professional schools, under their liberal environment, would boldly challenge the students' inclination for a purely practical training and the public's indifference to a general education both antecedent to and continuous with professional training, for "the separation of general and special training is an acute symptom of the disease of specialization by which we are now so sorely afflicted." [13]

Wilson's prescriptions for a cure of the disease were less revolutionary than these quotations might suggest. He was in fact asking that the theoretical and the practical be joined in the education for any profession. Thus his recommendations for an antecedent general training for doctors was a thorough grounding in chemistry, biology, and psychology, and for the theologian an education in the thought of his age and the literature of all ages. There is here, as there was in the prescriptions for the students at the University of Virginia, a suggestion of a separate kind of *general education* for every profession. Other essays by Wilson show that his whole view of liberal education was less circumscribed than this. Nevertheless the subsequent history of professional and vocational education requires us to take account of this view. As the colleges and universities came more to control the standards of professional education, they did require a broader knowledge of the disciplines related to the students' professional fields. The change marked the beginning, however, of comprehensive lists of prerequisites for admission to a professional school and, of course, requirements for degrees in the vocational schools. The preprofessional requirements were of necessity supplied by the colleges. By the first decade of the twentieth century, the content of preprofessional and vocational education at the collegiate level was pretty well prescribed. If a student acquired a general acquaintance with branches of knowledge outside his chosen field, he did it either because he exercised a wise choice of electives or because he attended a college which had not surrendered completely to the pressures for specialization and free election.

[13] *Ibid.*, pp. 225–229.

The organization of the college curriculum by departments was another application of the principles which divided the institution into several schools. To the extent that depth of experience in one subject matter became more important than the total intellectual experience of the student, departmentalization of the curriculum tended to destroy any conception of the unity of knowledge. In 1899, President Harper attacked the practices of departments as one of the sources of waste in education, saying that "teachers of science are ... doing just what teachers of the classics have been doing for many years ... they are dealing with the student in each department as if he were going to make a specialty of that department." The practice is injurious, he said, both to many students and to the departments concerned. But a worse fault lay in the failure to achieve an effective correlation between the different subjects of the curriculum:

> If a student does work in one subject after another and in one department after another, without discovering the interrelationship of the other subjects or departments, and all the while conceives these subjects and departments as distinct entities without relationship, he loses far more than one-half the value of his work. ... The division of the work into technical departments is an artificial and misleading one, but it is so fixed that, like the letter of the sacred Scriptures, it is by many supposed to be a part of the original creation itself. This vitiates in a greater or less degree the value of the entire college discipline, for it is the relationships of thought, and of life that a man ought to know, if he is to know anything.[11]

Both Wilson and Harper were aware of the price which liberal education was paying for the departmentalization of knowledge. In declaring that a liberal education is not a sum of a number of discrete parts but the power to discern the interrelationship of parts both within and without the student's field of specialization, they raised a question which lies at the heart of the concept of general education. Their ideas were related to Tappan's conception of a "philosophical" form of education which produces the capacity to relate all the fields of knowledge which enter into the well-being of society; and like Tappan, they considered a thorough general foundation in the major disciplines the basis for achieving this goal.

[14] "Waste in Higher Education," in *op. cit.*, pp. 97–99.

4

The controversy over the principle of free election has been re-corded in every history of higher education in America. Professor George Pierson has summarized the issues which precipitated the long conflict which followed Eliot's drawing up on the battle lines:

> Originally the sheer increase of learning had provided the powder to explode the traditional curriculum. At the same time a psy-chology of individual differences, together with the new voca-tional-technological pressures, had undermined the inherited ideal of unity in college studies. The consequence had been sub-division, but subdivision for varied purposes or governed by con-flicting interests. Wherever much specialization had been in-dulged, the educational authorities had had to decide who would shape the special programs—the professional faculties for profes-sional purposes or the students for their individual enthusiasms.[15]

Complete freedom of election did not gain universal approval, and it was not until 1895 that the principle of free election attained full control of the curricular requirements at Harvard. Nevertheless in varying degrees the idea of free election increased in favor through-out the remainder of the century. Full capitulation to absolute free-dom of election was challenged by defenders of general education and also by some advocates of specialization. In addition to the as-sertion that many students were lacking in either the maturity or the responsibility to be wise architects of their own course of study, defenders of a coherent plan of general education argued that the full exercise of the elective principle threatened the survival of liberal education. As the principle of controlled sequences within any given area of specialization gained wider approval, the most ardent ad-vocates of specialization also entertained doubts about unrestricted election.

One alternative to the principle of unrestricted election was an adaptation of the principle employed in the Amherst curriculum of 1827: alternate courses of study among which the students might freely choose. Once the choice was made, the student enjoyed a minimal power of election, since the course consisted of a general

[15] George Wilson Pierson, *Yale College: An Educational History, 1871–1921,* Yale University Press, New Haven, Conn., 1952, p. 305.

component common to all students and a specialized but required component which distinguished it from other courses. The continued expansion of the curriculum, however, made it increasingly difficult to secure agreement on a desirable common content. More attractive to some colleges was another version of the alternate course plan in which the vocational or preprofessional component was determined by the faculty, while the students were permitted considerable latitude in forming the remainder of their course. This procedure was essentially that which the University of Virginia had adopted from its beginning. The problem of allowing a reasonable exercise of individual freedom while preserving the balance and integrity of both the general and the special content was frequently under discussion as the century drew to a close.

In 1887, A. Lawrence Lowell, then a practicing attorney in Boston, examined the elective system in an article in the *Harvard Monthly*. The principles which should guide a student in his choice of electives could not be determined, Lowell said, apart from a consideration of the purpose of the college. This, he asserted, is "a general training of the mind as distinguished from the acquisition of specific information which is expected to be of any definite use in after life. Such a training of the mind may be looked at from two sides, one of which concerns the strength and soundness of the mental fibre, and the other the breadth and elasticity of the mind." [16]

In these general terms, the statement might have won the approbation of a defender of the classical curriculum. But where the latter would have stoutly defended the classics as the one proper source for securing the necessary strength of mental fiber, Lowell considered it a matter of secondary importance what subject the student selected for this purpose provided that it required hard mental work. "All branches of science are good, and so are the various forms of metaphysics and of law. Mathematics is excellent if one has any taste for it, and so are history and literature if they are really well taught." The important consideration should be that the student pursue the subject of his choice until he had mastered its principles. Concentration upon a single subject, however, could accomplish only one-half of the goal of a college education, since "a thorough education ought to make a man familiar with the fundamental conceptions that under-

---

[16] A. Lawrence Lowell, "The Choice of Electives," in *At War with Academic Traditions in America*, Harvard University Press, Cambridge, Mass., 1934, p. 5.

lie the various departments of human knowledge, and with the methods of thought of the persons who pursue them." [17]

To accomplish this objective, Lowell declared that the fundamental conceptions and methods could be divided into large classes, such as the physical sciences, literature, metaphysics, and history. Each student should devote a part of his time to study in each of these departments; nor should any student be allowed to graduate without a knowledge of the government of his country. There was no suggestion in this proposal for the construction of general courses in any of these departments; and apparently Lowell then thought that any of several courses in each area might serve the student equally well in securing a knowledge of the fundamental principles characteristic of the entire area. Lowell's article contained the basis of the principle of concentration and distribution which, in 1909, as the new President of Harvard, he was to introduce into the curriculum of that college as the corrective to the evils charged to the unrestricted elective system.

Another proposal, offered by President Hyde of Bowdoin in 1891, was based upon a distinction between two types of minds and related types of scholarly interest: the literary and the scientific. "The college should *by its required courses* insure to every student an acquaintance with the *first principles* in both these fundamental lines of study." [18] Ability to write correct English, to read both French and German, and a knowledge of the elements of political and economic science, psychology, and ethics should be the aim of literary studies, while appropriate courses in mathematics, chemistry, physics, and biology should form the content of scientific studies.

A few years later, President Hadley of Yale attacked the problem in a somewhat similar way. He classified college students according to mental types, distinguishing among three types: the scientific, the literary, and the administrative, or those interested in facts, in ideas, and in affairs. Each type inclined to one or another of several vocations, and rarely would a man change from one vocation to another which was incompatible with his mental bent. Hadley proposed that, instead of providing separate courses of study for each group, the

---

[17] *Ibid.*, pp. 6–7.
[18] "The Policy of the Small College," in *op. cit.*, p. 316. Hyde also pointed out that the standards for admission to college no longer took account of the realities of secondary school instruction. Italics mine.

same subjects should be taught to all students but by different methods —the methods appropriate to the mental disposition of each group.[19]

Woodrow Wilson offered a different approach to restoring the unity to the college curriculum which he considered to have been destroyed by the increase of modern scientific subjects and the elective system. In an article published in 1894 he wrote that the elective system had obscured the "idea of a balance between general and special training," and to restore the balance it was necessary to re-examine the idea of the general, i.e., that part of the curriculum which should be common to all students. He described the general content as that which deals with "the common experiences, the common thoughts and struggles, the old triumphs and defeats of ... men ... in the past: their dreams and awakenings; their ambitions, humours, confidences, liberties, and follies." [20] The core of a general education would therefore be the political and institutional history of our nation and the literature (in the broadest sense of the term) of the English-speaking peoples. There is, he said, no better corrective for the prevailing incoherence than "a wide acquaintance with the best books that men have written, joined with a knowledge of the institutions men have made trial of in the past," for the common problems of the present have their analogies in the past. "It is no new thing to have economic problems and dream dreams of romantic and adventurous social reconstruction." [21]

Apart from such a common training, carried throughout the undergraduate years, Wilson thought that each student should be free to choose his own way. This was a bold departure from the past modes of defining a common core. It proposed a unification of history and the products of human thought and imagination for a common end— the understanding of our society and our common humanity. It takes no great act of imagination to see in Wilson's proposals the principles which are the theoretical base of many contemporary "general courses" which bear the legends "social science" or "humanities."

Most of the attempts to solve curricular problems continued to be

---

[19] Pierson, *op. cit.*, p. 307. Professor Pierson's account is derived in part from an article by President Hadley, "Mental Types and Their Recognition in Our Schools," *Harper's Magazine*, vol. 111, 1905, pp. 123–129.

[20] Woodrow Wilson, "University Training and Citizenship," in *College and State: Educational, Literary and Political Papers (1875–1913)*, Harper & Brothers, New York, 1925, vol. 1, pp. 248–251.

[21] *Ibid.*, p. 253.

fundamentally quantitative—addition and contraction. The substance of the eventual sum depended very largely upon the concept of relative values entertained by its sponsor. There was simply not enough time to study all the subjects available, and each new subject fought for its place against the opposition of those who viewed it as a threat to the old. But the problems created by the multiplication of studies could not be solved by quantitative measures alone. At least that was the view of John Dewey in 1902:

> The problem of the multiplication of studies, of the consequent congestion of the curriculum, and the conflict of various studies for a recognized place in the curriculum; the fact that one cannot get in without crowding something else out; the effort to arrange a compromise in various courses of study by throwing the entire burden of election upon the student so that he shall make out his own course of study—this problem is only a reflex of the lack of unity in the social activities themselves, and of the necessity of reaching more harmony, more system in our scheme of life. This multiplication of study is not primarily a product of the schools. The last hundred years has created a new world, has revealed a new universe, material and social. The educational problem is not a result of anything within our own conscious wish or intention, but of the conditions in the contemporary world.[22]

The source of modern problems of education, as Dewey saw it, was the fact that the sciences had transformed society. The new sciences are not the product of self-willed men, bent upon forcing them upon the college curriculum; instead they are "the outcome of all that makes our modern life what it is." They cannot be denied their place in the curriculum, because everywhere they have serious application to life. They are not "a mere addition of so much bulk of information to what went before," for they represent "a profound modification and reconstruction of all attained knowledge—a change in quality and standpoint." The methods of the sciences have influenced the nature of humanistic studies and are in large measure responsible for the existence of the modern social sciences. One consequence of these changes is the necessity of defining the terms of organizing principles which will bring all branches of knowledge into a more harmonious relation.

[22] *Op. cit.*, pp. 85–86.

The body of knowledge is indeed one; it is a spiritual organism. To attempt to chop off a member here and amputate an organ there is the veriest impossibility. The problem is not one of elimination, but of organization; of simplification not through denial and rejection, but through harmony.... Until the various branches of human learning have attained something like philosophic organization, until the various modes of their application to life have been so definitely and completely worked out as to bring even the common affairs of life under direction, confusion and conflict are bound to continue. When we have an adequate industrial and political organization it will be quite time to assume that there is some offhand and short-cut solution to the problem of educational organization.[23]

Neither the elective system nor a patchwork assembly of a few common courses and a few specialized courses could solve the curricular problem until the relationship of all knowledge to the conditions of modern society as altered by the recent changes of knowledge was better understood. This view, Dewey argued, did not absolve the schools and colleges from continuing their efforts to impart a genuine general education to all their students.

I have previously quoted another passage from this essay of Dewey's in which he remarked that the function of general training is to give the student "a survey, at least, of the universe in its manifold phases" through which "he may get his orientation—his placing himself in the larger world." The words "survey" and "orientation" were shortly to become familiar as terms which identified new types of courses that broke down the rigidities of conventional departmental lines. Whether such courses were merely short cuts to the problem of educational organization or were genuine efforts to secure simplification in the organization of knowledge through harmony was to be a major issue in the discussion which they provoked.

In his Inaugural Address in 1909 President Lowell of Harvard restated the views he had expressed in 1887. He rejected the idea that the main object of a college education is vocational preparation and asserted that the American college must accept its responsibility for general education, a task which could not be left wholly to the secondary schools, since they were not then nor were they likely soon to be able to accept it. He renewed his argument for an educa-

[23] *Ibid.*, pp. 89–91.

tion which included depth in one area of learning and a breadth which covered all areas, the latter to be achieved through "a number of *general courses* in wholly unrelated fields." Recognizing the difficulties attending such a proposal, he said, "Instruction that imparts a little knowledge of everything is more difficult to provide than any other. To furnish it there ought to be in every considerable field a general course, designed to give to men who do not intend to pursue the subject further a comprehension of its underlying principles or methods of thought; and this is by no means the same thing as an introductory course." [24] General courses of this sort should be, he asserted, under the charge of a leading member of the department concerned, and his teaching should be supplemented by "instruction, discussion, and constant examination in smaller groups, conducted by younger men well equipped for their work." These observations constitute a landmark in the history of general education, for they are surely one of the earliest, if not actually the first explicit reference to the idea of a general course. This reference anticipated by nearly a decade the first successful experiments in this mode of curricular and subject-matter organization.

President Lowell's Annual Report for the year 1908–1909 sets forth the particulars of a plan for the modification of the elective system. The plan, developed by a faculty committee, was a scheme for concentration and distribution. Concentration might be in one department or in several departments covering related subject matters. Distribution (admittedly less simple to achieve) was to be secured by classifying all subjects taught in the college in four groups and by requiring every student to take something in each group. The groupings were based upon an assumption of common methods of inquiry in the courses or subjects assigned to each group. The groups were (1) the arts of expression—language, literature, the fine arts, and music; (2) the natural or inductive sciences; (3) the "inductive" social sciences; and (4) the abstract or deductive studies—mathematics and philosophy, including law and diverse kinds of social theories.[25] One object of the changes was to make the student plan his course of study as a whole, a principle presupposed in the elective

---

[24] A. Lawrence Lowell, "Inaugural Address," in *At War with Academic Traditions in America,* Harvard University Press, Cambridge, Mass., 1934, pp. 40–41. Italics mine.

[25] "From the Annual Report, 1908–09," in *ibid.,* pp. 239–240.

system, but by no means achieved in fact. There was, however, no further development of the idea of general courses in this Report.

The Annual Report for 1914–1915 stated that students must concentrate six of seventeen courses in one field and six more must be distributed among other subjects of knowledge after consultation with an academic adviser.[26] In the college, Lowell added, the problem of making the student the unit of education is more difficult than in other parts of the university because "general education is more intangible, more vague, less capable of precise analysis and definition." Nevertheless the distributional requirements were adopted for precisely the purpose of making the student rather than the course the unit of education.

Lowell's speeches and annual reports during the early years of his presidency show his deep concern for the problems of general education. For the cultivated man "no great region should be wholly a strange unexplored wilderness, traversed only by people who utter dark sentences in an unkown tongue." [27] In 1914, Lowell wrote that "democracies have the greater need of widely diffused general education, as compared with special training," since "all men partake of the character of rulers" and "ought to be trained in some measure for that duty." This means that everyone needs "an acquaintance with what are, not pedantically but correctly, termed the humanities, with what man has done, with the fabric of civilization." [28] These words echo the ideas President Chadbourne had expressed thirty-five years earlier.

Lowell's speeches also reveal a clear distinction between the idea of general education and liberal education. General education was, in his view, that part of a liberal education which contributed breadth of learning, whereas liberal education was the product of a learning which unites knowledge of the methods of many fields with a mastery of the content and methods of one field. The purpose of *concentration*, in this view, was not to be confused with vocational or professional specialization. Its goal was to secure disciplined minds. He challenged the defenders of vocationalism who found all subjects equally useful and strenuous and therefore equally liberal. "Any man who is to touch the world on many sides, or touch it strongly, must

---

[26] "From the Annual Report, 1914–15," in *ibid.*, p. 258.
[27] "Culture," in *ibid.*, p. 116.
[28] "The Selective Function of Education," in *ibid.*, pp. 104–105.

have at his command as large a stock as possible of the world's store of knowledge and experience; and ... bookkeeping does not furnish this in the same measure as literature, history, and science." [29]

The action of the Harvard faculty gave encouragement to other colleges, which recognized the principle as a means for strengthening the liberal objectives of their curriculums. Since concentration and distribution is still the guiding principle of curricular structure of nearly all American colleges, there is need to consider the reasons which led considerable numbers of educators to find its early practical applications lacking in effectiveness. Had it proved wholly satisfactory, some of the more recent developments undertaken in the name of general education might not have occurred. This question, however, anticipates a later stage in this narrative. It is sufficient to say that the extensive adoption of the principle of concentration and distribution marked a significant reversal of the trend in educational practice which dominated the last quarter of the nineteenth century. It was a serious attempt to produce a controlled curriculum which served both the specialized interests and general needs of the students, and therefore it was an important undertaking in the historical development of ideas about general education.

5

The transformation of modern society wrought by the phenomenal growth of the behavioral sciences has been in many respects as profound as that wrought by the natural sciences, and in no phase of life since the closing years of the nineteenth century has the influence of the behavioral sciences been more evident than in the field of education. The rise of the professional schools of education is but one manifestation of the power which they have exercised. No detail of the educational process has been left unexamined by the educational psychologists. Inevitably, therefore, their theories and techniques have had, both directly and indirectly, no little influence upon the history of general education. We are today, in fact, so deeply involved in varieties of educational experiments which have immediate bearing upon the meaning and practice of general education that it is singularly difficult to appraise them objectively.

As the science of psychology centered attention more and more

[29] *Ibid.*, pp. 108–109.

intensively upon phenomena of individual behavior, emerging facts and theories provided the bases for the reform of educational practices. The adjustment of educational processes to the needs and well-being of the individual became the first concern of the educational theorists. As President Lowell said, the student rather than the curriculum tended to become the center of education. Theories about the precise needs of the individual and about the proper means of securing his well-being multiplied rapidly, and the patterns of education as they pertained both to the content of learning and to the methods and habits of learning increased proportionately. At first the elementary and secondary schools were the important laboratories of educational experiment; and today more than one generation of our adult population are the products of practices which were first introduced in the schools in the late years of the nineteenth century. Since the work of the schools is universally acknowledged to be the foundation of all general education, it follows that these years of experiment had a profound influence upon the historical development of general education.

The influence upon the colleges has been only slightly less evident than that upon the schools. We have merely to compare the assumptions underlying the standard curriculum of 1800 with those which formed the bases of the curricular patterns at the end of the first decade of the present century to recognize the effects which modern social and psychological theories have produced. In the last five decades the differences have increased even more spectacularly. The doctrine of individual differences was pressed to the point that not only was the student allowed a remarkable degree of freedom in the determination of his program of studies, but often within a particular course he was encouraged to exercise considerable initiative in determining details of the content of the course. Theories concerning instructional guidance differed greatly. In some schools, students were encouraged to study only under the guidance of teachers; "homework" yielded to "supervised study." Individual and group "projects," planned jointly by student and teacher, took precedence over the traditional "recitation" procedures.

One of the most common criticisms of the uniform requirements of many current general education programs is that they make no allowance for individual initiative. The problem of flexibility in course and curricular structures has become an issue upon which the opinion of educators has been sharply divided. What degree of flexibility should be encouraged? At what points in the educational process should various forms of flexibility be introduced? Are there, amid all the accumulated stores of knowledge, any disciplines and any bodies of knowledge so fundamental that they cannot be excluded from the intellectual experience of a student who aspires to work of a collegiate level? Answers to such questions as these have had many consequences for the practice of general education.

Nothing illustrates more vividly the changes effected by modern educational theories in both school and college than a study of the place which linguistic and mathematical disciplines have occupied at successive periods during the last century and a half. Whether the theories which once established them as the heart of a liberal education were valid or not is irrelevant to the immediate question. The point is that the scope of experience with either of these disciplines has been materially reduced in large part as a result of educational theories which have gained favor during the last seventy-five years. I am not referring primarily to the study of foreign languages, either ancient or modern, although their study must be considered an important part of a total linguistic experience. Even more at issue is the place which the study of the English language has held, particularly with reference to the fundamental disciplines of grammar, logic, and rhetoric. As for the mathematical disciplines, the Bachelor of Arts degree has been awarded to students who have had little more than elementary arithmetic, perhaps at most an introductory course in algebra. Beyond this level the study of mathematics is often a matter of preprofessional requirement or of individual preference. That language and mathematics are still assumed to be the basic disciplines of liberal education is supported by the fact that almost all colleges employ some form of verbal and mathematical aptitude test among their criteria for admission. Modern psychology has contributed much to the development of these and other measures of aptitude and achievement. Yet colleges differ greatly in the level of aptitude and the extent of achievement they regard as minimal for admission, and they differ as much in general policies about what should be done to build upon the level of competence shown by the tests. Educational theories account for much of the difference.

The fact that English has been for many years the one subject which has been uniformly required of all students for as much as three or four years in high school does not disprove the foregoing observation. The study of English is not synonymous with the study of linguistic disciplines; and there is a reasonable doubt that training in the understanding and use of the English language is generally as rigorous today as it was even fifty years ago. At the same time it must be acknowledged that in few other subject-matter areas has there been as much experimentation with content and methods of instruction at the secondary school level as there has been in the English language. In fairness to the teaching staffs of the public schools and some of the large state universities it must be admitted that the growth of student population, unmatched by a proportionate increase in instructors, has made their task often grotesque and all but impossible to achieve.

If the schools and colleges have been unable to agree on any uniform policy with respect to the importance of the basic linguistic and mathematical disciplines in a general education, it is unlikely that they can agree about other disciplines. Distributional requirements for a general education have usually included some knowledge of the natural sciences, the social sciences, and literature and the fine arts; but there the agreement ends. Curiously enough the transfer theory, rejected as a just reason for the study of classical languages, was not altogether discarded as the distributional theory gained favor. Although President Lowell argued that some disciplines were more important than others in a general education, he also asserted that a knowledge of one branch of the natural sciences was adequate to give a student the means of exploring independently the content and methods of kindred sciences. This point of view is still widely held today; and many colleges allow students to choose any one of several courses in the natural sciences, the social sciences, and the humanities in satisfying general requirements. Since the courses are usually introductory courses in the subject matters of several departments, there are concealed in these options an assumption that the disciplinary skill acquired in one department can be successfully transferred to the solution of problems in another department.

From an assurance about the exact and proper content of a liberal education—an assurance so firm that it defied all challenges for generations—the American schools and colleges passed by degrees to uncertainty and disagreement. It is easy to account for the uncertainty in the light of the transformations that the increase of knowledge has produced upon modern society. But the relationship between expanding knowledge and cultural change in a social democracy is one of the problems to which the behavioral sciences, including the science of education, have addressed themselves. For more than fifty years the schools and colleges have been one vast laboratory for experiments aimed at discovering what students ought to know—as citizens and as individuals who must exist within a common culture. For the first time in history the techniques of the social sciences have been directed toward an improved understanding of individual behavior and how learning can be best adapted to the character and needs of the individual. And as the experiments have increased in kind, our agreement about the nature of the knowledge which the liberally educated should share in common has decreased.

Chapter 4

Two Decades of Curricular Reform
1909-1930

A retrospective view of American education during the last quarter of the nineteenth century can hardly fail to overwhelm anyone who contemplates the scope of the activity which was compressed into so short a period. The development on a nationwide scale of a system of state-supported secondary schools, the emergence of the first genuine graduate schools devoted to scholarly research in every branch of learning, the consolidation of technical and professional schools under the administration of the colleges and universities, the refinement of learning into a steadily mounting number of highly specialized departments which gave promise of stretching to infinity, the application of the techniques of the new sciences to the analysis of the process of education itself—all these lines of action unfolded with a rapidity that confounds the imagination. Place them in the context of a nation striving under the adverse conditions which were the heritage of a catastrophic Civil War toward a renewed political solidarity, of a nation entering upon the realization of the economic and cultural potentialities inherent in the great territorial expansion which preceded the war, of a restless nation made more restless by the waves of migrants from all parts of Europe attracted by the images of wealth or of political and social freedoms, of a nation whose values were changing—yet not perceiving why or how they were changing—under the very force of the new learning which the colleges and universities were themselves advancing. Place them in this context, and there is no reason for surprise that schoolmen or laymen should have failed to agree upon a philosophy which could give coherence to the whole of the vast responsibility which rested upon the educational institutions of the nation. Too much happened too fast.

The aristocratic image of a liberal education devised for those who had the wealth and leisure to pursue it had long been rejected. The image of another kind of liberal education so various in its parts that all free men could find and choose freely whatever suited their personal interests had now replaced it. To many men secure in the possession of social, economic, and political freedoms and to men striving to attain the material benefits which these freedoms promised, the image of an education comprehensive enough to provide an understanding of the principles which created and the means which preserved their freedom seemed, by comparison, unimportant. To the scholarly minded the challenge of isolating some new strand of learning became more engrossing than the principles which joined all strands in one complex fabric, and the tracing of each strand to some ultimate end was generally more exciting than holding fast to a knowledge of its origins. The temper of the times invited everyone to contemplate the present and the future and to be the master of his chosen intellectual or technical domain. In such an environment the concept of a general education did not flourish.

The concept could not flourish because it assumed the importance of our common humanity. It assumed that every man, though an individual, is none the less an individual *man*, and therefore united with his fellow men, past, present, and in the future. It asserted that as *man* he shared in the products of the accumulated wisdom of mankind and in the responsibilities that are the common obligation of all men. Though certain responsibilities must be discharged by each individual out of his special competence, others could be discharged only in the exercise of a kind of understanding which all men should strive to possess. Throughout the century, men had argued that such knowledge was indispensable to the preservation of a democratic society. The intellectual adventure, however, was no less competitive than the adventure of the market place; and the rewards seemed to fall to those who best cultivated their own special province of learning. No reasonable person protested the advances of scholarship and research, but there were a few who understood that if it were to be attended by the neglect of a common learning and indifference to the importance of an understanding of the interrelationships of the manifold parts of knowledge, society itself would be the loser.

The idea of a common learning shared by the liberally educated was embodied in the adjective "general." The word was always and obviously ambiguous since it referred to a subject matter or content of education and to a citizenry who would receive the benefits of the content. As terms such as "general education," "general studies," "general training," and "general culture" were used more frequently in the years that joined the nineteenth and twentieth centuries, the importance of the idea which they signified was more and more widely accepted. Though men might differ about the specifics of the content, they knew that the idea stood for something that was lacking in most of the educational practice of the time. They understood, too, that it denoted something that was no longer equivalent to the generally accepted meaning of the term "liberal education."

Dissatisfaction with the practical consequences of the free elective principle was recorded in vigorous demands for the restoration of a sound general education in the early years of the present century. It is significant that President Lowell, who defended the whole of his plan for concentration and distribution as a just plan for *liberal* education, defended the principle of distribution as a means to a necessary *general* education. It was Lowell also who pointed out that the multiplication of courses in colleges and universities was not necessarily and positively correlated with the expansion of knowledge. "The real reason for increasing the list of courses," he said, "though it is not often consciously recognized, is quite as much a desire to attract students as a belief in the benefit conferred on them after they come." [1] And he added that "for the undergraduates a comparatively small array of staple courses on the most important portions of the subject, with a limited number of others on more highly specialized aspects thereof" was sufficient.

Lowell's observations did little to check the increase in the number of courses, nor did they remove another objection to the actual operation of the distributional principle. In some areas the courses from which students were obliged to choose were in fact designed for those who planned to concentrate in the field, and little consideration was given to the needs of other students. Furthermore the plan assumed that courses designed by departments for departmental interests would provide a knowledge of methods sufficiently comprehensive to permit the student to employ them independently in the study of other related fields. Experience did not support the assumption.

[1] Lowell, "The Annual Report, 1915-16," in *At War with Academic Traditions in America,* Harvard University Press, Cambridge, Mass., 1934, pp. 264-265.

Although the distributional requirements did give assurance of greater breadth of intellectual experience than many students might have secured under the free elective system, the latitude of choice in any area was often so wide that the curriculum seemed in fact to differ very little from the system it sought to replace.

This is the impression one forms after examining the criticisms which grew in number and in vehemence in the years immediately after World War I. The evils of the elective system and specialization were a persistent theme. One of the most persistent critics was Alexander Meiklejohn, then President of Amherst. In one essay he attacked what he called "the fallacy of the scholar"—"the belief that all knowledge is so good that all parts of knowledge are equally good." It is a point of view, he declared, which runs through all varieties of the elective system, and is "the concerted statement of a group of men each of whom is lost within the limits of his own special studies, and who as a group seem not to realize the organic relationships between them nor the common task which should bind them together." [2]

Abraham Flexner, concerned that the professional student should have a truly liberal education as a background for his professional training, charged that the error of the elective system was not in the principle of flexibility which it introduced but in the lack of order or design operating within a flexible curricular organization. The expansion of the curriculum was an enrichment which kept pace with

> ... the enrichment and diversification of modern intellectual and social life. Individual capacity and preference had to be heeded, in order to utilize the abundance of opportunity thus provided. Experience showed, however, that many students lost themselves in the tropical wilderness; their capacities, even if developed, did not and could not instinctively appropriate and coordinate the most suitable courses of study; ... The elective system was introduced that the student might be free. But in what sense is he free, when, ignorant and confused, his choice alights on this subject rather than that? The elective system, meant as a wide-open opportunity to permit the student to organize his work, needs to be organized for him. [3]

[2] Alexander Meiklejohn, "What the Liberal College Is," in *The Liberal College,* Marshall Jones, Boston, 1920, p. 41.

[3] Abraham Flexner, *A Modern College and a Modern School,* Doubleday & Company, Inc., New York, 1923, p. 60.

M. L. Burton, President of the University of Michigan, writing in the educational supplement of the *New Republic* for 1922, declared that the "group" system, another name for the distributional plan, had failed to solve the defects of the elective principle and "the weight of undue specialization." Fragments of knowledge were presented to the student by a departmentalized faculty "with no conscious endeavor on its part to unify or correlate the fields of knowledge." [4] He continued by referring to a solution adopted by some institutions, the introduction of "general survey courses" by which "it is expected that every student will acquire a certain modicum of information, that he will secure at least a comprehensive, though superficial, view of the history of civilization and develop a tenable scientific point of view."

The introduction of experimental survey courses was the first material sign of the increasing reflection upon principles which governed the organization of courses. Some educators recognized, as Harper had declared two decades earlier, that the principles which determined existing departmental course structures were wholly arbitrary and that other organizing principles better adapted to general needs might be employed.

In the same issue of the *New Republic*, H. W. Chase, President of the University of North Carolina, criticized "departmental thinking" which, he said, has "supplanted thinking about education." He then turned his attention to two aspects of curricular organization: first, the relative values of subject matters in a liberal education for contemporary society; and second, the effective organization of that content which has a prior claim in terms of its liberal values.

> We must come to some clear conviction of what knowledge is, in the liberal education of today, of most worth; for there must be, for any period of history, *some* knowledge which is of most worth. Biological theory and the social sciences, for example, are two natural centres of value that suggest themselves in the world that our students will inhabit. But if the problem is really to be solved, such an evaluation is not enough. The artificial departmental partitions of knowledge must be cut through. History, for example, expresses itself in literature, in philosophy, in economics and social theory, as well as in events—and yet how many stu-

[4] M. L. Burton, "The Undergraduate Course," *New Republic*, vol. 32, Oct. 25, 1922, pt. 2, p. 9.

dents are ever brought to realize the relationship which exists between the literature of the nineteenth century, as taught by the English department, its political and social happenings studied in a course in history, the conceptions of its philosophers and its economists? Might not a better understanding of scientific method and achievement be gained if, let us say, instead of teaching chemistry and physics each as a separate speciality, "fusion" courses in natural science were developed, somewhat as algebra and geometry and trigonometry are now often fused into a single whole with an underlying unitary point of view? [5]

Early experiments in creating new patterns of courses began before America entered World War I. Reed College, which was established, as one of its historians says, in the heyday of the elective system (1911), imposed at first only two requirements upon students apart from the departmental sequences which constituted a "concentration." These two courses were freshman orientation courses called "College Life" and "Natural Science." [6] The natural science course was soon dropped in favor of traditional departmental courses, and the elective principle continued until 1921, when under the administration of President Richard F. Scholz, both the curriculum and the administrative structure of the faculty were reorganized.

Meanwhile another experiment in the organization of a new type of course was undertaken at Amherst under the leadership of President Meiklejohn. In his Report to the Board of Trustees for the year 1914, he wrote:

> The most significant feature of the educational changes which were put into effect in the fall of 1914 is the placing of an elective course in social and economic institutions in the Freshman year. The name of the course has been left in vague outline because its exact nature must be determined by the interest and method of the teacher who gives it. Its purpose, whatever form it may take, will be to serve as an introduction to the humanistic sciences. We wish if possible to make students, at the very beginning of the college course, aware of the moral, social, and economic scheme—the society—of which they are members. . . . Its functions are . . . (1) a sane, searching, revealing of the facts of

[5] H. W. Chase, "The Problem of Higher Education," *New Republic,* vol. 32, Oct. 25, 1922, pt. 2, pp. 4–5.

[6] R. F. Arragon, "The Development of the Reed Curriculum," *Reed College Bulletin,* no. 24, November, 1945, p. 3.

the human situation, and (2) a showing of the intellectual method by which these situations may be understood. It should be primarily an introduction to ethics, logic, history, economics, law, government, and not in any large degree an end in itself.[7]

Meiklejohn added that many members of the faculty and of the board regarded the experiment as of doubtful wisdom on the ground that it would not possess either the accuracy or the thoroughness needed to give the disciplinary quality which a freshman course ought to have. Though conceding the force of the objection, he argued that as the college curriculum was then given, a common result was that even the ablest students became aware of the human situation only near the end of their college days and had no systematic training in dealing with it. In addition, he asserted that the inexactness of content and looseness of method in the course he had proposed provided an opportunity to the genuine teacher, who could lead the students to a recognition that their own thinking was "a poor, silly, inept semblance of activity." Students would, he said, be brought face to face with the fact that before the genuine human problems their information was scanty and inexact and their reasoning confused and inconsistent. The arguments failed to convince, for the course was soon abandoned.

The issues raised by Meiklejohn pointed to the most serious problem which the new course at Amherst or any other new courses which departed from accepted departmental boundaries were to encounter. Arbitrary though departmental divisions and subdivisions were, they were arbitrary to a purpose. The principles which might determine any new patterns of courses would be no less arbitrary, and it was necessary that their purpose should be as clearly defined and logically defensible as that of departmental offerings. It was all very well to speak of "survey" and "orientation" courses, but the meaning of these elastic terms was often far from clear. Criticisms of the new types of courses appeared almost as soon as the first models were constructed. Nor were the criticisms by any means restricted to unimaginative defenders of the departmental point of view. An unsigned article in the *New Republic* in 1921, entitled "The Survey Course in College," began with some observations about a book by Barrett

---

[7] Alexander Meiklejohn, "A Course for Freshmen," in *The Liberal College*, Marshall Jones, Boston, 1920, p. 13. The term "humanistic science" should not be overlooked.

Wendell entitled *The Traditions of European Literature from Homer
to Dante* and a reference to a course of the same name given by
Wendell, which the author took to be a prototype of the general
course coming into vogue.

> The *general course* in literature in the American college is a prod-
> uct of the elective system. The unanswerable argument for the
> introduction of that system was the necessity of opportunity for
> specialization. But as the demands of specialization became more
> exacting, its requirements reached farther and farther back into
> the field of *general education* and more and more of that area
> was restricted to its uses. To replace courses preempted by the
> specialist student, and to give that student a chance to secure a
> summary view of fields other than his own, the general survey
> course was invented, not only in literature, but in history and in
> social and natural science. These courses were intended as a cor-
> rective to the over-emphasis of specialization, the concentration
> upon the unimportant, the absorption in detail. But the evil is
> that the general student, exercising his right of private judgment
> along the path of least resistance, tends more and more to restrict
> himself to such surveys.[8]

The author assumed that survey courses in literature (such as Wendell's) talked about literature but did not demand that the students
actually read the sources. "In the study of literature the general student is invited to a bibliography of criticisms, and a summary already
made, and is too often discouraged if he dissents from the accepted
view." His doubts were not without foundation.

The article did, however, direct attention to another significant
truth. If the first experiments were sometimes superficial, a very considerable measure of responsibility rested upon the specialists who demanded more time for their specialties at the expense of a more general education. The general courses were quite truly, in part, the
product of overspecialization and the elective principle. If it could
justly be said that some of them attempted to do too much in too
brief a time, the brevity of time was not entirely the fault of the
planners. And in their defense it must be said that they helped to re-
open the issue of the unity of knowledge which freedom of election
and intensive specialization threatened to destroy.

[8] "The Survey Course in College," *New Republic*, vol. 28, Sept. 28, 1921, p. 120.
Italics mine.

The decade from 1920 to 1930 was one of the most important in the history of higher education in America. For the first time since Eliot marshaled the educational resources of the nation in support of the elective principle, an intensive and concerted effort was made to review the idea of liberal education and to take constructive measures for restoring to the curriculum an integrity and a breadth of learning which had long been absent. The principle of curricular flexibility was not under attack, but its abuses were. The experimental general courses were the significant first step in curricular reform. The charge of superficiality did not apply to all of them, nor were the adjectives "survey" and "orientation," which were the early generic terms most often applied, always an accurate description of their content and methods. Some of them gained wide recognition and have had an unbroken history, modified only by the dictates of experience, as for example Columbia University's Contemporary Civilization course (1919) and Reed College's Humanities course (1921). These and others, e.g., a general course in the natural sciences called "The Nature of the World and Man" at the University of Chicago (1924), were models which influenced practices in curricular reconstruction in other institutions.[9] Some of the courses were planned for non-specialists, others (like the course at Columbia) were intended to serve equally well both the specialist and the nonspecialist. Some were required, others elective. As a rule the early experiments were planned by small groups of interested faculty members independently of any comprehensive scheme of curricular reform. This was not true of the

[9] Columbia University introduced the course in Contemporary Civilization in 1919 as a required course for all freshmen. The course grew out of one which was a required part of the educational program authorized by the United States Army for the Student Army Training Corps, a unit of the army established in the nation's colleges in 1918. That course, entitled "War Aims," was intended to deal with specific problems centering around the causes of war and the purposes for which the war was being fought. Following the armistice, Columbia (and a few other colleges) retained the course for the students who were returned to civilian life, changing the theme to "Peace Aims." The following year it became a permanent part of the curriculum under its present title. The staff was drawn from members of the departments of economics, history, government, and philosophy. A distinctive feature of the course was that it was constructed about actual problems of contemporary society. Perhaps the Army's requirement of the course called "War Aims" has proved to be one of the most significant contributions which that organization has made to education.

Humanities course at Reed, which was a part of a large plan of administrative and curricular reorganization embracing the entire college program.

Immensely important as these first general courses were in marking a new stage in the development of ideas about general education, they gave only a partial answer to a larger problem which engaged wide attention. A few isolated courses, planned without reference to the rest of the curriculum and often simply additions to an already lengthy list of distributional electives, could not contribute much to the creation of a genuinely integrated curriculum. The search for principles that would provide both breadth and coherence to the total intellectual experience of every student was as energetically pursued during this decade as were the experiments in the construction of isolated general courses.

In 1922 President Meiklejohn published an article in the annual educational supplement of the *New Republic* entitled "The Unity of the Curriculum." [10] It was among the most provocative criticisms of college education to be published in this period. He began by saying that it is impossible to talk about the unity of the curriculum without talking about the unity of knowledge, and that hesitation to speak about the unity of knowledge is the most striking feature of current educational policy. It is generally agreed, he said, that the present educational system allows students to make an education out of a few disconnected fragments of knowledge. But how to produce a unified understanding of knowledge as a whole out of these fragments is the question which educators face and about which there is so much hesitation in providing an answer. One answer is a flat assertion that knowledge as a whole has no unity. *Knowing* is a number of separate investigations, and the chief aim of instruction is the command of a "subject." The advocates of this position acknowledge that any subject is related to others in a similar group, as biology is related to chemistry and as economics is related to politics, and that every subject must be studied in relation to its practical applications; but beyond this they admit of no unity of knowledge, since no man can comprehend relationships more complex than those required for the control of his chosen subject. Some of this group, impressed by the idea of "the well-rounded man," encourage the student to explore

[10] Alexander Meiklejohn, "The Unity of the Curriculum," *New Republic*, vol. 32, Oct. 25, 1922, pt. 2, pp. 2–3.

other fields, "a little music, a taste of philosophy, a glimpse into history, some practice in the technique of the laboratory, a thrill or two in the appreciation of poetry." This is a protection against one-sidedness, but, he declared, "through it all there runs the quality of the devil at church on Sunday resting from the labors of a busy week," and in this point of view there is no pervading unity.

He placed the responsibility for the origin and influence of this view on the natural sciences:

> First, it is chiefly Natural Science which is responsible for the opinion that knowledge has no unity. Second, it is chiefly that view which has brought our college teaching into incoherence and confusion. ... The Natural Sciences deal with a type of content which invites and makes possible the isolation of problems to a degree not achieved in other types of investigation. If he have proper regard for related subjects, the scientific student can define his task as a separate and distinct piece of work, can adjust his technique to the dealing with it and can then go serenely about his labor knowing that it, by itself, will lead him as far and farther than he can ever attain. Wars may come and go, kingdoms rise and fall, schools of poetry flourish and decay, fashions bloom and fade, and through them all the egg-secretions stand secure.[11]

The sort of intellectual anarchy which is cultivated when every man isolates his own subject and lives in complete detachment from others does not fit the actual situation in the world with which we deal. President Meiklejohn continued:

> Out of the purposes and acts of many men, society must make a plan, ... such common dominating scheme as can be made. But just at present common schemes of thought have broken down. The sciences are not explained, not understood. Rightly enough, they will not knuckle under to schemes of thought devised before their principles were known. Thought must be made anew to take them in and give them proper place. But when they stand upon the ruins of an older scheme which they have smashed, and cry

[11] Elsewhere in this article, President Meiklejohn remarked: "It seems probable that the most important fact connected with the development of the elective system in America is that Charles William Eliot was a chemist. So far as I know he is the greatest leader in collegiate policy that America has had. But the modes of thought of his powerful leadership were predominantly the mechaniforms of chemical analysis."

"Down with the State; we'll have no state at all!" they talk familiar nonsense. Because another scheme of thought has broken down, they think that schemes of thought are gone forever, that unity in knowledge is a myth.

The search for satisfactory principles to bring knowledge into some kind of unity is the insistent task of modern scholarship, "not saying in advance what will be found, but trying to find the forms of unity which must be there if we can think at all. And teaching, liberal teaching, is just the attempt to put our students at work upon that task."

The article examined some of the methods which have been employed in curricular organization and in teaching as means of attaining a better and larger view of the unity of knowledge. President Meiklejohn thought the preliminary survey course had real but slight value:

> In general the plan is that as he approaches a group of subjects, a student shall be given an outline account of these, their problems, their procedures, their relations to one another. This is a device of which the social sciences are fond. I have heard the teachers of these sciences discuss with much eagerness the question, "How can the social sciences be unified?" May I record the opinion that in themselves these studies have no dominating unity? To tell of their relations to one another is not to unify them, unless it means to tell their common dependence upon other studies outside the list. Logic and ethics have, I think, the principles of unity for all our social studies. And if we seek for unity without them, we get a list of separate things quite shorn of all the deeper meanings which they ought to have. And so against the survey course which lists, describes and classifies a group of studies, I would suggest the analytic course which finds a method of thought and gives a student practice in it.

What is so very important about this distinction is that it contrasted two fundamentally different principles for the organization of general courses, that it made the contrast at a very early period in the history of general courses, and finally that the distinctions which it drew have been so generally disregarded in the thirty-five and more years which have passed since it was written. The distinction is between the general course which stresses "subject matter" or content rather than "method" and the general course which is analytical and which makes "method" an indispensable part of the "subject matter" of the course. "An introductory course should lead a student not so much by content as by method, not so much by answer as by problem, not only by external list of separate studies, but also by the dialectic of a mode of thought which seeks and finds the content which it feeds upon."

Recommendations of a practical kind bring the article to a conclusion. Here the author proposed courses of two kinds, one for beginners in college work and one for seniors "to bring the studies all together at the end." If a choice must be made, the latter, he considered, was the more important. This must surely have been one of the earliest suggestions for a kind of course which has in very recent years been widely adopted, the senior symposium, which under a variety of titles, has sought to perform a terminal integrative function and is a late extension of the idea of general education. I might add that these courses appear to be, in some cases, secular versions of the senior course in moral philosophy which was a standard requirement in the classical curriculum.

Shortly before Meiklejohn's article appeared, Archibald MacLeish declared the failure of the colleges to formulate a common and acceptable definition of liberal education to be a reflection of the "intellectual anarchy" which characterized the whole of contemporary society. "There can be no educational postulates so long as there are no generally accepted postulates of life itself. And there has been no real agreement as to the purposes and values of life since the world gave over heaven a hundred years ago." [12]

The assent given to the elective system was an admission of the loss of any common educational principles. It was "a system under which each individual student was to supply his own definition of education and set out to save his soul under the uncritical eye of a faculty which was to offer only what was demanded of it. He was master of his fate, and the learned gentlemen behind the professorial desks were merely to supply wind to his sails, concerning themselves not at all with the perils of his course." Under these conditions, liberal education lost any coherent meaning. "Perhaps it is the latitude permitted by this scheme which makes it possible for most of the institutions of higher learning in America, whether they are converts to election or not, to

[12] Archibald MacLeish, "Professional Schools of Liberal Education," *The Yale Review*, 10 vols., 1920, pp. 362–372.

proclaim through their catalogues that they provide all the essentials for a liberal education. So long as the phrase goes undefined there is no danger in the assertion."

The failure of modern education is the fact that there is in it "no sanction in the common experience of men." Our society will not, of course, revert to the creeds of our fathers, but:

> There are many men who hesitate before the first and most essential act of faith—the admission, that is, that the physical world is not the image of their own dreams, but real and substantial and in itself worthwhile.... Heaven is no longer our business perhaps, but this world is. And vague phrases about training for citizenship will not serve. Citizenship, with its connotation of purely political functions, simply blurs the issue. Rather must the universities set before themselves the task of training men to feel themselves members of a race which, as a race, consciously in part, in part unconsciously, moves forward towards its final realization. They must postulate the regeneracy of the race, the hope of the race, God in us.

Given such a postulate, the emphasis in teaching would shift, no longer concerning itself with static, self-contained units, e.g., with the present state of the knowledge of man under the heading of chemistry, "as though that condition, taken by itself, apart from its past or its trend, were of significance."

> No matter what aspect of the history of the development of man were in issue, whether his language, or his philosophy, or his arts, or the conditions under which he labored at all these things, or the structures political and social which he erected, the vitally important question would not be, what had he in 1215, but rather, how came he to his great age of architecture, and what do these arches and towers signify? Education ... is not the raw appropriation of results as results, but rather the comprehension of results through their processes.

If the regeneracy of man were genuinely accepted as a postulate for education, then the universities and the professional schools could devote themselves to the education of men for their chosen professions, secure in the knowledge that whatever a man's chosen profession, his total education must embrace far more than the technology of his trade. "A comprehension of the efforts of mankind to conquer death is more than a knowledge of medicine. It involves an under-standing of cowardice and superstition, faith that endures immeasur-able disasters, curiosity that pries into and beyond the grave, pity that can never rest. . . ." MacLeish's thesis dissolved the usual distinctions between general and specialized education, since in the terms of his postulates there could be no useful specialized or professional educa-tion which did not bring the knowledge of the techniques of any pro-fession into a meaningful relationship with the complex and ever-changing pageant of the society of men.

MacLeish's passion was not typical, of course, of the prodigious body of literature which was devoted to finding some principle that could restore a standard of values by which to judge the process of education. Yet that literature was not wanting in energy, and the energy which was generated during this decade was the force which gave birth to what is currently called "the general education move-ment." In this decade of inquiry, the new general courses were no more than instruments that might possibly be useful in achieving the larger goal. They did not, at least in the minds of the more responsible educators, constitute in themselves a general education; but each such course was conceived as a part, quite as much as any specialized course was a part, of a larger whole. It is likely that a later preoccupation with general courses, under whatever name they came to be called, eventually diverted the thinking of contemporary educators from the larger problem. At any rate when colleges speak, as they do, of "hav-ing general education" and point to an "interdepartmental" course as the sole evidence (a course which may be an elective among a long list of electives), it is fair to ask whether they have really considered the fundamental conceptual problem which historically has always been at the heart of the meaning of general education.

By 1930 experiments in various types of general courses had be-come commonplace. An article in the *Journal of Higher Education* in 1931 listed fourteen colleges which had made trial of one or more "orientation courses," but it gave no details about the variety of the courses or their content.[13] The list was certainly not complete. It is difficult to obtain reliable data on the content of many of the early

[13] Kathryn McHale, "Changes in the Colleges," *Journal of Higher Education,* vol. 2, 1931, pp. 289–294. The colleges listed are Mills, Pembroke, Rockford, Vassar, Colgate, Columbia, Dartmouth, Wabash, Bates, Beloit, Carleton, De-Pauw, Ohio Wesleyan, and Reed.

experiments. Some of them were *orientations* to the problems of college, home, and community life.

The University of Utah offered a course on Family and Religion and another entitled "Orientation through Social Ethics." The latter course, an elective for freshmen, was apparently first offered in 1910. An idea of its organizing principles can be gained from an outline of the five problems used in 1930. These were (1) our social inheritance, (2) human rights in relation to natural resources, (3) human conservation (public welfare and education), (4) rights of private property, and (5) public property. The unifying principle of the course was stated to be the ethical foundation of private and public action in human relations. In 1930, 600 students were enrolled in ten sections.[14]

The Nature of the World and Man, offered at the University of Chicago from 1924 to 1930, was organized around the concept of evolution. It consisted in a sequence of topics which included: (1) the nature and properties of matter, (2) the character of chemical properties, (3) the origin of the earth, (4) the evolution of the plant and animal kingdoms, and (5) the evolution of man. The course was taught by a combination of lectures and discussions. For the purposes of discussion, the class was divided into sections of thirty students each. At first the course was limited to a small and select group of freshmen; later the enrollment increased to a maximum of 225, and sophomores were admitted. The course was at all times an elective.[15] Two other survey courses were planned at Chicago at this time, but neither was established because of lack of faculty support in the appropriate areas. They had tentatively been entitled "The Meaning and Value of the Arts" and "Man and Society."

Some of the proposals for curricular reorganization went far beyond the planning of a single course. Among them were outlines for administrative as well as curricular reorganization touching the entire structure of an institution. Others outlined a conceptual structure which would, so the authors hoped, give unity or a coherent purpose to instruction. One proposal, which was published in *School and Society* in 1915, was a very early statement of the theories underlying

[14] Milton Bennion, "Orientation through Social Ethics," *Journal of Higher Education*, vol. 2, 1931, pp. 254–258.

[15] H. H. Newman, "An Orientation Course," *Journal of Higher Education*, vol. 2, 1931, pp. 121–126.

the instrumentalist psychology.[16] The article addresses itself to the problems of the nonvocational college or, as the author put it, colleges that "are for general education." It makes the usual criticisms of the abuses of specialization, but it goes on to declare that even if there were a reasonable return to "the more general courses of instruction" in the subject matters which were the core of the curriculum in the nineteenth century, "these subjects alone would not provide a sufficiently broad outlook on life for the student of the twentieth century." The key to the author's theories is "Know thy environment"; thus the task of education is to organize and present knowledge (including traditional subject matters) so that it brings the student into a close relation with his environment or rather so that it acquires significance through the light it sheds on environment. Since our society is an industrial one, says the author, the general education for all must include a knowledge of those processes which function significantly in our industrial environment. Specifically, the desirable content of such an education includes physiology, psychology, the methods and principles of the natural sciences, ethics, the organization of human society, the history of the race (socially and politically), and comparative religion.

It was inevitable that someone should find in history both the content and the fundamental disciplines in terms of which a complete curriculum could be organized. One such proposal was published in the *North American Review* in 1919.[17] A new use of history was proposed, which should be "the backbone" of the curriculum and by which the various subject matters could be assimilated. The author asserted that his proposal was not one for the expansion of the history department. On the contrary, he said, that would kill it. "I would rather take this enormous subject out of the hands of one department, which has found it impossible to teach it as a whole, which has been driven to reduce it to practical dimensions by omitting most of it, and I would put it into the hands of large groups of men. . . . We might create a Faculty for the Study of Antiquity, comprehending all men teaching anything relating to ancient life. . . ." Similar faculties for the study of medieval and modern life would be created. The

---

[16] A. C. True, "The Relation of the College Curriculum to Human Life and Work," *School and Society*, vol. 1, June 19, 1915, pp. 865–869.

[17] Roland G. Usher, "The Fundamentals of an Education," *North American Review*, vol. 210, 1919, pp. 778–786.

author was not insistent that there should be any prescription of studies. "The student might be restricted or left free. He might be required to take three or four elementary general courses, covering the fundamental notions of each group, and then be required to do enough work in the various phases of some one group until he had a well rounded notion of its meaning." With a historical principle for the unification of knowledge, the author declared, learning would be best related to *life*.

The classification of departmental courses into groups of related fields was the basis of President Lowell's distributional scheme. The group plan contained the germ of divisional reorganization schemes of which the division of subject matters into four fields, the biological sciences, the physical sciences, the social sciences, and the humanities, has become the most familiar. Given such a scheme, it was a natural next step to organize general courses in each of these divisions. There has never been any uniformity in the allocation of subject matters or departments to particular divisions; various schematisms appeared fairly early in this era of reform.

In 1923 Robert Morris Ogden, Dean of the College of Arts and Sciences at Cornell University, described a plan for complete curricular reorganization which he hoped would restore "general training" to liberal education.[18] Without some such plan, he asserted, the college of arts and sciences would certainly be superseded by the practical and coherent programs of the vocational schools. He proposed the following divisions of knowledge: (1) mathematics, (2) experimental science, (3) language and literature, (4) history and the social studies, (5) philosophy. He did not claim that these divisions were mutually exclusive in every respect or that there might not be other useful groupings, but he claimed that "a fair representation of each of these five divisions is desirable in any institution that aims to afford a liberal education." In each division there should be required courses. The descriptions of the required courses are extremely interesting:

> I. Mathematics: "Something of the mathematical point of view is essential to a liberal interpretation of life and being. But our required course of mathematics is not an ordinary course in geometry, algebra, trigonometry, analytic geometry, and the calculus. Instead I would have a general course in higher mathematics designed to serve as an orientation in the foun-

[18] Robert Morris Ogden, "A Curriculum for the College of Arts," *Educational Review*, vol. 65, 1923, pp. 208–214.

dations of mathematical reasoning, in the philosophy of mathematics, and in the applications of mathematics to life and conduct."

II. Experimental science: "Two general courses would be required under this rubric: one a course in physical science and the other a course in biological science. Each would be in a sense a popular course, covering the broad fields indicated by the division made. But to prevent a smattering of information in these subjects, each course must be rigidly experimental in its conception, with demonstrations and laboratory exercises sufficient to furnish a true scientific orientation." Mathematics was assumed as a prerequisite to the science courses, and both courses would be prerequisite to further work in either area.

III. Language and literature: This would embrace English literature and foreign languages. English composition was the province of the high school. "A general course on the philosophy of the language and literature is advocated to serve as an orientation both in the forms of verbal expression and in types of composition."

IV. History and social sciences: History was the most important general requirement of the social sciences. "A prescribed course in history would, therefore, occupy two terms, and would be in the nature of a general orientation—an outline of history—in which the study of man and his achievements would be discussed, with emphasis placed upon the meaning of civilization, the problems of human society, the discoveries of man, systems of government, economic aspects, and the cultural refinements of human life." This course would be required of all students and would be a prerequisite to additional work in the social sciences.

V. Philosophy: A two-term course was recommended and would complement the course in general history.

The required courses in this program would cover one-half of the student's undergraduate program. The author proposed that the student devote half of his remaining time to courses within one of the five groups, which would be his major. The remainder of his program should be freely elective. An unusual feature of this proposal is that the number of courses taken in any given term in the last two years should be limited to three; the assumption was that more time spent on fewer courses would produce better results. Proposals so comprehensive as Dean Ogden's were rarely tested. They cannot be disregarded, however, since they are unimpeachable evidence of the direction of educational thinking.

Two reforms, one undertaken at the beginning and the other at the close of this remarkable decade, deserve to be considered in some detail. In both instances a reorganization of the administrative structure of the faculty was made in order to secure a more effective operation of important curricular changes. The first was at Reed College in 1921 under the leadership of President Scholz. The second was at the University of Chicago in 1930-1931 under President Robert Maynard Hutchins.[19]

The principal administrative change at Reed was the replacing of a conventional departmental organization of the faculty with a divisional organization. The new divisions were (1) literature and language, (2) history and social sciences, (3) mathematics and natural sciences, and (4) philosophy, psychology, and education. The new curriculum imposed requirements in each of these divisions. The catalogue which announced these changes stated:

> The course of study for the first two years covers the general field of the evolution of man in nature and society. It aims to lay the foundation of a well-rounded liberal education and to provide for the orientation which will assist the student to an intelligent and wise choice of a major interest to be pursued intensively during the last two years of the college course. The elective principle is preserved, but it is made to subserve the synthetic idea of an inter-related and integrated curriculum.[20]

By the end of the second year, each student was expected to choose his major field of interest. The divisional or group structure of the curriculum permitted the student to choose his major field within the broad context of a division, subject to faculty guidance. In 1924 the curriculum for the first two years was organized around two courses

[19] For details of the reforms at Reed, see R. F. Arragon, "The Development of the Reed Curriculum," *Reed College Bulletin,* vol. 24, November, 1945. An account of the administrative and curricular reorganization at Chicago is given by Chauncey S. Boucher, *The Chicago College Plan,* University of Chicago Press, Chicago, 1935. An account of the historical background of this plan and subsequent modifications of it up to 1920 is given by Reuben Frodin in *The Idea and Practice of General Education,* University of Chicago Press, Chicago, 1951, chap. 2, pp. 25-99.

[20] Arragon, *op. cit.,* p. 4.

of study, (1) Letters—Social Science and (2) Mathematics—Natural Science. The theme for the first year was man's social and biological heritage and for the second year, contemporary civilization. The content for the two courses was stated in the catalogue for that year as follows:

LETTERS—SOCIAL SCIENCE GROUP	MATHEMATICS—NATURAL SCIENCE GROUP

FRESHMEN

History and Literature (To *c.* 1763) Including a supplementary section in	History and Literature (To *c.* 1763) Including a supplementary section in
A. Political, Economic, or Social Institutions, *or*	A. Political, Economic, or Social Institutions, *or*
B. History of Art or Music, *or*	B. French or German, *or*
C. History of Philosophic and Scientific Thought	C. History of Philosophic and Scientific Thought
Biology Including Human Evolution	Biology, *or* Chemistry, *or* Physics
Mathematics	Mathematics
Elective	Elective
A. Independent study under direction of instructors (reading or laboratory work), *or*	Independent study under direction of instructors (reading or laboratory work)
B. Foreign Language	

SOPHOMORES

Social Science Principles of Economics, *or* Comparative Government, *or* Social Theory and Institutions, *and*	Natural Science Biology, *or* Chemistry, *or* Physics
Literature	Mathematics, *or* Physical Measurements, *or* Auxiliary Natural Science, *or*
History (1763 to date)	
Elective	General Psychology
A. Additional Social Science	Social Science
B. Language, Ancient or Modern	Principles of Economics, *or* Comparative Government, *or* Social Theory and Institutions
C. History of Art or Music	
D. Chemistry, *or* Physics, *or* General Psychology	History (1763 to date), *or* Literature
E. Statistical Methods	Elective (at the suggestion of major professors, to meet individual needs)
F. Additional History	

As the program was originally planned, students were required to take in their junior year a course in the history and government of the United States, and in their senior year "a critical and summary course in Philosophy." The American history course was not successful and was dropped in 1924, but the senior Colloquium in Philosophy has had a happier and longer life. Since this was one of the earliest experiments with a senior integrative course, the description of its objectives taken from an early catalogue is historically noteworthy. Its aims were:

> ... first, to clarify the student's ideas concerning the nature of experience and knowledge and the concept of the universe, this to proceed from a synthesis of the various interpretations of contemporary society (historical, literary, biological, etc.) with which he has come in contact during the College course; second, to incite the student at least to face the question of his own "philosophy of life," involving, as this does, the persistent problem of right conduct and the values of life.[21]

As one studies the principles which underlie these courses of study for the first two years, one is reminded of the Amherst curriculum of 1827, since they are an application of similar principles of curricular organization, adapted to the social changes which 100 years had produced.[22] In general the courses seem to have been more conventional than many of the orientation courses introduced at this time. Orientation was apparently sought by means of a better balance of subject matters and closer articulation of courses rather than by means of the newer types of survey courses.

Because Reed was a small liberal arts college, many of its problems differed from those of an institution such as the University of Chicago. Although Chicago was founded as a university, President Harper's design included a strong undergraduate college. It will be recalled that he had firm ideas about the dual functions of a college. Consequently when the university opened its doors in 1892 the undergraduate division was divided into a Junior and a Senior College. The curriculum of the Junior College was, at first, largely required of all

[21] *Ibid.*, p. 9.
[22] Since Reed College is one of those whose current curriculum will be studied in chap. 6 of this book there will be occasion to consider some of the modifications of this early attempt to achieve a reasonable balance of the elective principle and a common core of subject matters and disciplines.

students, while that of the Senior College was determined by the students' special interests. The task of the Junior College was the continuation of the general education begun in the schools, while the work of the Senior College was regarded as the beginning of university studies. After President Harper's death, the distinction between the Junior and Senior Colleges, though formally retained, lost much of its original functional character, as specialized studies gradually crept into the curricular privileges of the Junior College. The quality of instruction, too, was subjected to severe criticisms as increasing numbers of graduate students were assigned to teach Junior College courses.

Following the appointment of Ernest DeWitt Burton as President in 1923, there was a renewed interest in undergraduate education, particularly in the improvement of the work of the Junior College. Under President Burton's guidance and later during the administration of President Max Mason, the faculty took the initial steps in planning the changes that were finally approved in 1930–1931. A faculty committee was appointed by President Burton to survey the educational needs of the university and to make recommendations for the reorganization of undergraduate education. The first experiment with a survey course for freshmen was undertaken, and the first of many far-reaching proposals for reform was tentatively drafted.[23] When President Hutchins took office in 1929, he gave enthusiastic support to the work which had been begun under Presidents Burton and Mason and urged the faculty to complete its plans for reorganization as rapidly as possible.

The administrative structure of the University of Chicago in 1929 was no less complex than that of most American universities, and in some respects it seems to have been more so. The heart of the undergraduate program was centered in The Colleges of Arts, Literature, and Science. Graduate and professional study was continued in nine different schools.[24] The plan adopted by the faculty in 1930 created

[23] The first suggestion that the Bachelor of Arts degree might appropriately be awarded after the completion of the Junior College was made by the committee appointed by President Burton. It anticipated by more than fifteen years the actual decision of the faculty in 1942 to award the Bachelor of Arts degree upon completion of the program of general education given by the college. The action of 1942 was revoked by faculty action in 1954.

[24] The Colleges of Arts, Literature, and Science was administratively a single unit, under one dean, despite the curious use of the plural "Colleges" in the

five divisions: (1) The college, the lower division whose primary responsibility was the general education of the students, (2) the division of the biological sciences, (3) the division of the physical sciences, (4) the division of the social sciences, and (5) the division of the humanities. Each of the five divisions was a ruling body with a faculty, a dean, and a budget. The School of Education became the department of education within the division of the social sciences, and the Medical School became a part of the division of the biological sciences. Other professional schools were not directly affected by the changes. The College of the University of Chicago henceforth signified that branch of the University specifically charged with the administration of and instruction in general education. At first the faculty of the college was drawn from the faculties of the four upper divisions, but in 1932 the dean of the college was empowered to make appointments to the faculty of the college without joint departmental or divisional affiliation. The upper divisions, through their several departments, assumed full responsibility for the curriculum and instruction in the last two undergraduate years; and since the departmental faculties were in fact graduate faculties, the effect, deliberately planned, was to integrate the last two undergraduate years with the graduate years. The divisions of biological science, physical science, social science, and humanities replaced the Graduate School of Arts and Literature and the Graduate School of Science. Until 1942 the bachelor's degrees continued to be awarded after the completion of the requirements of the new college plus two years of divisional work.

The administrative reorganization of the University of Chicago in 1930–1931 was the first instance in which an American university separated, in a legal sense, the officers of instruction responsible for general education from those responsible for education in specialized fields. The separation formally recognized and gave a form of legal sanction to an idea that had been widely accepted in principle since the middle of the nineteenth century, namely, that *general education should, by virtue of its unique function, be prior to and a preparation for specialized education.* By the same action it gave formal support

---

title. Each area of study (arts, literature, and science) constituted a "college" in the sense that there were three courses of study leading to three degrees, A.B., Ph.B., and S.B., respectively. In addition, each of these areas retained in theory at least the distinction between the Junior and Senior Colleges. Students who completed the Junior College were granted a certificate of Associate in Arts.

to the idea that the last two years of the traditional American college were properly within the sphere of university rather than collegiate studies. The curricular revisions at Reed were based on the principle that the first two years of collegiate work should be devoted to general education and the last two years to specialized education, but the administrative reorganization did not separate the faculty into an upper and lower divisional faculty. Such a division would have been impracticable in an institution the size of Reed. In a large university such as Chicago, however, the formal separation made possible the creation of a faculty which could give all or most of its energy to the problems of general education without impairing the activities of the departments. In an institution so greatly committed to graduate and professional education as is Chicago, it is probable that the formal separation of the general and the specialized functions was the best means of encouraging a professional interest in the means and ends of general education.

The policy of giving over all or part of the first two years of college to general education became the norm for most institutions which instituted general education programs in the years immediately following. The policy had considerable appeal to many junior colleges, which were entering upon a period of extraordinary growth. The pattern has, however, been challenged in recent years by a principle which holds that general and specialized education should run concurrently throughout the four collegiate years. This principle was given substantial support by the plan for general education adopted by the Harvard faculty in 1945.

The administrative reorganization at Chicago was, of course, accompanied by radical curricular revisions. The most significant was the provision that completion of the program of the college should be measured by the passing of seven comprehensive examinations, five of which were required of all students and which might be taken by a student whenever he was prepared to take them. Courses were planned to aid the student in his preparation for the examinations, but a student was privileged to take an examination at any scheduled examination period without taking the corresponding course. For the administration of the examination system, a board of examinations was created, consisting of members of the faculty, and a university examiner was appointed whose staff was responsible for the preparation of the examinations. Intellectual achievement independently measured rather than course credits was to be the criterion of academic progress.

The five examinations which all students were required to pass were English composition, humanities, social science, physical science, and biological science. In addition to these requirements, one year of foreign language was required, but this might be satisfied, and usually was, by submitting evidence of two units of a language taken in high school. To secure added depth of experience, students were required to pass an additional examination in any two of the four general areas. Thus a student might elect to take a second one-year course in biology in preparation for a second comprehensive examination in that field, and a three-quarter sequence in English poetry, drama, and fiction or a sequence in art history as preparation for a second examination in the area of humanities. Since the normal program for the college was four courses a year, and the comprehensive examinations a student must pass numbered seven, one-eighth of the time allotted to the college (i.e., the equivalent of three 1-quarter courses) was available for unrestricted electives.

The introductory courses in biological science, in physical science, in social science, and in humanities, each one-year courses and popularly called "survey courses," were the result of a year's work in planning by senior members of the faculty in each area. At first the instruction in each course was conducted primarily by lectures supplemented by one discussion period each week. The discussion sections were limited to about twenty-five students and were conducted by both senior and junior members of each staff. Weekly meetings of the staff prepared the members for the common enterprise of the week. In the natural science courses there was no laboratory work, but there were regular lecture-demonstrations. As the staffs of each course gained experience there was a reduction of the number of lecture hours and an increase of the discussion hours. Class attendance was not required, but frequent quizzes and end-of-quarter examinations, which were diagnostic and served an advisory function, helped prepare the students for the final comprehensive examinations given at the end of the academic year. There was no absolute rule fixing the order in which the introductory general courses must be taken; most students elected to take two of the survey courses in the first year and two in the second, filling in the remaining time in preparation for the English and foreign language requirements and second-year sequence examinations.

The revolutionary changes at Reed and Chicago, more comprehensive in scope than most of the experiments undertaken in this important decade of the twenties, undoubtedly had considerable influence upon the thought and practices of many other colleges and universities. Yet on the whole they proved to be more important as signs of the nationwide interest in the correction of the abuses of the elective system and the dangers of overspecialization than as models of administrative and curricular organization useful to other institutions. Within a few years after the University of Chicago had completed its reorganization there were a number of other equally bold and unorthodox educational reforms aimed at the same general goals, for example, the development of the General College at the University of Minnesota and the total reorganization of St. John's College which accompanied the introduction of its program of liberal education. At the same time reforms were occurring more gradually in many other institutions. At Columbia, for example, the Contemporary Civilization course expanded into a two-year course, an introductory general science course as an alternative to optional departmental courses was organized though never offered, and in the mid-thirties the first course in humanities was opened, to which a second year was soon added. By 1940 much of the first two years of work in Columbia College was devoted to fulfilling general requirements.

Yet when one compares even these few examples, the most striking fact is the great diversity in the content of these programs, their methods of instruction, and the administrative measures adopted to facilitate their operation. The idea that a liberally educated man or woman should possess considerable breadth of intellectual experience was a premise common to all these experiments. It was easy to state in general terms what that breadth should consist of. But attempts to particularize upon the specific content which should form the broad experience were less successful, and ideas about the best methods of instruction differed greatly. The emphasis on the "survey" or "orientation course" tended to make many of the early experiments descriptive and informational in substance. To this extent they were often open to the charge of superficiality. But the business of defining principles to guide the organization of knowledge in new terms and for purposes different from those which determined the content of departmental courses was no easy task and necessarily proceeded slowly and painfully. Nevertheless the conviction that the task was of paramount importance to the future of education increased. One significant sign of rising interest was the devotion of the entire proceedings of The Institute for Administrative Officers of Higher Education in 1934 to the subject of general education.[25] This was probably the first major educational conference to take this topic for its central theme.

It was also the occasion of a remarkable speech by Henry M. Wriston, then President of Lawrence College and later President of Brown University. Concerning the meaning of "general education," he asserted that it identifies a *quality* inherent in education and that it cannot be expressed by any measure either of time or of quantity. "Whatever measures in either one of those two respects we may adopt are arbitrary; they are dictated by prejudice, or interest, or finance, or some other practical consideration. Whatever their character, they are essentially irrelevant to the basic concept of general education." [26]

The quality which we seek to identify by the term is *universal validity*, "an education useful to all who possess it, at all times, and under all circumstances." There must be common elements which are so vital in character and so unchallengeable in validity that everyone should have the opportunity for general education. Those who have such an education are equipped for living in a sense in which they would not be equipped without it. The values of such an education must have permanence. Permanence means continuing value but does not mean fixation, which is the antithesis of education.

> If general education must be something which gives the mind freedom, whence arises its quality of permanence? This characteristic cannot be said to be inherent in the *facts* which constitute the body of instruction, for the facts themselves, except in an extraordinarily limited field, and upon a very elementary level, are not themselves stable. Whether there be place names

[25] *General Education: Its Nature, Scope, and Essential Elements, Proceedings of the Institute for Administrative Officers of Higher Institutions*, vol. 6, University of Chicago Press, Chicago, 1934.

[26] Henry M. Wriston, "Nature, Scope, and Essential Elements in General Education," in *ibid.*, pp. 1–16.

in geography, or theories of the atom, or historical movements toward successive frontiers, or the growth of political parties, or even good usage in English, verily they shall pass away. The man with flawless memory who learned the theory of the atom thirty years ago would today be ranked as ignorant rather than educated.... *The quality of permanence which we seek, therefore, must lie beneath and behind these manifestations. I suggest that the essence of permanence must be found in disciplines.*[27]

The values expressed in the concept "general" should be not only universal and permanent but should be dynamic. To those who claim that the end of general education is the adjustment of the individual to society, Wriston answered that this view lacks dynamic quality. Too often adjustment has meant placement, a form of fixation. "We should be interested not so much in adjustment as in capacity for continuous readjustment and vigorous adaptation." Knowledge of environment is inadequate for the reason that environment changes. *"Ever since the overthrow of the formal discipline concept we have suffered for want of a generally accepted organized concept which might give a dynamic quality to general education."*

Conceding that the term "discipline" had for years been a football in educational discussion, Wriston defined it as "the essential mode of thought in a field of study, the inherently characteristic mental method of attacking that kind of problem." Each discipline is "a type or category of intellectual experience involved in a successful or fruitful approach to a problem of knowledge." His exposition listed four basic disciplines: (1) the discipline of precision, (2) the discipline of appreciation, (3) the discipline of hypothesis, and (4) the discipline of reflective synthesis.

The discipline of precision is the most elementary of basic disciplines. It lies at the root of mathematics and fields in which approximations are worthless. The natural sciences, grammar and vocabulary (to the extent that precision rather than approximation in meaning is essential), and history demand the discipline of precision. Of history, Wriston said: "If the substitution of approximation [in the order of events] for precision ... puts the effect before the cause, there is no history."

The discipline of appreciation is the "assertion of the validity of emotional experience as worthy of recognition on a parity with the

---

[27] *Ibid.,* pp. 1–2. Italics mine.

intellectual life. It is founded upon the fact that emotion has the quality of cultivability." It is, however, the least understood of the disciplines. Its province is, of course, art, poetry, and music. For those who have not cultivated appreciation, he asserted, the arts do not exist.

The discipline of hypothesis might be called the "discipline of opinionation." It is "the construction of coherent patterns of thought from available data." It is the most difficult of the disciplinary concepts, because the patterns of thought which are constructed by its application are not demonstrably true. Yet this discipline has, as one of its major functions, "to awaken the students to a recognition of not only the necessity but the genuine validity of tentative conclusions. The discipline of precision shows the relatively limited range of the absolutes. The discipline of opinionation exposes the enormously wide expanse of the relative." It is fundamental to the natural sciences as well as to the social sciences. It has been more readily acceptable to the so-called "exact sciences" than to the social sciences, where there is a tendency to insist that one form of political or economic organization is right and all others are wrong. Yet nowhere is the need for the exercise of this discipline greater than in the social sciences.

The discipline of reflective synthesis is the highest of all disciplines essential to a general education.

> It looks to the validity of the intellectual experience itself. It has in common with the discipline of opinionation the creation of patterns and hypotheses. Its distinguishing difference is that the data have to do not so much with observed phenomena of an objective, tangible, and external character as with ideas and concepts themselves. It is the synthesis, if one may so speak, of all the patterns built up through opinionation. It is the effort to give reality not merely to observation but to experience itself.[28]

The summary of President Wriston's address is a fitting conclusion to this account of the historical background to contemporary thought and practice in the field of general education. If by 1934 renewed interest in general education was sufficiently widespread to warrant a conference of national scope to consider its problems, there was none the less need for such an address if the experiments were to be rescued from superficiality and a too great emphasis upon

[28] *Ibid.,* p. 14.

factual information. Categorical divisions of subjects were rather clearly established. But there was still need for much reflection upon the functions which each division should serve in a general education. By defining the content of general education in terms of kinds of problems and the types of disciplines necessary for their solution, President Wriston offered a direction to thought which could aid in removing many of the ambiguities which result when content is considered quite simply in terms of "subject." In this respect, his observations were an extension of ideas which had already been touched upon though less systematically by President Lowell, President Meiklejohn, and Archibald MacLeish. For the next quarter of a century there would be no more important problem for general education than that which was the central problem of President Wriston's address.

Part 2

Contemporary Problems
of General Education:
A Study of Ends and Means

Chapter 5

Content and Organization:
Some Theoretical Distinctions

Since 1935 the history of the general education movement has largely been a record of the adoption by a steadily increasing number of colleges of ideas and practices which had already been tried experimentally and the refinement and improvement of practices through continuous experiment. To complete the record we must take note of the abandonment of some experimental projects after admitted failures to achieve the success which faculties and administrations had anticipated.

The numerous problems which have marked the course of the expanding movement can be divided, for analytical purposes, into two kinds: (1) problems of theory, that is to say, those which arise in any attempt to define the ends and means of general education; and (2) parochial problems—those which are created by the necessities of adjusting a program of general studies to the entire and often complex academic program of any individual institution. The fundamental differences among the programs of the General College of the University of Minnesota, St. John's College, and the University College of Michigan State University are differences in the solutions of a problem of educational theory.[1] There are no doubt many details

[1] These three programs, which will figure prominently in this study, are among the older of modern general programs, dating from 1932, 1937, and 1944, respectively. I have stated in the Introduction that St. John's does not use the term "general education" in official documents, preferring instead the term "liberal education" to designate the content and ends of its curriculum. I am claiming the sanction of history, however, in placing it among the contemporary experiments in general education. The most energetic defenders of the traditional ideal of liberal education throughout the nineteenth century argued for its superiority over the newer concepts of liberal education precisely because the traditional ideal was a more general education.

of each program which are consequences of local and accidental circumstances. In every institution, educational theories suffer modification from such factors as the lack of the right personnel to do a particular job, lack of financial resources, conflicting interests of different administrative units, the size of the faculty and the student body. In the analysis of contemporary programs of general education, it is important to consider the details in relation to both theoretical and accidental determinants.

If one asks how much actual change the interest in general education has wrought upon the practices of colleges and universities since 1935, the answer must be that the degree of change has been by no means uniform. In some colleges, changes have been slight; in others, changes have been very great. Although talk about general education has exceeded performance, there is no doubt that the total effect has been very considerable indeed. There have been numerous subtle changes which have affected institutions that still disclaim any interest in "the general education movement."

It is well to bear in mind the point of departure for most of the changes in the last thirty years. By 1935 the majority of American colleges had adopted some form of the system of distribution and concentration. It will be recalled that the distributional plan was initially introduced to ensure a better general education. Most of the curricular reforms subsequently associated with the general education movement were directed toward the improvement of the distributional principle. The reforms sought to achieve this in part by reducing to some extent the time allowed for concentration and, more importantly, by improving (so it was hoped) the means of employing the distributional principle. With almost no exceptions (St. John's is the most notable) the colleges continued the principle of concentration with minor modifications, while they attacked what seemed to be the major defects in the actual operation of the distributional principle.

Two assumptions were implicit in the distributional plan as it was conceived by President Lowell: first, that the numerous departmentalized subject matters which formed the college curriculum could be classified by groups, the subjects which formed each group being related by common principles and methods of inquiry; and second, that the principles and methods of each group were of sufficient importance to warrant their study as a part of each student's degree program. Some of the problems in the operation of the plan derived from the first of these assumptions. First of all, the principles in terms of which subjects could be grouped had to be determined. Although the group plan was widely adopted, there was not and never has been any uniform principle of classification of departmental subject matters. Furthermore, although President Lowell had suggested the possibility of a general but nonintroductory course in each *group* of subjects, the idea was not immediately adopted. Instead, a further assumption was often made, namely, that the study of any one or two courses in a group was an adequate introduction to the principles and methods of the whole group. Criticisms of this assumption, supported by the evidence gathered from actual operations of the plan, were the immediate forerunner and cause of the first experiments with *general courses*. Because the introduction of these courses was an occasion of great significance in the history of general education, it is important to remember that their use was not a rejection of the distributional principle but rather an attempt to make the principle more effective.[2]

The general courses were devised to eliminate the defects in the

[2] I have used the term "general course" throughout this section to designate the new types of courses whose subject matter is more inclusive than that usually contained within any one of the courses of a single department. It seems to me to be the least invidious of the many collective terms which have been employed for this purpose. I use it, however, with the understanding that it is a relative term, dictated by convention and convenience. Only the fact that the normative terms for designating courses derive from the departmental divisions of knowledge accounts for its usage. The history of changing usage of other collective terms for these courses sheds a few rays of light on shifting concepts of their structure and purposes. The earliest terms, "orientation" and "survey," suggested a synoptic view, informative in character, of the subject matter of the departments within any group. The term "survey" suggested superficiality. Later the term "integration course" was used to signify an emphasis upon principles and methods thought to be common to a group of subjects. The motive was laudable, but the results were not always so. Other terms, long familiar, are "interdepartmental" and "interdisciplinary." The first betrays the force of habit which holds the departmental division of knowledge to be a necessary rather than an arbitrary principle. The latter term has often been used as a synonym for interdepartmental, albeit more erudite, on the assumption that each department represents a unique discipline. The assumption is misleading, since there is no department which does not engage students in the exercise of several disciplines. It can be safely argued that a single course in English literature will require the exercise of historical disciplines, aesthetic disciplines, and of course linguistic disciplines. The least defensible of terms

distributional plan, but the construction of these courses introduced many new and serious problems. Since these problems are still stumbling blocks upon which many a projected general course or program falls, they require thoughtful consideration. So long as students were allowed, under the distributional plan, to choose one of several courses within a group of studies, the principles by which each division or group of studies was formed did not become a serious source of trouble. But as soon as a faculty was faced with the task of constructing general courses which undertook to secure an effective relationship of the disciplines of the sciences or the humanities, the principles which determined the allocation of departmental subject matters to any group could not be ignored. It did make a difference whether philsosphy and history were regarded as social sciences or as humanistic studies. The task was often complicated by the temporal limitations imposed upon a course. The fact that most of the faculty members engaged in constructing new courses were products of the rigid departmentalism of the graduate schools often hampered their ability to see the full scope of their problem.[3] Yet these were problems which had to be solved if the concept of the general course was to be proved valid and useful in a planned program of general education.

The historical significance of the general courses, which have become almost the trademark of the contemporary phase of the history of general education, does not lie merely in the quality of the courses themselves. As one might expect, the quality has been uneven. Much more important is the fact that they signified a reversal in the trend of educational thought which had dominated curricular organization for nearly a century, specifically the division of knowledge into an ever-increasing number of departmental units. The departmental fragmentation of knowledge has not been halted nor can it be; but the more successful experiments with general courses have demonstrated

---

that has gained some prominence in recent years is "courses in general education," since it implies that general education is a discrete subject matter.

[3] There is no doubt that many of the early general courses were "general" in name only. They achieved no unity of their own when they merely strung together a series of highly abridged departmental units, and they frequently did the subject matter of these departments a disservice through their oversimplification of the materials with which they dealt.

that educators can also think in terms of the relationship of subject matters which have long been studied in isolation from one another. This may be the most important contribution which the contemporary interest in general education has achieved.[4]

Preoccupation with the development of general courses had some unfortunate consequences. The chief of these was a tendency to mistake the means for the end. It is an unhappy fact that many colleges even today apparently believe that they have introduced general education into their curriculum simply by introducing a single general course. The practice, which some colleges have adopted, of setting general courses apart from other basic requirements by designating only the general courses as "courses in general education" has distorted the true meaning of general education; it can never be defined in terms of any one type of course. General courses have proved to be, at best, a means to a larger end, and that end is still the one which Lowell had hoped to achieve through the distributional system and which other educators (e.g., Dewey, Harper, Meiklejohn, Ogden, and Wriston) had in mind when they proposed means of bringing various kinds of knowledge into an integrated experience for every student.

The one activity which, more than any other, stands out as the most significant enterprise in the recent history of general education is the planning of coordinated general programs that are statements of a desired common intellectual experience and are based on philosophical principles which define the integrity of the desired experience. Probably never before in the entire history of higher education in America has there been so much concerted interest among the colleges in self-appraisal. Some colleges which have rejected the *name* of general education have none the less sought to restore something of the ancient ideal of liberal education. The fact is that they have been

---

[4] It is no exaggeration of the truth to say that the experience gained in the planning of general courses for general education programs has materially influenced curricular revision in the areas of concentration. The *departmental major* no longer holds the absolute dominion it once had. Witness the number of area-study courses, interdepartmental and divisional majors, and degree programs in "general studies." Some of the more recent "departments" are actually the result of a merging of subject matters previously separated into two or more departments, as for example, the departments or committees of American studies.

striving toward the same end that has always been the ultimate goal of general education.[5]

Three distinct aspects of these programs must be examined:

1. The educational principles which have been invoked in determining the content and aims of the programs
2. The administrative structures designed to make the operation of the programs effective
3. The pedagogical methods adopted for the better implementation of the programs

It is only for analytical purposes, of course, that these factors can be separated. In practice they are inseparably bound. The *characteristics* of any principles, administrative structures, or pedagogical devices can easily be determined. *Why* they have been adopted is much more difficult to determine. Principles are as often the consequence of the overriding influence of an administrative structure as administrative structure is the consequence of educational theory. Instructional methods may impede the operation of a program just as they may contribute to its success. The countless variables which arise from the parochial characteristics of an institution are major determinants of the ways in which these factors are related to one another in the development of a program.

Regardless of the effects of these variables, the nature of the principles which define the scope and purpose of a general program is the first and most important consideration in appraising the meanings which have accrued to the term "general education." It is a matter of principle when one institution declares that a required part of every student's education must include study that will lead to an insight into the nature and forms of mathematical thinking (abstraction, symbolic expression, and the structure of mathematical systems) and into the uses of mathematics in the statement, organization, and communication of ideas. All questions of how this experience can be worked into a crowded academic program are subordinate to the question of why it is an essential experience. On the other hand, the absence of requirements for any mathematical knowledge beyond the minimum prescribed for entrance to college is also a tacit statement of principle. Even if the answer to queries about the omission

[5] See Table VI in the Appendix for a list of some of the self-study reports which are products of this activity.

is simply that there is not time for any additional mathematics, the answer implies that in a hierarchy of values a more mature mathematical knowledge is relatively low. Principles as divergent as these (and they are not hypothetical) must be examined and debated.

It is altogether too complex a problem for this study to examine the variety of principles which have determined curricular policy with respect to the place of foreign languages in a general education. Many liberal arts colleges impose some requirement, though there is nothing approaching uniformity with respect to either admission or graduation. Most undergraduate professional and vocational schools have no foreign language requirement of any kind.[6]

Analysis of principles, however, reaches much further than questions about the presence or absence of any single subject matter in a general curriculum. The most important questions of principle concern the organization of a program. For illustration let us take three examples (somewhat but not altogether hypothetical). One college may state that all knowledge is essentially *one*, and that the goal of general education is to grasp the unity of knowledge. A general education is an education which discloses to the student *the great ideas of mankind* (which is really the sum of man's knowledge) as they are represented in the monumental works men have produced. Formalistic distinctions among these works are less important than an understanding of the particular truths which each author was seeking. Human institutions, science, and human arts have been shaped by these ideas, and the best approach to institutional and cultural development proceeds from a study of ideas found in great books. The techniques of the laboratory and the disciplines of mathematical and linguistic systems are important as instruments of learning and communication by which these ideas are understood.

---

[6] The place of foreign language in general education is one of the most disputed of current issues. In my opinion it is an important element; but neither the schools nor the colleges have reached any agreement, nor have they been able to give a convincing argument in defense of the one or two years that they most often consider sufficient for a general requirement. There have been a few signs of genuine concern about present conditions of language instruction in the secondary schools and even a few efforts to begin instruction in the lower grades. Dr. Conant's discussion of the issue and his recommendations are both interesting and pertinent. See James Bryant Conant, *The American High School Today*, McGraw-Hill Book Company, Inc., New York, 1959, pp. 69–73.

Another college may assert that knowledge proceeds by statements, and that the statements differ in terms of the kinds of problems to which they are addressed. From this principle, the college proceeds to an organization which recognizes three kinds of statements and problems: one kind which relates to the solutions of problems that explain the operations of natural phenomena, one which concerns problems related to the organization of society and to social action, and one which addresses itself to problems of the appreciation of the products of the arts. From this come familiar classifications of knowledge, the natural sciences, the social sciences, and the humanities. The key to such an organization is the concept of *problems*.

A third college may begin with the proposition that knowledge is meaningful only to the extent that it functions in the daily activities of men. The effective organization of knowledge depends therefore upon first determining kinds of life activities which constitute our common human experience. The subject matter of a general education can then be defined and organized in terms of its utility in any of these activities. The home and the family might be the theme of one such sphere of activity, and around it might be grouped courses in household economy, child psychology, the chemistry of foods, and interior decoration. The natural and social sciences and the arts are thus drawn into the curriculum in ways that are relevant to the functional purposes of the unit. The arts and sciences may also have a place in other units, but the content will always be adapted to their functional ends.

A superficial reading of curriculums based on these and other organizing principles may lead one to the conclusion that there is very little difference in their actual content. A more careful study usually reveals that there are very great differences. For example, it is a fact that the reading lists of many courses, designed to introduce the student to the great literary achievements of Western man, differ in no important respect. But it is also a fact that the points of view, i.e., the organic structure of the courses, often differ radically for reasons which are implicit in the principles which define the purposes of the entire program.

There is another difference in the structure of general education programs which derives from basic principles. Since in most colleges what is described as the general education program constitutes only a part of the total undergraduate program (rarely more than half), there is the necessary problem of articulating the curriculum of the general education program and that of the numerous areas of concentration. On the assumption that a good general education is the best preparation for a wise choice of a field of concentration and probably on assumptions borrowed from the German distinctions between the functions of the *Gymnasium* and the university, nearly all the early experiments with general programs were restricted to the work of the first two years of undergraduate studies. In most institutions this practice still holds true. In recent years, however, another view has gained in favor. This view begins with the conception that general education is a continuing process throughout life and that collegiate studies may contribute to but never complete a general education. Accordingly, the student's program of general studies should be carried on simultaneously with his specialized studies throughout the collegiate program. Though in practice the greater part of the first two years may be devoted to the general aspects of a student's education, at least some part of every year is specifically reserved for general studies. In theory at least, the principle provides for an increasingly mature level of general studies in the later years. One specific by-product of this principle has been the very considerable increase in recent years in the number of "senior symposiums."

These two principles of curricular organization touch very closely upon concepts about the proper structure of the American college; the first tends to separate more or less decisively two educational functions, and the other, though acknowledging their existence, treats them as complementary and continuing. The first concept has sometimes led to a division of the college into a "lower" and "upper" college or "junior" and "senior" college. These concepts have greatly influenced the administrative structure of several colleges and universities.

The translation of a program of general education from its theoretical formulation to a practical operation introduces many problems, not the least frustrating of which are those concerned with the means of administration. If the achievement of an effective program of general education is worth all the labor which has been expended in projecting theories about its ends and means and in devising new types of courses for their better realization, then the conditions under which the program is administered deserve an important place in the deliberations of college administrations and faculties. The administrative patterns which have been developed merit careful examination. Most of them will be illustrated in the practices of the colleges we are about to study. Actually there appear to be no more than three basic administrative structures, although each has numerous minor variations. These are:

1. An autonomous faculty specifically created for the purpose of administering a program of general studies. Such a faculty under the direction of its own administrative officer has power to formulate its curriculum, subject to the approval of the entire faculty of the institution. It has its own budget, can make appointments to its faculty, and can recommend promotions independently.

2. A committee on general education. Usually this committee is formed from members of the various departments or divisions whose subject matters are in some manner represented in the general curriculum. The committee sometimes has an operating budget, but has little or no budgetary control over salaries and rarely has the power of appointment to the faculty. It may act as a supervisory committee in directing curricular reforms, but neither the committee nor the instructional staff is empowered to make major revisions in the course offerings without general faculty consent. It may request the services of faculty members for instructional duties from appropriate departments, and in some colleges it may reject an instructor offered by a department if he is not considered desirable by the committee.

3. Decentralized administration. Usually the several parts of a general program are assigned to the administrative charge of separate departments or divisions of the faculty. General courses, requiring the services of faculty members from more than one department, are usually administered by the staffs teaching the course; such staffs differ in the degree of freedom they have in devising the content of their courses and in adopting appropriate instructional procedures. Courses such as English composition, foreign language, or mathematics, when regarded as part of the general curriculum, are under the administrative direction of their respective departments. In general, budgetary control resides in departments as does the power of faculty appointment. General supervision or review of the whole curricular structure often is assigned to a college curriculum committee, either a standing committee or a temporary committee appointed at periods of crisis in operational procedures.

Only a very few institutions have adopted either the first or second of these procedures, and usually they are universities with a comprehensive program involving all or very large portions of the student body and requiring a large faculty for instructional duties. Small colleges have tended to decentralize the administration of their general program, and some universities prefer this method. Obviously the size of an institution and the instructional and extracurricular duties of the faculty are vital factors in determining administrative organization. Tradition is also a strong factor, as is the experience and competence of a faculty with reference to performing a particular administrative or instructional task. Generally, however, the decentralization of administrative responsibility has often resulted in an uneven development of the various parts of the program and has not infrequently led to a withering of general faculty interest because of a lack of communication among the various departments concerning their common interests.

In the early years of this century severe criticism was frequently directed against the instructional methods which were almost uniformly employed throughout the entire undergraduate program. From the freshman year to the senior year the common practice was to rely upon the lecture except in language and mathematics where instruction was more often in the form of "recitation." Objections usually were supported by the contentions that the lecture method was not always suitable for younger students and that it did not permit the active participation of students in the examination of issues raised by a course.

It is impossible to assert with any assurance the precise degree of influence which the general education movement has had upon the introduction of new pedagogical methods or upon the injection of some refreshing vigor into old methods. Yet the new types of general courses created conditions which made necessary a close scrutiny of established habits of teaching. In origin and nature they were a cooperative enterprise, and they brought their instructors together on new terms. It can be said with little risk of contradiction that where instruction in general courses did not in fact become cooperative, the experiments failed. Teachers were obligated to instruct one another, even as they all shared in instructing the students. Staff conferences were almost mandatory, and comparisons of instructional devices were inevitable. Where the achievement of students was measured, either wholly or in part, by a common examination, staffs discovered new problems in the construction of tests which would be at once fair to the students and to the objectives of the course.

A great deal of study was given to ways of bringing the values of lectures and discussion techniques into effective relationship. If the results of some of the experimentation have sometimes been less than miraculous, there have been enough successes to credit the general education movement with some very valuable contributions to the arts of teaching. A complete study of the current trends in general education cannot disregard the pedagogical instruments which it has employed.

Against this brief analysis of the movement as it has matured during the past twenty years, we may turn now to the study, in some detail, of a representative group of colleges which have shared in varying degrees and in various ways in the contemporary concern for a vigorous and effective general education. The programs of these eighteen colleges differ sufficiently in both theory and practice to afford a reasonable image of the range of contemporary meanings associated around the idea of general education.

Chapter 6

The Colleges Speak
for Themselves

The colleges which have supplied the data essential to this study are:

Amherst College, Amherst, Massachusetts
Antioch College, Yellow Springs, Ohio
Berea College, Berea, Kentucky
Brooklyn College, Brooklyn, New York
Goucher College, Baltimore, Maryland
The University of Louisville, Louisville, Kentucky
Macalester College, St. Paul, Minnesota
Michigan State University, East Lansing, Michigan
Mills College, Oakland, California
The University of Minnesota, Minneapolis, Minnesota [1]
The University of Notre Dame, Notre Dame, Indiana
The University of Oregon, Eugene, Oregon
Reed College, Portland, Oregon
St. John's College, Annapolis, Maryland
Saint Xavier College, Chicago, Illinois
San Francisco State College, San Francisco, California
Stanford University, Stanford, California
Washington State University, Pullman, Washington

The data have been obtained through the study of available documents describing academic programs and through visits to the institutions and conferences and correspondence with members of faculties and administrative officers. It has been the general design of this study to limit the analysis to liberal arts colleges, both independent colleges and the liberal arts divisions of universities. The absence in this list of an institution which is primarily concerned

[1] The study of the University of Minnesota includes both the General College and the College of Science, Literature, and the Arts.

107

with teacher education does not signify a lack of interest in the problems of such colleges; instead it derives from the conviction that general education has a significance for these institutions of such importance that the subject should be considered in a separate investigation. For somewhat similar reasons, the list does not include a representative technological institution. The place of general education in technological training has been very much under discussion in recent years, so much so, indeed, that it has seemed wise that this, too, should be a separate field of study. It is true that three land-grant colleges are included in this account—the University of Minnesota, Michigan State University, and Washington State University —but each of them maintains a college of liberal arts which is among the largest of the institution's undergraduate colleges. There are occasional references, for purposes of comparison, to programs of other colleges, some of which have been rather widely publicized for several years.

Eleven of the institutions are supported by funds from private sources. The remaining seven are supported primarily by state or municipal taxes. Two of the institutions admit men only; three admit women only; and the remainder are coeducational.

Nine institutions are colleges in the strict sense of the word and describe themselves as "liberal arts colleges." Most of them offer only the baccalaureate degree, though a few offer a one-year course in education beyond the undergraduate level which leads to a master's degree in education. Two colleges offer a variety of graduate programs leading to the degrees of Master of Arts and Master of Science, but do not award the Ph.D. The remaining seven are universities which unite several undergraduate schools, professional schools, and graduate schools, and which award all academic degrees and several professional degrees.

Two of the private institutions are supported by agencies of the Catholic Church; one is closely affiliated with and receives support from the Presbyterian Church. The remaining eight claim no specific religious affiliation at present, although some of them were founded by and received their initial support from Protestant churches or agencies. Some still assert the cultivation of the Christian faith to be among their educational aims, while they disavow any denominational affiliation.

One of the extraordinary characteristics of higher education in

America is the enormous range in the size of our institutions. The range between the smallest and largest institutions of this group of eighteen comes close to the maximum range for accredited institutions in the entire nation, i.e., from slightly more than two hundred students to over twenty thousand.

In addition to classifying these institutions by various principles which establish certain common interests, I have deemed it wise to consider aspects which give a unique character to each and which are also important determinants of educational policy and practice. That the oldest college in this group was founded in 1784 and the youngest in 1930 is by itself of little significance. But the weight of tradition is strong, and it would be unwise not to take account of the intellectual currents which attended the birth of each institution. No college wholly escapes the conditions imposed by its charter, a fact which often lends legal sanction to the force of custom. The place of theology and religion as formal subjects of instruction—their presence or absence—is often explained by tradition, by local law, or by both. The educational policies of Antioch are still influenced by the ideas of Horace Mann, the college's founder and first President; and many of the principles which give Berea College its particular identity are directly traceable to the social reform movements of the nineteenth century.

All the foregoing differentia and no doubt several others unite to give an institution a combination of circumstances which affect theory and practice in every phase of its educational program. It is impossible to trace precisely their effects, but it will be well to recognize their importance in contributing to the great variety of educational patterns which constitute the sum of ideas embraced in the term "general education" today.

Colleges are seldom reticent in recording the educational goals which are their reason for being, and the colleges which have contributed to this study provide no exceptions. The intellectual travails through which some of the faculties have passed in arriving at their present conceptions of their educational means and ends have been recorded in reports of committees and in published self-study monographs. Through their annual catalogues they inform the student, in different degrees of explicitness, of what they hope to achieve through his cooperation. Statements of objectives, however, do not as a rule clarify educational philosophies. All the colleges and universities whose undergraduate programs we are about to survey state that a primary purpose of their programs is to contribute to the *liberal education* of their students; and most of them declare this to be their one all-important objective. All other objectives are subordinate, as stages or elements in the learning process which, when realized, constitute the college's contribution to the liberal education of the student. The colleges and universities would not hold that they initiate and complete a liberal education, but they would very probably agree that every type of activity represented in their liberal arts curriculum is appropriate if not essential to a liberal education.

Despite the unanimity about the primary purpose of the college, there are represented in this group of institutions two widely different conceptions of liberal education, and fortunately for this study, the theoretical bases of these opposed conceptions have been succinctly stated in various official documents. The concept of liberal education held by seventeen of the colleges embraces a dualism of functions in the learning process which is acknowledged in their curriculums by two kinds of requirements: some type of broad distribution of subject matters and a concentration in one relatively limited field of study. In short, they adhere to a conception of liberal education at the collegiate level which has been dominant in America for over fifty years. One college (St. John's) explicitly denies that concentration, as it is conventionally understood and practiced, has a place in liberal education, and it argues that concentration or specialization at the collegiate level has corrupted the true meaning of liberal education. We shall examine the theories advanced in support of both conceptions in their proper contexts.

The objectives of the dualistic conception of liberal education are stated very simply in the Catalog of Macalester College (1955–1957) which says:

> The student who selects Macalester College has a right to expect that the college will help him to answer two questions:
>
> 1. How can I build a life that will be competent, happy, balanced and qualified to meet the responsibilities of a free citizen in a free world?
> 2. How can I prepare myself for a career that will make me a self-sustaining member of society, with joy and pride in my work and a sense of usefulness and achievement?

If the reader were told from what source comes the right of the student to expect answers to these questions, he would have a clearer idea of the philosophic base of Macalester's conception of liberal education. However, whether one believes this to be implicitly a right of the student or not, it is evident that sixteen other colleges share with Macalester the belief that they have an obligation to satisfy the two kinds of needs presented in these questions. Although the basic need stated in the second question is not always couched in such candidly vocational terms as the Macalester phrasing, the means of satisfying it are fundamentally the same, i.e., *concentration* in a major field of study selected by the student in accordance with his interests and aptitudes. Despite President Lowell's conviction that the end of concentration was to strengthen the "mental fibre" rather than to prepare students for vocations, most colleges seem not to trouble to make that distinction.

The means by which the student is helped to answer the first question are also in a broad though superficial sense identical, i.e., they all represent some form of comprehensive distribution of studies. The most commonly recurring phrase which describes the objective to be attained through distribution is "broad foundation." Thus Macalester "insists that every student must have a *broad foundation* of knowledge, personal competence, and constructive purpose." Brooklyn College states that "the Liberal Arts curriculum leading to the Bachelor of Arts degree is designed to provide a *broad foundation* for a liberal education and to give the student preliminary preparation for the field of his special interest." Goucher College says that "the first two of the four years in college (Lower Division) are devoted to courses in general education which aim to lay a *broad foundation*," while "the last two years (Upper Division) afford opportunity for intensive specialized study." Michigan State University asserts that "the aim of the Basic College is to strengthen and enrich specialized training by supporting it with a *broad foundation* of general education." Reed College refers to its "general basic courses introductory to *broad fields of knowledge* ... designed to provide an informed world view."

From these references, if references were needed, it is evident that the chief concern of this study must lie with the activities which the several colleges have employed for the realization of the first of the two objectives, i.e., the building of a broad foundation; for this is the area of educational activity which, either by direct statement or by implication, is accepted as the area of general education. What these colleges do by way of helping their students to acquire a broad foundation represents their conceptions of the nature and the extent of their responsibility for general education and their ideas about the best practical means of discharging it. The colleges which regard general education as a part but not the whole of liberal education may be expected to reveal the relative value which they attach to this aspect of their commitment partly by the amount of time they allow for it but more importantly by the substantive character of the subject matter which constitutes the "broad foundation of knowledge." We shall be interested, also, in their views on the relationship of the general to the specialized, for it makes some difference, conceptually, whether they regard the broad foundation as simply preparatory to the special, or as equal but disjunct aspects of liberal education, or as complementary and continuing elements which serve in different ways to achieve a more unified view of knowledge.

In the comprehensive description of each college program I have sought to include statements of objectives and, where obtainable, statements of theory which have been determinants of the curriculum. The greater attention is given to that part of the curriculum requirements which falls legitimately within the meaning of general education, broadly defined. I have also attempted to give a summary view of the total requirements for the baccalaureate degrees in liberal arts programs. The terminology used in identifying the general (as distinct from the specialized) part of the program varies considerably and includes such terms as "the program in general education," "the general curriculum," "all-university requirements," and "the comprehensive basic studies."

The accounts are based upon evidence gathered from a variety of sources. First in importance have been conferences with instructors and administrative officers in each institution. Self-study monographs, reports of faculty committees, published articles, course syllabi, and annual catalogues and bulletins have provided statements of objectives and principles, accounts of curricular structures, and administrative organization. Histories of some of the institutions have provided useful records of the evolution of curriculums.

Although I have sought to give a factually accurate account of each curriculum and each program, seeking and receiving the assistance of a responsible officer of each institution in checking the statement for accuracy, the reader will understand that college curriculums and administrative procedures rarely stand still. At the time the study began, three of the colleges were engaged in major revisions of their undergraduate programs which have materially altered their general education program. At least three others have begun the task of revision since then, a task which is only partially completed. All accounts have been checked against official announcements for 1958–1959, and some against those for 1960–1961. Nevertheless the details of any one institution's program will, like a timetable, suffer change without notice. The concepts and practices which prevailed within the span of time devoted to the study still have value, for each of them reflects some attitude or problem—no doubt several problems—which are constant. The procedures of any one of the colleges, even though they should be abandoned tomorrow, will still be those of another college or may become so in the future. Although I have raised questions concerning theory and procedures, at no time have I intended any reflection on the merits of any course in itself. I have avoided visiting classes on principle, for I am convinced that only continued visitation over an extended period of time justifies a judgment about the excellence of a course.

On the other hand, it is proper, I think, to raise questions about the relevance of a course within the context of stated objectives or within the structure of the entire program. It has seemed to me proper likewise to ask about the absence of certain subject matters within the limits of the general education requirements and to inquire into the success or failure of certain kinds of course organizations and such procedural matters as course staffing, instructional methods, and testing practices.

I have arranged the accounts of the programs in alphabetical order because this seemed to me the simplest and fairest order. If they give a representative record of what general education means in theory and practice in these middle years of the twentieth century and if they bring attention to bear upon some of the unresolved issues which must continue to be subjects for critical reflection, this section will have served its purpose.

AMHERST COLLEGE

Amherst College, the second oldest of the colleges included in this survey, was founded in 1821. This fact is important because its birth coincided with the first stirrings of revolt against the classical curriculum of American colleges and because the record of its adjustments to the various pressures created by that revolt is one of the most interesting in the history of higher education in America. It has steadily sought to preserve the integrity of the four-year independent liberal arts college, resisting most of the various compromises with the university system to which many institutions founded both before and after Amherst yielded. The history of more than a century of national concern for general education is epitomized in the history of Amherst. A comparison of the motives which prompted the curricular reforms of 1827 with those which produced the most recent reforms, introduced in 1947, illustrates the great reversal of trends. The curriculum of 1827 sought to achieve what the faculty regarded as a greater and more useful flexibility while preserving the essentials of a common intellectual experience. The curriculum introduced in 1947 sought to redefine and restore these essentials which had been all but lost in consequence of curricular fragmentation.[2]

The following facts, though generally well known, are useful to bear in mind in studying Amherst's present program. Amherst is an independent liberal arts college for men, offering the Bachelor of Arts degree. Its student body numbers slightly more than one thousand. The majority of its students come from New England and the Middle Atlantic states, though there is a substantial number from all parts of the nation. Almost 95 per cent of entering students graduate from the college. The majority of Amherst graduates pursue

[2] For a detailed account of the work of the committee on long-range policy, which drafted in its principal details the 1947 curriculum, see Gail Kennedy (ed.), *Education at Amherst,* Harper & Brothers, New York, 1955. The report of this committee is one of the most penetrating self-studies produced by an American college. For details on the curriculum of 1827, see Part 1 of this study, pp. 13–16.

careers in business or in the professions. Students are admitted on the basis of high school records, personal interviews, and the College Entrance Examination Board aptitude and achievement test scores. Academic preparation for admission is strongly recommended in the following fields: English (four years), mathematics (three years), foreign language (two, preferably three years), history (one year) and a laboratory science (one year). In some subjects, admission with advanced placement is granted to students who have achieved satisfactory grades on the College Entrance Examination Board advanced placement tests.

The Catalog of Amherst College for 1955–1956 states that "Amherst's courses are confined to the liberal arts and sciences and lead only to the Bachelor of Arts degree; no vocational or specialized studies are offered." This statement is followed by a reference to its *general curriculum* "under which all students follow a prescribed program of studies during the first two years, and 'major' or take 'honors' work during the last two years in 'area' or departmental studies." The suggestion that departmental majors do not constitute specialized studies is most unusual. It is very interesting, therefore, to find in the Catalog for 1958–1959 a remarkable revision, particularly since no important curricular change had occurred. "The curriculum of the College, key features of which were first introduced in 1947, was designed to put more emphasis on participation by the student, and to provide a body of common knowledge that would serve as a basis for later specialization in any field." The dropping of "general curriculum" for "body of common knowledge" merely exchanges an empty academic term for one that is more precise. The reference to specialization, however, appears to be a contradiction of the former view of area and departmental majors and invites speculation upon the reasons for the changes.

The theoretical justification of the Amherst curriculum is also presented in the following brief statement in the Catalog for 1958–1959:

> The curriculum is based on the view that an important goal of liberal education is to develop the student's power of using abstractions in a way that will enable him to deal with a great diversity of experience. A Policy Committee of the College has described the relation between the curriculum and the contemporary world as follows: "It has become more important than

ever before that individuals be able to comprehend intelligently as much of the enormously complex and rapidly changing society in which we live as it is possible for them to do. . . . Between the education of infancy and childhood, which should be primarily a matter of acquiring essential skills by direct participation, and the subsequent training that one receives by the direct method of apprenticeship in technical and professional schools, there lies a period of late adolescence and early maturity when at least the ablest and most gifted members of their generation should be given the opportunity to develop the kind and quality of interests that will enable them to understand how their specific functions as businessmen, teachers, artists, lawyers, physicians, engineers, etc., fit into the whole complex changing pattern of the Great Society."

The subject matters of the entire college curriculum are divided among three divisions: division I, humanities; division II, social studies; division III, mathematics and the natural sciences. The humanities division comprises fifteen departments or subject-matter areas; the social studies, five; and the natural sciences, nine. Anthropology and psychology, frequently grouped with the social sciences, are at Amherst grouped with the natural sciences. History is grouped with the social sciences.

The *general curriculum,* or as the more recent Catalog refers to it, "the body of common knowledge" which is required of all students, is organized on the same divisional lines, although the tabular view of the requirements separates the foreign language and public speaking from the humanities. Briefly the general curriculum requires two years of natural science, two years of history, two years of humanities, one year of foreign language, and one year of public speaking. The curriculum contains both general and departmental courses. In the freshman year all students are required to take Science 1 and 2 (a course which unites mathematics and physics), Humanities 1 and 2, English Composition, European History, and a foreign language unless excused by qualifying tests. If the language requirement is waived, the student exercises elective privileges. In the sophomore year the program admits of greater flexibility. The requirement for a second year of science may be met in two ways. The student may take a two-semester sequence in chemistry and biology, or a semester course in organic evolution (Science 23, formerly called "Evolution of the Earth and Man") followed by a semester course in chemistry, geology, astronomy, or psychology. In humanities the student must take three semester courses from a list classified in three groups: (1) philosophy, religion, classical civilization; (2) music, fine arts, dramatic arts; (3) literature, either English or foreign. The student may take one course in each group or two courses in one group and the third in either of the other groups. One of the courses may be deferred until the junior year. The social studies requirement of the sophomore year is Problems in American Civilization. Public speaking is also required in the sophomore year, though the course meets only one hour per week throughout the year. In addition to these second-year requirements, the program allows for an elective course each semester. The total requirements of the general program are approximately 60 credit hours out of a minimum total of 128 required for the baccalaureate degree, or slightly under one-half of the total.

"The body of common knowledge" which constitutes the general curriculum is a combination of general courses required of all students [Science 1–2, Humanities 1–2, European Civilization (History 1–2), and American Civilization (American Studies 1–2)], a limited number of optional courses for meeting second-year requirements in science and humanities, and a common requirement in English composition and foreign language.

Some aspects of the general program in the natural sciences at Amherst are in remarkable contrast with the usual pattern of science programs in other institutions. The history of general courses in the sciences has been very spotty. As a rule they have been less successful, at least in the judgment of those responsible for their planning, than courses in the humanities and the social sciences. Furthermore, the record of success, generally, has been greater in the biological sciences than in the physical sciences. At Amherst the reverse seems to have been true. The general course in mathematics and physics has experienced continuous success both for science majors and nonscience majors. This is all the more unusual because of the high level of the mathematics (problems in analytical geometry and calculus) from which the course starts. A general course called "Evolution of the Earth and Man" has fared less well. Originally a two-semester course which united materials from biology, geology, and astronomy, it was eventually reduced to a one-semester course, and now has become or been replaced by a one-semester course called "Organic Evolution." At first this course was intended for nonscience majors, but the privilege allowed these students of choosing between the general course and the chemistry-biology sequence placed it in a competitive position.³ Whatever reasons may account for this lack of success, the present requirements in the natural sciences at Amherst make it possible for students to take at least three semesters of mathematics and physical sciences, while a minimum of one semester of biology will satisfy some degree requirements. A combination of organic evolution and psychology is the only two-semester sequence in biology now available for nonscience majors.

The first year of the humanities sequence is described as a course in the "great books" of Western culture. Actually it is a half course which meets twice a week in the first semester and three times a week in the second. It is carried concurrently with a half course in English composition. Intended to illustrate various stages in the development of literature in the Western tradition, it is one of the most familiar types of general humanities courses. Since it is allotted about half the time usually given to such courses, its reading list is less extensive than most, and the current trend is toward increasingly intensive reading. Instruction is conducted through the medium of small discussion sections of twenty to twenty-five students, supplemented by occasional lectures.

Because the second year of the humanities sequence allows a limited degree of freedom in the choice of courses for fulfilling the requirements of the sequence, it is proper to examine some of the sequential patterns that are permissible. It is, for example, possible for a student to choose two courses in English literature and one in philosophy, thereby excluding any experience with music and the visual arts. English 21–22 which is a required sequence for all English majors may be taken in satisfaction of the humanities requirements. On the other hand, a student may elect a semester each of music and art and one course in religion, with the result that his total experience with the monumental works of literature (as taught from the humanistic tradition) may be limited largely to the half course in the freshman year. A not improbable pattern might be one course in philosophy, one course in religion, and a foreign language literature course.

One significant change in the humanities program since 1947 has been the abandonment of an "integrated" course in the fine arts, music, and dramatics, originally an elective in the second year. The

³ See Gail Kennedy (ed.), *ibid.*, pp. 214–217.

course was dropped chiefly because of the dissatisfaction of the teaching staff. In its place the departments have introduced one or more semester courses which they considered most appropriate for the purposes of general education.

The distributional structure of the second year of the humanities sequence presents a question which will recur frequently in the course of these pages. How broad should a general experience of the humanities be? By virtue of the required first-year course, Amherst has declared that some knowledge of Western man's great literary achievements is imperative. The fact that two of the three groups of studies from which students may elect courses to complete the second-year sequence are specifically concerned with subject matters which find expression in literary forms confirms the high priority which is set upon literature. Can a program which permits the exclusion of the fine arts and music provide an adequate view of the humanities? The answers to these questions vary considerably.

The two courses which constitute the social studies sequence offer interesting similarities and contrasts both in the planning and in the teaching of the courses. An appraisal of them is given in *Education at Amherst* which illuminates their different approaches to the social sciences.[4] The first-year course is titled "The Development of Western Civilization: A Survey of European History and an Introduction to the Social Studies." It is a modification of an elective history course offered before 1947, and it was planned and is still taught by the history department. The second-year course was introduced in 1947 on the recommendation of the long-range policy committee. It was planned by members of the departments of economics, English, history, philosophy, and political science, and it is still taught and administered by the department of American studies, itself an "interdepartmental" department. The course is called "Problems in American Civilization." [5]

[4] In addition to the report of the committee on long-range policy, *Education at Amherst* contains a report of a review committee, submitted in 1954, as an appraisal of the first eight years of the new program as approved and modified by subsequent faculty action. See *ibid.*, pp. 218–229, for a review of the social studies sequence.

[5] The department of American studies is an excellent example of the type of interdepartmental staff or committee which is becoming increasingly popular in American colleges. The activities of these staffs cannot be dissociated entirely from the general education movement, for though they are primarily

Both courses purport to give an introduction to the nature and scope of the social sciences. To an observer who has been obliged to draw conclusions chiefly from descriptive accounts of the structure of the courses, it seems likely that the second-year course has been more successful or at least more attentive to the problems of integrating the disciplines of the several social sciences into a course which is basically constructed upon a historical framework. Neither course is a conventional survey of history. Both are organized in terms of topics which center upon major problems or crises. The second-year course distinguishes between "historical problems" and "contemporary problems," and at least five of the ten or twelve problems studied in the course of a year concern contemporary issues.[6]

An issue which has been debated by most staffs engaged in the construction of a general course in the social sciences has been: Should a theoretical foundation in the separate disciplines of economics, political science, and sociology precede the practical application of the techniques of analysis to social problems? The answers given by the Amherst staff are that the social sciences, unlike mathematics and the natural sciences, do not depend upon a logical and sequential order in the learning process and that "neither chronological sequences nor syllogistic systems provide a satisfactory approach to the social studies." One of the arguments most frequently advanced in support of a distributional system which permits students to elect *any one* of introductory courses in economics, political science, anthropology, sociology, or geography is that it is better for the student to be well grounded in one discipline than to receive a smattering of several. This ignores, say the respondents, the real nature of most concrete problems of social action, whose complex dimensions require their consideration in terms of more than one discipline. Upon this issue, the course in Problems in American Civilization asserts:

---

concerned with programs for "majors," the spirit which motivates the organization of their programs for concentration is the same as that which seeks to organize a "core curriculum" for all students. Just as the general "core curriculum" may demand of each student experience of natural and social sciences, literature, and the arts, so the interdepartmental program may contain a core of courses including history, political science, literature, and philosophy.

[6] Several volumes of readings, edited by the staff and prepared to illuminate the topics developed in Problems in American Civilization, have been published by D. C. Heath and Company, Boston.

Many students never have an opportunity for advanced work in the social studies or a special study of the techniques of analysis used in connection with them, although as citizens they will have to deal with these and similar problems. This course, though it cannot give the student a mastery of the formal studies, can at least give him some appreciation of the need for careful analysis and of the importance of exposing and considering assumptions. On the one hand he will gain an appreciation of the contributions which the experts may take toward analyzing certain aspects of experience; on the other he may acquire a healthy skepticism of the competence of such experts to select the values or assumptions from which their chains of reasoning seem to follow.[7]

One of the urgent recommendations of the committee on long-range policy concerned instructional methods, evidently with the intention of reducing excessive reliance upon lectures. To secure increased active participation by students in the classroom, the committee urged the use of "laboratory" or seminar techniques in as many courses as possible. Lectures still play an important role, and in many of the courses in the general curriculum, a dominant role. Humanities 1–2, however, is conducted chiefly by discussion; laboratory work is an important part of the natural science courses; and Problems in American Civilization conducts a two-hour seminar every two weeks.

The administration of the general curriculum is assigned to the various staffs responsible for teaching the courses; this means that for the most part administration is under the direction of the departments responsible for each course. The staffs of Natural Science 1–2, Humanities 1–2, and Problems in American Civilization are interdepartmental. Other courses are almost wholly in the charge of a single department. There is no standing committee for the administration of the general curriculum, nor are there permanent divisional committees for the supervision of the three sequences. Departmental control of the curriculum is strong and is apparently reflected in some of the modifications of the original recommendations of the committee on long-range policy.

The organizing principle of the general curriculum is in its general divisions similar to that of many colleges. The basic skills of communication are represented in the requirements in mathematics, English,

[7] Gail Kennedy (ed.), *op. cit.*, pp. 228–229.

and foreign language. The broad division of knowledge and disciplines into the natural sciences, the social studies, and the humanities is now a commonplace. Though the two-year requirement in each area is called a "sequence," the principles which have determined the sequential structure of the two years do not stand out with equal clarity in the three areas.

In social studies, the sequence obtains a measure of continuity through a historical framework. History (past and in the making) provides problems of social action which can be understood in terms of the choices men have made and can make and in terms of the bearing of economic, political, and social interests upon those choices. In the natural sciences, there appears to be a deliberate ordering in the sequence by proceeding from mathematical concepts to a view of certain key concepts in the physical nature of matter, thence to a chemical view, and finally to a biological view. This structure, however, is broken for those students who elect organic evolution in the first semester of the second year and geology or psychology in the second semester. The guiding principles of the humanities sequence are less clear. There is, in so far as literature is concerned, a procedure from the comprehensive and rapid view which embraces poetic, philosophic, and historical forms in the first year, to a more intensive and particularized view of works in any one of these genres in the second year. There is also a movement from the broad sweep of Western man's literary achievement to a more limited national and linguistic view (English literature or that of another nation and language). Given the nature of the options provided in the sequence, the inference one must draw is that in the general education of any student, a knowledge of the fine arts and music may be expendable, but a knowledge of the major literary genres is not. I point to this fact, not so much in criticism as for the purpose of fixing attention upon a scale of values. In every curricular structure, choices have been made between the more and the less valuable. No doubt this is unavoidable. But the differences among the colleges in their order of values are many; and the reasons why *this* and not *that* is given preference are often difficult to determine. Yet they are one of the most important objects of reflection as we review the practice of general education at the present time.

ANTIOCH COLLEGE

Antioch was founded in 1853, and Horace Mann was its first President. The ideal of social responsibility which characterized Mann's educational philosophy still permeates the college. The unusual degree of student participation in the conduct of the affairs of the college is an extension of Mann's doctrines. Although the faculty has final authority over matters of educational policy, great responsibility is granted to an administrative council consisting of nine members. Six members are from the faculty and three from the students. The students are elected by the college community, which consists of the faculty and student body. Two faculty members are elected by the community, and three by the faculty only. The dean of the college is a member *ex officio*. The council participates in decisions affecting both policy and personnel. In addition it elects seven of the twenty-seven members of the board of trustees, and confers with the board in the appointment of a new president. The administrative council also appoints subcommittees which advise on various policy matters, such as admission standards and college development. Student representatives are members of these committees. Responsibility for the extraclassroom activity of the Antioch community is delegated to a community council which consists of six students and three members of the faculty, all of whom are elected by the entire community. The faculty of Antioch College say that student participation in all the activities which engage the society which is Antioch College is as much a part of its program of general education as the formal curriculum.

Antioch College is coeducational. Its present enrollment is approximately twelve hundred students, nearly evenly divided between men and women (55 per cent men and 45 per cent women). It offers both the Bachelor of Arts and the Bachelor of Science degrees. Antioch's cooperative or study-plus-work plan has gained national attention for many years. Just as Antioch believes that the full range of campus activities is a useful educational laboratory in community living, so it asserts that the combination of formal studies and on-the-job learning

123

constitutes the best means of developing individual competence and the liberally educated person. At any given time during the academic year about 60 per cent of the students are in residence and the remainder are engaged in many kinds of jobs which have been arranged cooperatively by the college and business, industrial, and professional employers throughout the nation. Cooperative credit, required for a degree, is granted for work on the job. To achieve the goals of its unusual and ambitious study-plus-work plan of liberal education, the college allows a normal period of five years for the completion of degree requirements.

The essential ideas of the study-plus-work plan were conceived by Arthur E. Morgan who became President of the college in 1920 and immediately undertook a thorough reorganization of the entire academic program. The college credits President Morgan with introducing the basic principles of its program of general education in the new curriculum of 1921. It is historically noteworthy that this was the same year that the new President of Reed College, Richard Scholz, led his faculty in the inauguration of a new curriculum designed to give a better general education. President Morgan's writings indicate that he viewed with equal distaste an education that was wholly academic and traditionally "cultural" and one that was wholly technical. His aim was to secure a "symmetry" in the education of the student through the union of the two.

The academic year 1958–1959 was an important year in the history of Antioch. The program of general education which began with the reforms of 1921 was subjected to a revision which the faculty regarded as "the most fundamental one in the college's curriculum since Arthur E. Morgan's introduction in 1921 of its emphasis upon educating 'generalists,' a slogan which . . . was stressed here before the term 'general education' had come into vogue." [8] The revisions are indeed fundamental. Antioch therefore provides us with an opportunity to compare the principles and basic assumptions of two curriculums, one which had been tested for many years and the other in the first experimental stage.

In terms of total academic credits required, there is little difference in the programs. In both, about half of the students' academic work is

[8] Morris Keeton and Ruth Churchill, "Antioch Redesigns Its General Education Program," *Journal of General Education*, vol. 10, July, 1957, pp. 145–149.

allotted to the program of general education. Both programs permit students to obtain credit for general education requirements by passing achievement examinations or, without receiving credit, to gain permission to take advanced courses in an area in which they have demonstrated a specified level of competence. Rigorous grade standards control the operation of the achievement test program.

The divisional organization of subject matters for the entire college curriculum has been changed in several important respects, and these changes are reflected in the structure of the general education program. Originally subject matters were divided into four areas: humanities, life sciences, physical sciences, and social sciences. This divisional structure is a familiar one, but some of the subdivisional groupings gave the scheme an unusual character. Life sciences, for instance, included biology, education, family studies, psychology, and health and physical education. The new divisional structure consists of the humanities, the physical sciences, and the social sciences. Biology is now treated as a subdivision of the physical sciences. Education, psychology, and physical education are grouped with the social sciences; and history has been shifted from the social sciences to the humanities. The changes raise some questions for which there are no clear answers immediately available but which invite much speculation.

In the new program no course is specifically required of all students. This is the most significant change adopted by the faculty. In the program which it displaces, nine of the fourteen courses which constituted the general education curriculum were required of all students, and the remaining five were selected from a very small list of optional courses.[9] At least one required course in each of the four divisions was a general or "interdisciplinary" course. In addition to the common courses in each of the four divisions, two "communications" courses were required: Fundamental Concepts of Mathematics and Current Reading and Writing. The former course and all the general courses have been retained in the new program, but all are electives in one of the three new divisional groupings. Current Reading and Writing has been abandoned; and responsibility for instruction in writing and for maintaining acceptable standards is now shared

[9] All references to curricular details are taken from the Antioch College catalogs for 1955–1957 and 1958–1959.

by the entire faculty. By the end of the third year each student is expected to have given proof of his competence in writing to a faculty committee appointed from the department of literature. The proof will be found in a selection of papers written for various courses, cooperative reports, or other written material. No student may graduate who has failed to establish his competence in the judgment of the committee. Skills tests in mathematics and reading are employed at Level I only.

The curriculum which forms the new general education program is divided into three *levels*. Courses designated as "Level I" are intended to be taken during the first two years, and no more than two may be deferred until the third year. In each of the three divisional areas, Level I courses are subdivided into two groups, A and B; and a student must earn not less than 5 credits (usually the equivalent of a one-term course) in each group in the three major fields, i.e., a minimum of 30 credits distributed among the six groups of Level I courses. Level II courses may be taken whenever a student has completed course work for Level I and has passed at least one of the two achievement examinations. Only one Level II course may be deferred until the year of graduation. Ten credits or two 1-term courses in each of the three areas are required in Level II. Level III consists primarily of the Senior Seminar and the Senior Paper.

The significance of the differences between the old and the new programs can be judged by a comparison of the requirements in the area of the humanities. In the old program all students were required to obtain credit either by achievement examinations or by successful work in the following courses: Introduction to the Arts, Introduction to Philosophy, and either Landmarks of Western Literature or Survey of English Literature. In the new program the student must obtain credit for one course in Group A and one in Group B, each course to be elected (with the advice and consent of his adviser) from the following offerings:

Group A	The Historian and Western Civilization
History and	Ideas and Institutions in European Civilization
Philosophy	American Civilization
	Reflective Thinking
	Present-day Religion
	Cultural History of Mexico

Group B	Design and Materials
Creative Arts,	Introduction to Dramatics
Languages,	Introduction to Music
Literature	Music Theory I
	French III
	German III
	Spanish III
	Elements of Poetry
	Techniques of Fiction
	Contemporary Writing
	The Novel and the Modern World
	Self and Society in the Novel
	The Language of Science
	Advanced Spanish (Mexico)
	Arts of Mexico
	Music and Dances of Mexico

To obtain the 10 credits in humanities required at Level II, the student may elect any two of twenty-one courses, subject to the approval of his adviser. The variety of the offerings may be judged by the following selection from the list:

> History of Western Art
> The Baroque Era in Music
> Twentieth Century French Drama
> Introduction to German Civilization
> Europe in the Nineteenth Century
> Twentieth Century America
> Tudor and Stuart England
> Landmarks of Western Literature, I and II
> Shakespeare
> Introduction to Philosophy
> Philosophy of the Physical Sciences

The latitude of choices in the humanities is greater than in either the physical sciences or the social sciences, but in each division the principle of allowing guided election from a considerable list of courses is observed. The break with the past—with a curricular structure which prevailed for a quarter of a century—is therefore radical. It is not, however, an innovation. It is, in its major outlines, a return to a conception of general education against which many colleges including Antioch reacted vigorously twenty-five years ago, a return to the original conception of the distributional scheme. Whether it avoids the problems which brought about the educational reforms of the twenties and thirties will largely depend upon the success of two instruments intended to secure a wise distribution of courses and a breadth of knowledge greater than any combination of courses forming a single general program can give. The first instrument is the advisory system and the second is the achievement examination.

With the aid of a general education syllabus, which explains the objectives of general education and the detailed operation of the Antioch program, each student begins the planning of his program in his first year. Placement examinations, given during orientation week, serve as a diagnostic measure of aptitudes and achievement. Exceptionally high scores admit a student at once to Level I achievement examinations. High scores on these examinations allow students to waive certain courses or to receive credit for them. Satisfactory scores indicate a minimal level of achievement required for graduation but do not permit the waiver of a Level I course in the area of the examination. Unsatisfactory scores may lead to extra course requirements. On the basis of placement tests and achievement examinations, if the student has been permitted to take any, the student then begins planning his program of general studies. During the winter or spring quarter of his first year he must submit a detailed outline of his program of general studies, his examination schedule, and the jobs which he hopes to undertake. With the syllabus as a guide the adviser must approve or modify the program, and the student may not register for further courses until the program has been approved. An outline for a program of studies in a field of concentration must be filed in the second year, and this, together with the outline of the general studies program, forms the student's degree program. The burden of responsibility placed upon the adviser who must see that the objectives of a general education can be realized by every program is obviously very great.

It is intended that the achievement examinations shall provide evidence that the objectives have been obtained. The Catalog for 1958–1959 describes the function of these examinations as follows: "One aim of the general education program is to enable you to obtain a broad understanding and insight into the fields of human knowledge without obliging you to take courses in each academic department. However, you are required, regardless of the courses that you select, to demonstrate this broad knowledge through examinations that set standards for each group, area, and level in the program."

The scope of the achievement examinations will, it seems likely, be the ultimate measure of Antioch's conception of the "breadth" of a general education. Yet the large number of courses from which students may elect their programs and the restricted scope of the content of some of the courses will certainly raise some doubts about the adequacy of many combinations of four courses in any of the three general areas to prepare the students for an examination which deals justly with the methods and the range of content which define these areas. The doubt is particularly acute with respect to the humanities where the range of choices is large and the content of many of the courses is highly specialized. Professors Keeton and Churchill state that the faculty proposes to put renewed stress upon the integrative function of general education. It is not intended, they say, that "these courses should all be explicitly interdisciplinary in the primary content studied but that they should relate facts through principles with wide-ranging implications and sensitize students to the interrelatedness of things and to the values of methods and perspectives of different disciplines." [10] The intention of stressing the integrative function of general education is consistent with aims which have been traditionally expressed throughout the history of the idea of general education. It may be difficult, however, for a student to develop a sensitivity to the values of methods and perspectives of different disciplines even within the field of the humanities if he is permitted to satisfy the whole of his Level I requirements in that field by taking two courses dealing with the cultural history and the arts of Mexico, a combination which is apparently possible.

One point of general interest in the new program is the role of foreign languages. The great majority of liberal arts colleges require the equivalent of at least one year of study in a foreign language at collegiate level for graduation. The old general education program at Antioch was an exception. By admitting three modern foreign languages as electives in the new program at Level I of the humanities courses, the faculty admits them as acceptable though not essential constitutents of a general education. They cannot be regarded as essential skills, since the faculty has named those skills and set standards of competence in their use which all students must meet. Their

[10] *Op. cit.,* p. 147.

relevance to general education is therefore located in their subject matter and is presumed to serve a function similar to courses in literature in the English language. It must be noted that the approved courses (French III, German III, and Spanish III) are two-term courses which may not be taken without previous training equivalent to an introductory course in the language. Students who elect a foreign language in satisfaction of Level I, Group B requirements may sacrifice the opportunity for any experience with the creative arts unless their field of concentration requires it, or unless they use elective credits for this purpose.

I have observed previously that in the reorganization of the curriculum, history was transferred from the social sciences to the humanities. Two courses, formerly listed among the social science requirements, have been retained as electives in Group A of the humanities program, American Civilization and The Historian and Western Civilization. To these another has been added, Ideas and Institutions in European Civilization. The courses in European civilization and American civilization appear to be roughly parallel to the two courses which constitute the sum of the required general studies in the social sciences at Amherst. The resemblance is not superficial. Like the Amherst courses, the courses at Antioch are organized around a selection of topics which stress key problems of their respective subject matters. The description of the American civilization course at Antioch states that it treats of the development of the political, economic, and cultural aspects of American society; this suggests that the objectives of the two courses are similar.

The significance of the parallelism is that it draws attention to the ambiguity characteristic of the principles by which colleges have classified subject matters. A generation of students at Amherst and Antioch have learned that the study of history is an important part of their study of the disciplines of the social sciences. For some students it may well have been the only formal study of the social sciences at the collegiate level. Now a new generation of students at Antioch will learn through much the same courses that they are studying basic humanistic disciplines. From its beginning, the concept of distribution of studies was founded upon the idea that subject matters could be classified in terms of a relationship in the kinds of problems which they evoked, the methods of solving the problems, and the ends which were served by the kinds of knowledge they yielded.

Whether general education proceeds by means of a common core of studies required of all students or by an optional-course distributional structure, such as Antioch has now adopted, or by a combination of the two, as Amherst has chosen, the assumptions which determine all divisional organizations of knowledge will be of paramount importance to the clarity of a program if not to its success.

If a knowledge of history were all that was involved in the example before us, the differences in classification would be of little importance, since in either case the students might obtain the desired knowledge. But more than history is involved, as the passage I have already quoted from Professors Keeton and Churchill makes abundantly clear. History is now one instrument by means of which the interrelatedness of those things which we call "the humanities" shall be understood and by which the values of methods and the perspectives of different humanistic disciplines shall be comprehended by Antioch students. On the other hand, it is no less an instrument by means of which Amherst students are to perceive the relatedness of those disciplines we call "the social sciences." I am not questioning the right or wrong of either of these classifications. I am concerned with the more fundamental question of our success in conveying to our students any reality in the meaning of those concepts in terms of which we have persistently classified knowledge, classifications which have been made solely for the purpose of imparting a greater sense of the integrity of knowledge. The theoretical bases which have determined the divisions and subdivisions of subject matters that are the foundation of all programs of general education are the least explored of all the themes which form the contemporary body of literature about general education. It is quite possibly the most important theme, for to the extent that this theme is unexplored all talk about integration is idle talk.

By way of summary three aspects of the Antioch program require further consideration. First, the program of general education runs collaterally with concentration throughout the entire college program, with more time allotted to it in the early years than in the later years. This practice is almost mandatory (as it was in the old program) because of the study-plus-work program. It is an essential element of the educational philosophy of Antioch that academic training, both general and specialized, and on-the-job learning are complementary parts of the educational process at all times.

The second aspect is the adoption of highly individualized programs of general education in place of a "common core" curriculum. The reasons for so radical a change have not been easy to determine. A suggestion of a reason is given in the article by Professors Keeton and Churchill. No longer, they say, will a teacher be obliged to carry on a famous course created by a predecessor simply because it is required and someone must teach it whether he believes in it or not. This observation points to a problem in the construction and teaching of the staff-taught general courses which differs with the size of the institution. In large institutions, staff-taught courses have almost always been the work of many men and have required the services of large teaching staffs. No one person could claim credit for their conception, and at no time was the normal displacement of the faculty so great that it disrupted the continuity of the course. The best of such courses, or at least those which have withstood the stress of time, have always been modified; but the modification has been the work of staff members who have worked together long enough to achieve a common understanding of the organic structure and aims of the course. The conditions which have made possible the long history of such courses as Columbia's Contemporary Civilization and Chicago's humanities sequence do not always exist in smaller colleges. One cannot discount the importance of cooperative planning and staff continuity as factors in the success of general courses.

Another possible cause of the change is one that goes much deeper into educational theory, namely, dissatisfaction with a program which admits or seems to admit of a minimum of flexibility and individual initiative on the part of both teacher and student. As the historical record has shown, this has been a critical issue throughout the history of American education. The task of finding a satisfactory balance between the desire to obtain a common intellectual experience and a desirable and useful flexibility in curricular structure has been the most difficult of all problems in the history of general education. Since evidence of the persistence of the problem will increase as we continue the exploration of current practices, we shall return to a consideration of its current implications at a later point.

It is appropriate here, however, to point out that many champions of freedom of choice within a limited distributional program do not defend the principle in the areas of concentration with equal ardor. Some programs of concentration in the Antioch curriculum permit less freedom of election than is currently encouraged in the general education program. The reasons for required courses in areas of concentration are obvious and just. But there is need to consider why the principle is not equally desirable in the sphere of general education and whether it is any less invidious to the intellectual integrity and independence of the students than in a field of concentration.

The third feature of the new Antioch program is a provision for a standing committee on the general education curriculum. The functions of this committee are to "define for faculty approval the criteria for courses acceptable for general education credit, and [to] act as a steering committee for meetings of general education course instructors." [11] The adoption of this administrative instrument has been the result of faculty dissatisfaction with a lack of central administrative direction in previous years in which the old curriculum "seemed to undergo piecemeal changes without a clear governing purpose or general faculty understanding of the changes." The nature of the new program is such that it will undoubtedly place heavy responsibilities on this committee. The enlarged number of departmental courses admitted to the general curriculum has reestablished an old principle. It will be difficult, in the light of some courses already approved, to justify the exclusion of others of a parallel kind. If, for example, the Cultural History of Mexico is acceptable at the first level of a general education program in the humanities, it will be difficult to find reasons for excluding a cultural history of India or China or Russia. If Self and Society in the Novel is admissible, on what grounds can a variety of other themes in fiction be excluded? The criteria employed by the committee will be an illuminating mark of Antioch's newly adopted conception of general education. The committee will surely know that the road of curricular fragmentation has been traveled before with results less than encouraging.

[11] Keeton and Churchill, *op. cit.*, p. 148.

BEREA COLLEGE

Berea admitted its first students of collegiate rank in 1869, though like many colleges west of the Alleghenies, it was an outgrowth of an older precollegiate institution. It is a privately endowed, nonsectarian, and coeducational college, located in Berea, Kentucky, on the western rim of the Cumberland Mountains. In 1958 it enrolled 1,273 students, nearly evenly divided between men and women. It awards the Bachelor of Arts and the Bachelor of Science degrees. It has long been known for its unusual admissions policies and its labor program. Ninety per cent of the students are selected from the mountain regions of eight Southeastern states. The labor program is a corollary of the admissions policies. A condition of admission is that a student needs financial aid to obtain a college education. To meet a portion of his expenses, each student is expected to engage in some work; the labor program has been developed to provide jobs, the return from which is applicable to the student's expenses.[12] Many of the jobs, including those in the Berea Student Industries, constitute a useful vocational apprenticeship. The labor program, however, is unlike the Antioch work-study plan in that it is not incorporated into the academic program in the same way or for the same ends. The planned homogeneity in the social, cultural, economic, and geographical background of the student body distinguishes Berea from the other colleges in this study.

The character and needs of the student body explain some of the features of the curriculum which are not common to most liberal arts colleges of the size of Berea. In addition to the customary departments and programs for which the B.A. degree is granted, Berea maintains departments and offers the B.S. degree in agriculture, industrial arts, business administration, home economics, and nursing. To compen-

[12] Berea does not charge tuition. The college depends upon endowment income and gifts to meet the difference between the students' payments and the total operating expenses. Most students carrying a normal academic load earn enough to pay for one-eighth to one-third of their expenses. A few who have greater financial need may carry a reduced academic program and may undertake a special work program which requires a minimum of twenty-four hours of work per week.

134

sate for the considerable disparities in the secondary school preparation of the students, the college provides instruction in basic composition, literature and reading, mathematics, geography, and American history and government. Students whose placement test scores indicate deficiencies in any of these areas must take appropriate courses without credit. The content of these courses is therefore regarded as a part of the general education of the students which normally should be supplied by the secondary schools.

The curriculum of the college is subdivided into a general college curriculum and a senior college curriculum. The former is a core curriculum which engages most of the time of the students during their first two years and which is required (with a few minor qualifications) of all students regardless of their degree programs or vocational interests. The senior college curriculum includes the various departmental offerings from which the students select their "majors" or fields of concentration. Most degree programs provide for some guided or free elective courses. The nearest approximation to area studies or interdepartmental majors are three programs for prospective high school and elementary school teachers in science and social studies. Listed as general studies at the senior college level are three courses which might conceivably form the nucleus of an area-studies degree program: Problems of the South and a two-semester sequence called "Rural Reconstruction in Underdeveloped Areas." At present these courses, which are interdepartmental in the scope of their subject matter, are applicable to various departmental degree programs in the social sciences but are elective.

In addition to the core curriculum requirements of the first two years, students are required to take one course in philosophy elected from the department's offerings in their junior or senior year. The total requirements of the general curriculum constitute a little less than one-half of the minimum 120 semester hours (exclusive of physical education) required for a degree. A working knowledge of a foreign language is required of all candidates for the A.B. degree except those in elementary education. It is waived for all B.S. programs except certain programs in business administration. It is not regarded as a part of the core curriculum. The achievement of a satisfactory working knowledge is measured by a proficiency examination when the student enters college or by the completion of the second-year course in a language.

The normal distribution of the core courses in the first year covers English composition, including library usage, elementary psychology, the history of Western civilization, the literature and religion of the Hebrews, physical science, physical education, and health. In the second year the required courses are humanities, social science, New Testament literature, biological science, speech, and physical education. Humanities is a two-semester course of four hours each semester. English composition is a two-semester course of three hours each semester. All the others are one-semester courses except physical education, which grants one hour of credit in each of the four semesters. The minor exceptions to the requirement of the entire core curriculum of all students are in the Bachelor of Science programs. Students in the professional curriculum in agriculture (designed for prospective teachers of agriculture), for example, are excused from the second semester of the humanities course. For students in the nursing program, departmental courses are substituted for the general courses in the physical and biological sciences, and the course in Old Testament literature is waived.

The core program thus consists of a combination of departmental courses and general courses. The general courses follow the familiar division of subject matters into the humanities, the social sciences, the physical and biological sciences. Aside from these general courses, there is no divisional grouping of subject matters and departments either in the general or in the senior college curriculum. The History of Western Civilization is classified neither as a humanities course nor as a social science course. It is intended to be equally useful as a preparation for the humanities and for the social sciences; this explains its place among the requirements of the first year.

The present program has evolved over a period of several years. The first general courses were introduced in 1947 and have been periodically revised. Primary importance is attached to class discussions, which are supplemented by lectures and, in appropriate courses, by laboratory work.

The single semester allowed for each of the general courses except that in humanities is perhaps the source of one of the most serious problems in the curriculum. There is evidence that the faculty members, at least some of them, have felt the inadequacy of time acutely. The staff of the history course has recently requested that the course be extended to a full year, meeting three times a week, and that it be granted 6 credit hours instead of the present 5. The request invites consideration of the relation between the learning processes and the distribution of time allotted for courses, a problem which is often ignored in curricular planning. Effective assimilation of content probably proceeds at a slower pace in some subjects than in others; hence the distribution of available time may be as important as the gross number of hours allotted to it. The enduring values of a course in the history of Western civilization may possibly be better achieved in a course meeting three times a week for a year than in one meeting five or six times a week for a semester. Although it would be difficult to prove or disprove this assertion, especially if the only proof were comparisons of grades, it is nevertheless true that, while the bare facts of history can be memorized under pressure and retained for a short period of time, the assimilation of the meaning behind the events of history and the ideas which have determined the character of Western culture cannot be achieved effectively without adequate time for reflection and discussion. In any event, it is important in comparing programs of general education to give some thought to the quantitative scope of the courses. The fact that two programs bear close resemblance in the number and kinds of courses is not a sufficient test of their similarity. General courses, which attempt some form of synthesis or integration of wide areas of knowledge, impose very difficult problems of organization. However competent the instruction, a one-semester course in physical science or in the literature of the Western world can scarcely achieve as much as a course which is allotted a full academic year.

The one-year course in humanities at Berea is an approach to the integration of literature, visual arts, and music. The principles which organize the course differ sharply from those which have been employed in most attempts to unite these subject matters in a comprehensive, single-course view of the arts. Among the earliest general courses in humanities, the most common type was a survey of Western civilization which embraced political, social, and cultural history. In such courses it has been customary to place strong emphasis upon the study of selections of monumental works of art and literature from all principal epochs. Rather infrequently some attention has been given to music. In some instances two parallel courses, one treating of political and social history and one with the arts, mainly literary, were developed; but in all historically oriented courses principal consideration has been given, as a rule, to the arts as an expression of the culture which produced it. The integration of the arts on principles other than historical has been rare. One of the most ambitious is the first of three general courses in the humanities given at the University of Chicago which aims at developing an appreciation of literary, visual, and musical arts through a study of the formative elements characteristic of the three great media of artistic expression and the uses and effects achieved in the individual works of great artists in each field and from all important historical periods.

The humanities course at Berea is organized around several functional units. Each is concerned with a sphere of human activity, e.g., creative man, social man, contemplative man, worshiping man. Each unit includes a selection of works in each medium—literature, visual art, and music—which expresses the interest of the artists with the theme of the unit. The staff for the course is drawn from members of the English department, the art department, and the music department. Each staff member is responsible for instruction only in the field of his special training. The staff, under the direction of a chairman, works as a unit in the organization of the whole course, a task which demands close cooperation in the ordering of the units and in the selection of instructional materials. Creative activity in each medium, particularly in the visual arts, is an important part of the course. The art studio is an important laboratory in the course.

The two courses in Biblical literature in the general curriculum reflect the historical background and traditions of the college. Among many privately endowed colleges whose origins owe much to the Protestant traditions of Christianity, the study of religion or the literature of the Old and New Testaments has never yielded place as a uniform requirement, even in the heyday of the elective system. With the adoption of a distributional plan or a core curriculum the requirement quite naturally became a part of the general or core program. Practices now vary considerably in the application of the requirement. In some colleges the courses in religion are grouped with those in philosophy, and students are granted an option, as in the Antioch and Amherst programs. The requirement of both philosophy and religion, as at Berea, is less common today among colleges of Protestant origin. This is noteworthy since Berea is nonsectarian. Required courses in religion are more likely to occur in colleges which maintain a close denominational affiliation.

BROOKLYN COLLEGE

Brooklyn College is one of the four 4-year institutions of higher education which form a part of the municapal college system of the city of New York. In addition there are three 2-year junior colleges. Founded in 1930 as a coeducational college, it is an outgrowth of branches of the College of the City of New York and Hunter College, established in Brooklyn in 1926 for men and women, respectively. It is the youngest of the colleges in this study, but its growth in recent years, typical of municipal and state colleges, now makes it one of the largest of the group. The total enrollment in 1960–1961, exclusive of the division of adult education, was 19,877 students, 8,728 of whom were in the College of Liberal Arts and Sciences, the division with which this account is concerned. The School of General Studies, an evening school which enrolls chiefly part-time students, was slightly larger; and the division of graduate studies enrolled 2,347 students, full and part time. Of the students in the College of Liberal Arts and Sciences, 45 per cent were men and 55 per cent were women. The college offers courses of study leading to the Bachelor of Arts and the Bachelor of Science degrees.[13] Brooklyn is a nonresidential college. Most of its students are legal residents of New York City, but the college presently admits some students from outside the city. The latter pay a part of their tuition and their home counties pay the balance. In one important respect Brooklyn College is an example of a phenomenon of American education in the twentieth century— a collegiate institution whose services reach far beyond those of the traditional liberal arts college but which does not undertake to embrace all the functions of a university.

Though the college is open to legal residents of New York City,

---

[13] In addition to the Bachelor of Science programs in the usual scientific departments, the college offers B.S. degree programs in accounting, physical education, and health education. It also offers an Associate in Arts degree. The School of General Studies also offers the baccalaureate degrees, and the division of graduate studies grants the Master of Arts and the Master of Science in Education.

its admissions requirements are sufficiently rigorous to impose a degree of selectivity which exceeds that of most tax-supported institutions as well as many private ones. Students are admitted only upon evidence of meeting a required average of class ratings in academic subjects completed in high school. Of the minimum 16 units of high school studies required for admission, 11½ are prescribed in the following distributional pattern: English, 4 units; American history, 1 unit; one foreign language, 3 units; mathematics, 2½ units; natural science, 1 unit.[14]

This prescription is an affirmation that the foundation of a sound general and liberal education must be laid in the secondary school. So specific a list of prerequisites is rarely found among American colleges, and in fact it signifies a doctrine that is contrary to that accepted by most colleges. It is true that most colleges recommend a distribution of secondary school subjects similar to this as advisable in preparing for college, but few impose any fixed number of units in these subjects except in English, for which 3 or 4 are sometimes required. The characteristic view which many colleges have adopted for more than a quarter of a century is well stated in the Reed College Bulletin for 1958–1959: "Over the years Reed College has maintained an attitude of flexibility in relating the particular courses which an applicant has taken in secondary school to the question of his fitness and preparation for the college's academic program. The college expects to continue the attitude and to judge each applicant as an individual." A similar statement comes from Macalester College: "An applicant is not required to present specified units of credit for admission, since Macalester believes that the quality of scholastic performance is more important than mere subject matter requirements as a criterion for selecting its students." Brooklyn College maintains that quality need not be sacrificed by imposing specific admission requirements.

Contained in the views represented by Brooklyn, on the one hand, and Reed and Macalester, on the other, are different conceptions of both the nature and the means of acquiring a general education. The views have immediate consequences for the practice of general education at the collegiate level, yet the effect of these views upon the total conception of general education has been almost entirely ig-

---

[14] Students in the pre-engineering curriculum may be admitted with 2 units of a foreign language and 3 units of mathematics. The science unit must be either physics or chemistry.

nored in contemporary discussions. If general education is the common concern of the schools and colleges, which few educators seem to question, then the problems of prerequisites and the continuity of studies from school to college are acutely important. They have become more important as the curriculums of both the schools and the colleges have expanded.

The theories which currently dictate the attitudes of most colleges toward the substantive character of a proper preparation for college need a thorough reconsideration. No one would deny the importance of the quality of scholastic performance among the criteria of acceptability for admission to college. The distinction, however, between scholastic performance and "mere subject matter requirements" is unrealistic. Scholastic performance is always a performance in subject matters. If some subject matters were not more important than others as a foundation for college studies, colleges would not strongly recommend (as do Reed and Macalester) that high school students concentrate their studies in English, foreign language, mathematics, history, and science. If they believe that a prior knowledge of history is highly desirable, why is it not proper to make this an explicit requirement for admission? Failure to do so often results in a severe handicap to students, and it complicates the curricular and instructional problems of the college. But there is more involved than mere preparation for college. The larger issue is that of the joint responsibility of school and college for the general education of the student. If the modern liberal arts college is to remain committed to the dual functions it now accepts—a "broad foundation" and a "concentration" leading to some vocation or professional training—it will need more support from the schools in laying the broad foundation than it now customarily receives. The issue here is less concerned with the competence of the schools than it is with deliberate and coordinated planning toward a common purpose.

Of course every student admitted to college should be judged as an individual, but the cultivation of a wholesome individuality is surely no more impaired by specific requirements at the secondary school level than it is by specific requirements, in a well-distributed pattern, at the collegiate level. The undeniable fact is that the practice of recommending subject matters without imposing any specific quantitative distribution of secondary school studies tends to impair the student's general education. The student who can distribute his time freely among five or six academic subjects may allow a special interest to absorb an undue amount of time at the expense of other needed subject matters; in fact, he is often encouraged to do just this. Despite official statements that it is "quality of performance" rather than subject matters that are significant indexes for admission, the student knows that to qualify for certain degree programs he must meet some prerequisites in secondary school subjects. He knows that 2½ to 3 years of mathematics and 1 year of either chemistry or physics are virtually mandatory if he expects to major in any field of the natural sciences. He knows that 2 to 3 years of a foreign language are desirable if not necessary if he expects a degree in literature, history, philosophy, or the arts, and that if he does not complete this in high school he will have to make up the loss in college at the expense of other courses which might enlarge his view of knowledge.

The student who is least sure of his vocational interests is no less injured by the ambiguous statements of admissions requirements. Free to distribute his time among the various academic subjects as he inclines, he may wholly neglect some disciplines and begin others at unpropitious times. Every college adviser is familiar with the student who has studied one or two years of a foreign language in his freshman or sophomore years of high school, but is unprepared to pass a qualifying test in the language when he enters college two or three years later. If general courses in physics are justly open to criticism for their superficial character, it must be said in their defense that they have to be planned with the foreknowledge that many students will have only a minimal knowledge of mathematics and perhaps no more than an elementary general science course.

It is quite true, as the Reed College Bulletin says, that the opportunity to pursue certain studies in secondary schools varies greatly with the location and size of the schools. The colleges ought, however, to ask very seriously whether their own lack of firmness in establishing precise though minimal prerequisites in those secondary school subjects which are admittedly important elements of a general education has not proved to be a significant factor in the deterioration of secondary school instruction in some fields. If all colleges suddenly imposed Brooklyn's requirement of three years of secondary school training in one language the immediate effects would be devastating, since there are many high schools unprepared to offer so much and a few which offer none. Until the role of languages in liberal education is more clearly determined and the joint responsibilities of school and college for instruction are firmly fixed, the present unhappy conditions of language instruction in the schools will prevail, conditions which can lead only to injustice to the students who have a serious purpose and to an unpardonable waste of both the students' and the teachers' time and energy.

No college need be so rigid in its standards of admission that it cannot adjust regulations to individual cases where circumstances warrant, but the theory that high school students should enjoy great latitude in the distribution of college preparatory subjects can be as great a fetish as any mechanically rigid system of prerequisites. The notion that a reasonable but clearly specified distribution of high school subjects is harmful to the individuality of the student is controverted by the practices of every vocational and professional school which explicitly specifies those subjects which each considers a prerequisite to vocational studies. Medical schools have not been charged with injuring the individuality of prospective doctors by requiring all applicants to present evidence of specific preparatory training in chemistry, biology, and physics. The fact is that the prevailing policy among most colleges has encouraged early specialization at the expense of a well-ordered program of general studies.

The courses of study leading to all baccalaureate degrees in the College of Liberal Arts and Sciences at Brooklyn consist of three parts: (1) a core curriculum, (2) courses forming a functional major, and (3) free electives. In 1949 the college introduced an experimental curriculum for a limited number of students. This experiment sought to strengthen the regular liberal arts curriculum: (1) it provided some integrated courses in the freshman year and reduced the number of first-year courses; (2) it strengthened the functional major by reducing the number of prescribed courses, with minimal interference with a good general education, and by extending opportunities for free election; and (3) it introduced a system of exemption examinations which would allow superior students freedom to pursue advanced studies within the area of the major or to enlarge the scope of their studies in other areas. Of the total of 128 credit hours required for graduation, the number prescribed in the core curriculum ranged from about 50 to 77. A minimum of 36 credit hours was required in a functional major and from 17 to 42 might be freely elected. The differences in range in the credit hours required in the core depended in part upon previous training and in part upon certain options in the core. Differences in the hours required for a major and those available for election depended in part upon the requirements in the major and in part upon the core program. It is probable that for most students completion of the core requirements normally requires about two years, unless the time is reduced by the exemption examinations.

The prescribed courses which constituted the experimental program of general studies were by no means all of a general or integrated type. The principal experiments in developing integrated courses were in the natural and social sciences. The integrated course in the natural sciences was called "Science in the Modern World." It was a three-semester course especially planned for and restricted to nonscience majors and carried 12 credits. Science majors were required to take introductory one-year courses in specified departments for a total of 16 credits. All students in the experimental program were required to take the one-year general course in the social sciences, which was called "Our Contemporary World." Several of the required courses in the old program were retained with little or no change.[15]

In 1956 the experimental program with some modifications was approved as the standard required core of general studies for all students entering in the fall term of 1957 and thereafter. There have been some important revisions since 1957. Nonscience majors may now choose between the three-semester integrated course or a combination of introductory courses consisting of one year each in the biological and physical sciences. They may also choose between the one-year course, Our Contemporary World, or three introductory departmental courses: Economic Institutions, Introduction to American Government, and either Introduction to Sociology or General Psychology. These options represent the judgment of the curriculum committee that students should have the opportunity to choose between different prescriptions. As at Antioch College, however, the optional provision indicates a shift away from the single general course as a uniform requirement. Other core requirements are:

> Art or music. Either History of Art or Introduction to Music.
> One year, 3 credits
> Classical civilization. Greek and Roman Classics in Translation.
> One semester, 3 credits

[15] A detailed analysis and evaluation of the new curriculum is given in the report of the self-study committee whose work was supported by a grant from the Fund for the Advancement of Education (1954).

English
1. Literature and Self-expression. One year, 8 credits
2. (For non-English majors: Second year)
   Literature and Self-expression (a third semester) *or* a course in English literature. One year, 4 credits
3. (For English majors: Second year)
   History of English Literature. One year, 6 credits

Foreign language
One semester in the literature of the language studied in high school in addition to the minimal entrance requirement. Students who cannot meet the minimal requirement, as established by a placement test, must take such preparatory courses as may be needed to make up the deficiency. Students who wish to begin a new language must meet the entrance requirement and complete two years in the new language.

History of Western civilization
Social and cultural history from the feudal age to the present. One year, 6 credits

Mathematics
Any one of six courses designed to meet different degrees of previous mathematical training and different interests. One semester, 3 or 4 credits

Philosophy. Knowledge and Values. One semester, 3 credits

Speech. Oral Communication. One semester, 2 credits

Physical education. One year, 3 credits for men; 2 credits for women

Health education. One semester, 2 credits

The College of Liberal Arts and Science is organized by departments, and the curriculum follows a departmental pattern. The integrated courses in the natural and social sciences have been developed by and are taught by interdepartmental staffs. The breadth of the core curriculum is noteworthy. In terms of credit hours and variety of content, the subject matters which are generally regarded as humanistic are emphasized in the core requirements more than others and more than is usual in most general education programs. The requirements in English language and literature, foreign language, classical civilization, art or music, and philosophy are a formidable part of the whole; and this list omits the requirement in the history of Western civilization, which is grouped with the humanities quite as often as it is grouped with the social sciences.

An account of the operation of the core program at Brooklyn cannot disregard the exemption examinations. These are open to all students and are given in all courses except those which are designated freshman sequences and physical education. Exemption from prescribed courses up to 9 credit hours may be achieved by superior scores on the tests. There is no limit on the number of credits which a student may earn in elective courses. Students may also qualify for exemption without credit, which enables them to take more elective courses and fewer required courses. Students prepare independently for the examinations with the aid of study guides. The examinations are given once a year at the opening of the fall term.

The similarity in purpose of the exemption examinations and Antioch's achievement tests points to a practice which has gained considerable popularity in recent years. One criticism of comprehensive general programs which allow few options among courses has been their inflexibility. The purpose of various forms of achievement tests which may be taken independently of course registrations and which permit either acceleration or an opportunity for greater freedom of election is to provide flexibility for those students whose knowledge and capacity for independent study merit the freedom and are best prepared to benefit from it. In principle these tests also are an answer to another criticism of modern collegiate education, particularly in America, namely, that students fail to acquire habits of independent study and often depend too much upon the instructor and course lectures. The use of qualifying examinations in so-called "tool subjects" such as English, mathematics, and elementary language courses has long been a practice, but the use of placement tests and various kinds of achievement and comprehensive examinations in so-called "content courses," which permit students to benefit from independent study, has received its chief encouragement and has been most thoroughly tested in a few general education programs during the last two decades. The University of Chicago was one of the first institutions to employ the principle when it adopted the system of comprehensive examinations in 1931–1932 as the sole measure of achievement in all its general courses and abolished all requirements of class attendance. Extensive use of the independent exemption test is currently made by several of the colleges in this study. Exemption tests can be abused by students who are looking for a quick and easy way to satisfy quantitative requirements; and their wise use demands great skill on the part of the instructors and examiners charged with preparing the tests, since such tests will defeat their purpose if they demand less rigorous application than the courses they replace. Nevertheless the basic principle deserves thoughtful consideration. Where properly employed it can help to cultivate the independence and self-discipline that is claimed as a sign of the liberally educated person. Colleges faced with the prospect of increasingly large enrollments may well find that the encouragement of independent study attended by study guides and the occasional counsel of faculty members plus sound achievement examinations may be an important means of alleviating some of the troublesome instructional problems in certain types of courses and for superior students.

GOUCHER COLLEGE

Goucher College was founded in 1885, under the name of The Woman's College of Baltimore City, as a liberal arts college for young women. According to its charter its purpose was to provide an education "under auspices distinctly favorable to the maintenance of the faith and practice of the Christian religion." There was, however, a provision that all departments of the college should be open to students of any religion or sect and that no religious tests should be imposed on trustees, faculty, or students. In 1910 its name was changed to Goucher College in honor of an early benefactor and president of the institution.

Goucher is today an independent, privately endowed college for young women. In 1957–1958 it enrolled 713 students of whom 685 were candidates for the Bachelor of Arts degree. Seventeen were candidates for the degree of Master of Education, the only other degree offered, and the remaining were students at large. According to recent estimates, approximately 70 per cent of entering freshman students graduate from the college. Of the 140 graduates in the class of 1958, a large majority planned to enter upon full-time employment following graduation or to continue with graduate studies or some form of vocational training. The most-favored career was elementary school teaching. Other vocational choices were widely distributed. Although the majority of Goucher's students come from the Middle Atlantic and New England states, all sections of the nation are well represented in the student body.

Graduation from high school is a normal condition of admission, but since 1951 Goucher has admitted a number of carefully selected students who have completed two or three years of high school, providing they give promise of the intellectual competence and social maturity adequate to the demands of college life. Of the 16 units of high school studies normally required of high school graduates, 4 must be in English. The remaining 12 may be selected from four groups of studies: foreign languages, mathematics, natural science, and social studies. Applicants are urged to present either

148

three or four years of a foreign language and at least three years of college preparatory mathematics. Entrance credit is not given for less than two years of a foreign language. All applicants must take the College Entrance Examination Board aptitude tests and three achievement tests. One of these must be the English test. Others may be in any subject, but not more than one foreign language test may be offered and only one in either mathematics or natural science.

At the time that this study was initiated Goucher, like Antioch, was engaged in a major revision of its curricular requirements; and the revision of its general education program was a primary object. Stanford University, also, had just approved a new undergraduate program with similar ends in view. Although the inclusion of these colleges had been decided upon prior to any knowledge of impending changes, the coincidence seemed a happy circumstance because it suggested the possibility of ascertaining whether there might be any identifiable direction or goal toward which colleges were moving. At Antioch and Goucher the analysis was complicated by the fact that the points of departure were almost at the extreme of opposites. Antioch was clearly moving from a conception of general education based upon a common core of uniformly required courses to a conception of curricular flexibility within a controlled distributional framework. Goucher, on the other hand, was moving away from a program of extreme flexibility with no specific courses required except one in religion which met a charter stipulation. Under the curriculum revision of 1957 Goucher has moved to a clearly defined distributional framework, with a limited, though relatively large, option of courses in each of three subject-matter areas (or faculties) into which the curriculum is divided, namely (1) languages, literature, philosophy, and the arts; (2) history and the social sciences; (3) mathematics and the natural sciences. The number of options in each area is smaller than that permitted in the new Antioch program. In addition to the distribution requirements, the revised curriculum of 1957 has defined levels of achievement in English composition and foreign language which a student normally meets by taking a two-term course in expository writing and one or more courses in a foreign language.

Prior to the reorganization of the curriculum which became effective in the autumn of 1958, the last major curricular revision at Goucher had occurred in 1934. Part 1 of this study referred to the widespread reforms which were taking place in the decade beginning about 1930 in the name of general education. The reform at Goucher in 1934, like so many others, was intended, so its designers believed, to provide an improved approach to the problems of general education. It was, nevertheless, radically different from the trend which sought a reduction in the number of courses open to freshmen and encouraged experimentation in new types of general or survey courses, since it sought not to reduce but to increase the number of courses open to freshmen. The curriculum adopted by the faculty in 1934 may be characterized as a free elective system, but the one which it replaced has been described as "regimented and controlled for the first two years by course requirements," and as having "induced an academic lockstep that kept students from stepping out at their own pace and in their own direction." [16] Also the charge was made that it favored some departments to the nearly total exclusion of others.

The faculty began its reform measure in 1934 by drafting a definition of the goals of general education; these were stated in the form of eight objectives. Each student was expected to make reasonable progress toward the attainment of these objectives through a program of studies of her own choice, subject to the advice of her guidance counselor, who emphasized the interdependence of all branches of knowledge and encouraged a distribution among the arts and sciences. The ultimate checks upon the student's progress toward the desired goal were the sophomore examinations. These examinations, which provided a measure of progress toward the achievement of the eight objectives, were taken at the end of the sophomore year. They were important, together with the student's cumulative grade record, in determining admission to the Upper Division. The objectives, as they were originally stated in 1934, were:

1. To establish and maintain physical and mental health.
2. To comprehend and communicate ideas both in English and in foreign languages.
3. To understand the scientific method in theory and application.
4. To understand the heritage of the past in its relation to the present.
5. To establish satisfying relations with individuals and with groups.

[16] *Report of the Curriculum Committee of Goucher College, 1956.*

6. To utilize resources with economic and aesthetic satisfaction.
7. To enjoy literature and the other arts.
8. To appreciate religious and philosophical values.

The Report of the Curriculum Committee submitted in 1956, which presented the proposals subsequently adopted, gave its approval to the conceptual framework of the 1934 curriculum, but described in detail the disparity between concept and practice that had revealed itself in the twenty-two years intervening. "The extreme reaction against required courses and the faculty's failure to define a pattern of education that could be freely administered apparently combined to heighten the departmentalism that the new program [of 1934] had sought to avoid. It also tended to fragment the student's learning rather than to integrate it." The Report quoted extensively from the College Bulletin of 1956 to show the variety of ways by which each of the objectives might be achieved, the consequence of which, it says, is "to make the lower division program of many students a potpourri of introductory courses." The Report added that the old curriculum failed to encourage the degree of initiative and freedom of which it boasted. In support of this a study of course elections revealed a nearly standardized pattern of election. This was due in part to the fact that English composition, one foreign language, introductory courses in history, physiology, and bacteriology, and a course in religion which was specified by the college charter had become virtual requirements. The remaining courses, though distributed somewhat unevenly among the three divisions of subject matters, were chiefly introductory courses in the various departmental fields. Choices among these were to some extent guided by the character of the sophomore examinations.

The curriculum committee, whose labors extended over a period of several years, had given encouragement to some experiments before it submitted its final report. Four general courses, which Goucher calls "interdepartmental courses," were introduced in the curriculum of the Lower College in 1953—in the humanities, the social sciences, the biological sciences, and the physical sciences. The history of the interdepartmental two-term sequences at Goucher is interesting and perhaps reflects a decentralized procedure in the planning as well as differences in attitudes among the faculty groups responsible for their construction and teaching. Of the two science sequences which were developed, that in the biological sciences was given only once, and that in the physical sciences failed to materialize because of a lack of sufficient registration to warrant its being given. The sequence in the humanities was offered from 1953 to 1956, with registration increasing steadily during the first three years. Thereafter registration languished to such a point that the course was dropped in 1957. The highly successful sequence in the social sciences took a longer period of time to establish itself but it was dropped in 1960, when it became clear that it was not being used to reduce and replace introductory departmental courses in sociology, political science, and history, whose content it was to a large extent duplicating. Neither of the sequences in the humanities or social sciences had been successful in meeting the problem of staffing; the original idea had been that, within a reasonably short period of time, the courses would be given by one faculty member rather than three. At the time the sequences were dropped from the curriculum they still were using three faculty members who were present at all meetings of the classes. The curriculum committee had observed in its Report of 1956 after three years of observation of the interdepartmental courses that "it is doubtful whether the courses have yet achieved their two-fold aim: (1) to introduce students to the methods and/or characteristic problems of the three broad fields of knowledge; and (2) to reduce the number of introductory courses by integrating where integration is possible and desirable."

The experience of the Goucher faculty with respect to the short-lived interdepartmental courses in the sciences is not uncommon. As a rule, general humanities courses have fared somewhat better than similar courses in the natural and social sciences. This may be partly due to the nature of the subject matters and the problems which attend their organization. It may be that the range of differences in the backgrounds of students in the sciences, particularly the natural sciences, is greater, which would make it more difficult to plan a single integrated course properly adapted to the capacities of all students. It may be also that differences in professional motivations have been important factors in the comparative success of the humanities staffs. Teachers of literature, the fine arts, and philosophy have long been accustomed to the presence of students who are not majors in their fields. The enjoyment of great works in every field of the arts attracts many students who have no professional interest in the humanities. Instructors move with considerable freedom through the literature and arts of different ages and of different nations, and they have one advantage of great significance; they are always dealing with individual works which can speak directly to the student in some degree. In the sciences, and again more particularly in the natural sciences, professional interest is the primary factor in attracting students to courses; hence the courses tend to be planned with a view to professional demands.

The unsuccessful effort to develop a general course in the physical sciences at Goucher invites speculation upon the role of the sciences in women's colleges, especially those with enrollments under one thousand. It is not surprising that in most such institutions the enrollment in the natural sciences is proportionately much lower than it is in men's colleges or in coeducational colleges. An a priori judgment might hold that women's colleges would be a natural ground for many experiments in the development of courses planned especially for the large number of women who have no professional interest or initial enthusiasm for this field. There is, however, another factor which must be considered. Precisely because there are few science majors, teachers quite naturally exert themselves to make their courses as strong as possible both in the interest of their majors and with a view to sustaining the professional standing of their departments. Because the staffs are likely to be small, there is often little time available for planning and teaching courses especially designed for students whose interests lie in other fields.

The attentive observer of the recent history of general education will have, I think, great sympathy for the teachers of science who undertake the planning of a science curriculum that meets the needs of the nonmajor, for he is aware that many of the students will be poorly prepared for the kind of instruction which would be most valuable. His sympathy will not prevent him from reminding the teachers of science that while they have recommended and even required prospective science majors to make adequate preparation in high school by taking specified courses in mathematics and laboratory sciences, they have been generally indifferent to the kind or amount of preparatory studies in science and mathematics essential or useful for the nonprofessional student. If knowledge of the methods of science is part of a liberal education, then the training of most students will have to differ from that of preprofessional students. There is just ground for dissatisfaction with a great deal that has been attempted at this level. There are equally just reasons for believing that one or two introductory courses in departmental fields are unsatisfactory for the needs of the nonmajor. Each branch has grown much too complex to justify the belief that an introduction to a single science can yield a truly liberal understanding of the problems of other related fields. The important task of giving the proper kind of education in science to the nonspecialist is a challenge to the imagination of teachers of science—a challenge which has yet to engage the amount of interest which it deserves.

The particular changes, recommended by the curriculum committee in 1956 and later approved by the faculty, which concern directly the general education requirements may be divided into two categories:

1. *Administrative organization.* For both administrative and curricular purposes, the faculty is organized in three divisions:
   Faculty I —languages, literature, philosophy, and the arts
   Faculty II —history and the social sciences
   Faculty III—the natural sciences and mathematics
Each faculty is under the direction of a chairman, though this office does not eliminate departmental chairmanships. The academic year continues, as in the past, to be divided into three terms, and a normal course load for each student is three courses per term. Most courses are for one term; some are for two.

2. *General education requirements.*
a. A proficiency requirement in English composition, which is normally satisfied by passing a two-term course, English 1–2. Students of superior achievement, as measured by placement tests, may satisfy the requirement by taking the second term or by taking an advanced course in expository prose.
b. A proficiency requirement in a foreign language, unchanged from the old curriculum. Students may continue a language begun in secondary school or begin a new language. Placement tests indicate the extent of continued study required of each student. Students who elect to begin a new language are normally expected to complete four terms of study.
c. A one-term requirement in religion (Knowledge of the Sacred Scriptures). This is a charter requirement. It may be met by taking either of two courses in the Bible or by satisfactory achievement on an exemption examination.

d. Area distribution requirements. In each of the three faculties, students must elect one 2-term sequence or two 1-term courses which are sequential in character. An exception to this rule is that in Faculty III where the equivalent of four 1-term courses is required, with two of these a sequence and with at least one course chosen from either the physical sciences or the biological sciences. The departments have retained the long-established one-term introductory courses intended for nonmajors and for those who enter college with no prior experience in the field. The sequences that have been established to replace the interdepartmental sequences are all departmental.

In Faculty I the English department offers a two-term sequence and two sequential one-term courses in literature which are acceptable in meeting distribution requirements. The fine arts, music, French, Spanish, and philosophy also offer two sequential one-term courses. Faculty II, in addition to a sequence in history, offers two sequences in the social sciences, economics, and sociology, although in each of these fields the first term of the sequence may be taken independently. Political science offers two courses, sequential in character, dealing with problems of the American national government. In the biological sciences, besides a newly planned introductory course, there is a sequence in the history of science, a sequence in psychology, and a course in physiology and hygiene, all optional. In the physical sciences, there are several combinations of sequences in each of the departmental areas of chemistry, physics, mathematics, and astronomy. The several combinations have been carefully planned in order to adjust the content to the previous experience of the students in each of these fields. One of the mathematics courses, Language and Concepts of Mathematics, is planned primarily for the student whose major is not in mathematics or the physical sciences but is interested in the history of mathematics, its concepts and symbolism, and its cultural connotations.

Any or all of the distributional requirements may be met by satisfactory achievement on exemption examinations. In addition to the use of placement tests in English and foreign language and the exemption tests, the sophomore examinations are continued in the revised program; they are, however, diagnostic tests which serve as instruments for guidance in future work. Since 1955 the graduate record examinations area tests have been used for this purpose.

In 1960 the faculty, following recommendations of the curriculum committee, took the last step in the curriculum study that had been going on since 1950 by fitting the curriculum into three sequential levels of demand and responsibility, each level demanding greater independence of study and thought by the student. A fourth level is that of the senior thesis, an independent project extending over two terms, the work of which is of an advanced character, requiring more initiative and power of organization than are usually expected of undergraduate students. The last of these changes became effective in 1961–1962.

Although it is impossible to assess the significance of all the curricular changes which have occurred during the four years since the curriculum committee's first proposals were adopted, several things are clear. The net result has been the adoption of a more firmly organized program of distribution and concentration. The optional-course distributional plan, which provides the foundation of the student's general education, is balanced in so far as it ensures some experience with the major fields of knowledge. This is the function of the first of the three sequential levels of the new curricular structure. Since all the courses in this level are departmental sequences, following the dropping of the interdepartmental courses, there is no provision for a comprehensive view of the relationships of the several disciplines, except in so far as the instructors conscientiously guide students in discovering them. There seems to be little doubt that the latest changes will materially strengthen the departmental majors. We shall meet with a similar direction of changing ideas in the recently revised curriculum of another woman's college, Mills College, which like Goucher has made important administrative and curricular changes during the same period.

THE UNIVERSITY OF LOUISVILLE

The University of Louisville is a municipal institution, although it receives some financial support from private sources as well as from the state of Kentucky. Resident students are defined as those who hold or whose parents hold legal residence in Jefferson County, Kentucky; and the great majority of its students are legally residential students.

Like a number of other institutions which have grown gradually in larger American cities, the university is the result of the merging of the resources of several local institutions. It traces its origins to the Jefferson Seminary, founded in 1798, and to other local schools, including the Medical Institute of the City of Louisville. In 1846 the several schools were merged and chartered under the name of the University of Louisville. In the same year a School of Law was established as a division of the university; other schools have been added in succeeding years. At present the university consists of the College of Arts and Sciences and the Schools of Medicine, Law, Dentistry, Music, Business, Social Work, the Graduate School, and the Speed Scientific School. In addition there are several affiliated institutes. The College of Arts and Sciences is the principal under-graduate division. Other schools which offer baccalaureate degrees use the services of the College of Arts and Sciences for instruction in courses outside their professional fields. The program of general education reviewed here is that offered by the College of Arts and Sciences.

The College of Arts and Sciences enrolled approximately three thousand students out of a total of about eight thousand in 1958–1959 in all divisions of the university. It is coeducational, but the ratio of men to women is higher than in many similar institutions. The college offers the Bachelor of Arts and Bachelor of Science degrees and the Associate in Arts to students who complete a two-year program which includes the general education requirements and either twelve semester hours in one department or eighteen hours in one division. Like Brooklyn College, it does not admit all graduates of accredited high schools who meet the legal residential requirements. Applicants

157

for admission must rank in the upper 50 per cent of their high school classes, or if their ranking is lower, they must give evidence of superior promise on the admission tests, which are given to all entering students. Of the 15 units of high school studies normally required for admission, 12 must be in academic subjects. There is no specific requirement governing the distribution of the 12 courses. Like Goucher College, the University of Louisville has for several years admitted to the College of Arts and Sciences a small number of exceptionally qualified students who have completed three years of high school upon the recommendation of their principals and superior achievement on the admission tests.

The admission tests are a form of placement and exemption test. They include scientific and literary aptitude tests, tests of reading and writing ability, and general culture tests covering the social sciences, history, literature, art, the natural sciences, and mathematics. Students with high scores on the tests qualify for exemption from the general education course requirements in the appropriate areas, with the exception of the course in English composition. The qualifying standards are high; as a rule not more than 10 per cent earn exemptions. Exemption by admission test scores also earns exemption from the sophomore comprehensive examinations. Unlike the Goucher College sophomore examination, the passing of the sophomore comprehensives is one requirement for admission without qualification to the Senior College. The tests, however, are not based upon the courses in the general education program but are standardized general culture tests.

The division of the college into a Junior and a Senior College is chiefly a curricular device for distinguishing and emphasizing the general objectives of the first two years from the more specialized objectives of the upper two years. All courses in the curriculum are designated as either Junior or Senior College courses. There is no division of the faculty or administrative officers corresponding to the curricular division. The faculty is organized by departments, and the departments are grouped in three divisions: the humanities, the social sciences, and the natural sciences. Administrative direction of both the Junior and the Senior Colleges is vested in the Dean of the College of Arts and Sciences, and there is no other administrative officer or faculty committee whose specific duty is the supervision of the program of general education.

The basic required courses in the Junior College, which are called courses in general education, are both departmental and divisional. These courses, required of all candidates for the B.A. degree, unless excused by the admission test scores, are:

1. English Composition   one year (6 credits) freshman year
2. Problems of Modern Society one year (6 credits) freshman year
3. Introduction to the Natural
 Sciences   one year (6 credits) freshman year
4. History of Western Civilization one year (6 credits) sophomore year
5. Introduction to the Humanities one year (7 credits) sophomore year

The natural science course is divided into two parts; the first semester deals with the physical sciences, and the second with the biological sciences. The humanities course is also subdivided. One semester is given to a course in world literature which grants 3 credits. In the other semester students may choose two courses from the following subjects: art, music, and philosophy.

1. Art
 Introduction to Architecture *or*
 Introduction to Painting
2. Music
 Introduction to Music
3. Philosophy
 Introduction to Philosophy

Each course grants 2 credits. Physical education and a series of orientation lectures (freshman lectures) are required in the freshman year. Two years at the collegiate level of a foreign language are required of all students in Bachelor of Arts programs. The requirement may be met by a qualifying examination or by completing a second-year course. Language requirements vary in the B.S. and pre-professional programs from none to one or two years. In science and certain preprofessional programs, equivalent departmental courses may be substituted for the general courses in humanities, social science, and natural science.

The basic general program was introduced in 1932 and has, in its general details, undergone little change. It is one of the oldest continuing programs in American colleges. In addition to the basic program, which is normally completed in the first two years, all degree programs require that students shall take one or more courses at the Senior College level outside the department and division of their concentration. Though students may elect these courses, several departments recommend courses or areas of study in other divisions which will contribute to a well-integrated degree program. The college regards this requirement as a legitimate continuation of the general education of students beyond the core curriculum of the Junior College.

The required introductory general courses in natural science, the social sciences, and the humanities are regarded as divisional rather than departmental courses, and they are taught by staffs drawn from several departments. Each division offers divisional courses at the Senior College level, and the humanities division offers a divisional major. A recent addition to the curriculum is an International Studies Area Program which offers a major and is directed by an inter-divisional committee. Among the Senior College divisional courses are the following: in the humanities—four courses on epochs of culture and four courses on the great books of the Western world, arranged in a chronological sequence; in the natural sciences—a course on the history and philosophy of science (required of all science majors); in the social sciences—a course based upon the contributions to social thought made by leaders in all major fields of the social sciences.

The principle of the divisional major and the interdepartmental course has gained general favor in recent years and it must be included as an extension of the basic purpose of general education which aims at disclosing principles and methods by which related subject matters can be more fully apprehended. No single introductory course in the humanities, however well conceived and taught, can successfully comprehend in any depth the variety of materials and disciplines which constitute the humanities. A well-planned major which embraces literature, the fine arts, and philosophy in a historical or critical context can give a meaning to the humanities which no departmental major can hope to do. The divisional major has by no means displaced the departmental major and minor, but it has an appeal to many students who wish to explore a broader range of subjects and disciplines than a departmental major permits.

In the absence of a faculty committee or an administrative officer whose principal task is the coordination of the several parts of the core program at the Junior College level, considerable responsibility at Louisville rests upon the divisional and departmental faculties. English and the history of Western civilization are the responsibility of their respective departments. Each of the general courses is in the charge of a chairman who obtains his staff from members of the appropriate departments. Instructors in the various sections of all core courses have considerable freedom in adapting materials of the course and are solely responsible for the grades of students in their sections. For students who pass these courses with a grade of C or better, the sophomore comprehensive examinations are chiefly diagnostic. Those whose grades are below C must pass the examinations with a grade of C as a prerequisite to admission to the Senior College. Practice varies from staff to staff with regard to teaching assignments in the core courses. In some departments teaching in a core course is frequently assigned to young staff members; in others older and more experienced teachers insist upon teaching regularly.

The staffing of general courses in large institutions where there is no central administrative authority and policy has often been a major difficulty. The problem is unlike that of the small college or even that of the large institution where the general course is an elective and the number of sections remains small. The chairman of the course often faces the task of approaching departmental chairmen annually to request the release of time for one or more members of their staffs. The policy frequently results in a rapid turnover of staff, and occasionally it leads to an assignment of the least experienced members of the departments. In either case it militates against the development of an effective *esprit de corps* which is essential to staff-taught courses.

The principal question provoked by the core program of general education at the University of Louisville is, once more, that of the relation of the time available to the scope of the subject matter. Exclusive of physical education and the freshman lectures, the program amounts to thirty-one semester hours or the equivalent of a little more than one academic year's work for a student carrying a normal load of fifteen semester hours. One semester of physical science and one semester of biological science is the sum of the assured experience for nonscience majors. These are lecture courses, supplemented by required and recommended readings, but without laboratory work. It is not uncommon among colleges to limit the basic requirement in natural science to one year, as the Berea College program and others yet to be reviewed show. It is less common to reduce the requirement in literature to one semester. There has been some discussion among the faculty of permitting students to choose one 3-hour course in the area of art, music, and philosophy. The semester course devoted to world literature does not attempt a comprehensive survey of all epochs of Western literature, and currently it places greatest emphasis upon the literature of the nineteenth and twentieth centuries.

The general course in the history of civilization presents another instance of extreme compression of content. The first semester treats Near Eastern, Hindu, Chinese, Greco-Roman, and European medieval civilizations. The second semester covers modern European history from the Renaissance to the present, stressing the global expansion of European culture and the revolutionary aftermaths of two world wars. In the expansion of the subject matter of this course, there is an illustration of an acute problem concerning the role of history in general education courses. Since the end of World War II events have forced an acknowledgment that history is in truth global. The issue which now arises is how to deal effectively with the history of civilizations in its global dimensions. We have only to recall some of the early discussions of general education to be reminded of the high priority which has long been placed on history as an indispensable part of a general education. For some leading educators at the beginning of this century, European and American history were regarded as the central discipline around which all others might be grouped. But it is doubtful that the minimal foundation can henceforth be safely limited to European and American civilization. If history is to have an important place in general education in the future it seems likely that a fresh approach to the organization of the content and methods of instruction will be necessary.

The severely compressed general courses in the Louisville curriculum would be more open to criticism were it not for the requirement that students must devote some elective time to courses outside the division of their major. Elective courses especially designed for nonmajors at both the Junior and the Senior College levels are provided in most departments. Majors in English, for example, must include twelve semester hours of study in *either* or *both* the natural sciences and the social sciences, six of which must be at the Senior College level. It would be unfair, also, to fail to mention the unusually effective use of the limited available time which both the art department and the music department have made of the resources of the university and the city in strengthening their contribution to the general humanities course. Through the Allen R. Hite Institute the general humanities course has had at its disposal original sources in visual art often denied to colleges. The audio-visual department and radio station operated by the Louisville Free Public Library maintain a direct FM service for all Louisville schools. The music department, which provides staff members for the music sections of the general humanities course, is well equipped with listening rooms and classrooms which are directly connected with the FM station and can secure upon request the excellent resources of the library's musical library.

MACALESTER COLLEGE

Macalester College was founded in St. Paul, Minnesota, in 1885 as a liberal arts college for young men; in 1893 it became coeducational. From its beginning it has been affiliated with the United Presbyterian Church, U.S.A. In 1958–1959 it enrolled 1,659 students of which 726 were men and 933 were women. The college offers the Bachelor of Arts and the Bachelor of Science degrees; the latter is awarded only to students specializing in business administration, elementary education, art education, medical technology, and a functional major related to nursing. It offers one advanced degree, the Master in Education.

Macalester draws the great majority of its student body from Minnesota and the bordering states. A large number of students are residents of the St. Paul–Minneapolis metropolitan area. It is primarily a residential college, but it unites characteristics of the residential college and the urban college for commuters.

Although Macalester admits graduates of accredited high schools upon evidence of quality rather than upon fulfillment of any specified credits in prerequisite courses, applicants are strongly urged to include in their preparation three years of English, two years of foreign language and mathematics, and one year each of history and a laboratory science. Despite these recommendations the college finds it necessary to offer a noncredit course in elementary algebra for students who have had no high school mathematics.

I have previously referred to the twofold conception of functions which Macalester acknowledges as its educational goal—the provision of a broad general education and of the foundations of a specialized education leading to a career. General education is not identified by the college with any particular kind of course or with any specific courses; nor is it regarded as restricted to the first two years. The college regards its provisions for elective courses in the upper years as the means by which general education can be continued throughout the four years. There is, however, a distributional requirement amounting to slightly over one-half of the total credits required for the bachelor's degree which are described as "basic requirements

164

for cultural distribution." The basic requirements for the Bachelor of Arts degree are distributed in the following manner:

Freshman English   6 credits
   A one-year course in communication skills.

Foreign language   6 to 14 credits
   One year in addition to two years of high school study or two years if the student has no high school preparation or wishes to begin a new language. The requirement is waived for students with four years of high school work in one language.

Literature   6 credits
   Courses in English literature or a foreign language literature at the third or fourth year level, or a general humanities course.

Science or mathematics   12 credits
   Group A: astronomy, biology, geology
   Group B: chemistry, mathematics, physics

   The distribution of credits in the sciences is quite flexible. Students may elect 8 credits in either group and choose the remaining 4 from the other. Since there are optional courses in most departments, it is possible to satisfy the 8-credit requirement either by taking one 8-credit course or by taking two 4-credit courses. The provision for 4-credit courses gives an opportunity to distribute courses among two departmental fields in either group.

Social science and psychology   12 credits
   At least four of the following introductory courses
   Economics   Political science
   Geography   Psychology
   History   Sociology
It should be observed that no options are offered within a department of the social sciences, except history, where the choice between Modern Civilization and Modern American Civilization is permitted. All courses are semester courses.

Philosophy   3 credits
   Optional courses at the second-year level are offered.

Religion   8 credits
   A somewhat complicated plan of optional courses is offered, but at least six hours must be studies in the English Bible, either Old Testament history or a survey of Biblical literature.

Fine arts   2–3 credits
    One course to be chosen from two in art, two in music, and one
    in speech.
Senior Symposium: Great Issues of the Modern World, one semester

Physical education   2 credits

The requirements for the Bachelor of Science degree are modified slightly by a reduction in the foreign language requirement, a reduction in the number of options in the social science requirement, the omission of the fine arts requirement, and by making psychology a uniform requirement. The number of formal courses in the natural sciences is reduced, and additional courses of a functional type are substituted.

The organization of the distributional requirements does not conform strictly to a divisional or group plan or to a departmental schematism. The social sciences and the natural sciences follow a conventional group plan, but subjects that are often grouped under humanities are divided into four groups, two of which are strictly departmental and two which are interdepartmental. The subdivisional classifications in the natural sciences are also puzzling. It is not clear why biology, astronomy, and geology should be grouped together, unless the purpose is to make possible a greater variety of one-semester course offerings. The options and the grouping apparently permit a student to omit any study of biology. We must take notice, however, of one use of the optional-course plan which is unusual. Biology 101–102 is an advanced introductory course for students who have had previous experience in biology. These may not take Biology 109 which is a one-semester course for students without prior training. Similar alternatives are offered in chemistry and physics. A noncredit course is required of students who have not had elementary algebra or its equivalent. A special course in English writing and speech is an alternative for foreign students to the regular freshman English course. All these provisions are evidence that the college recognizes some consequences of the generally poor coordination of high school and college curriculums. Given Macalester's policy in regard to admissions, it is commendable that the college makes such provisions. Many colleges do not. But whether Macalester's unwillingness to name specific prerequisites as conditions for admission is a wise one is altogether another question. It is shared at present by the majority of liberal arts colleges. In the account of the curriculum of Brooklyn College I have indicated my own conviction that the large issue of planned articulation and continuity of school and college studies needs a thorough discussion such as it has not had for many years.

The core of the general education program at Macalester is a limited optional-course distributional plan. Only freshman English is uniformly required. This course is so organized that the more able students are assigned to sections meeting three hours per week while the less competent are placed in sections meeting five hours in order to permit time for more intensive study of fundamentals of writing and reading. The only courses of a general or interdepartmental type are the introductory course in biology and some courses offered by the division of humanities. Two courses at the sophomore level are concerned with classics of the Western tradition, one with major works of Greek and Roman antiquity and the other with a selection of drama, fiction, and poetry of the nineteenth century. A third-year course unites literature, art, and music in an organization which deals with the formal characteristics of each medium and with the uses of these in the context of a variety of themes.

Two other interdepartmental programs, which do not fall within the scope of the distributional requirements, are nevertheless important extensions of the interdisciplinary objectives of general education in the upper years of the college. These are the Area Studies Program and the International Studies Program. The Area Studies Program is a cooperative project developed by Macalester and three other colleges in the St. Paul–Minneapolis community: Hamline, St. Catherine, and St. Thomas. Russia, Asia, the Middle East, and Latin America are the areas included; and a one-year course open to juniors and seniors is given in each area. The courses undertake to give a comprehensive view of political, social, and cultural characteristics of each area. The program of international studies is a cooperative enterprise of the division of social studies and offers a functional major.

Like many liberal arts colleges located in urban areas with a substantial number of nonresidential students, Macalester experiences a considerable attrition of its student body. State-supported institutions expect this as a consequence of statutes governing admission. Many are able to adjust to the condition by offering two-year programs leading to an Associate in Arts degree. For the private liberal arts college the problem is more serious. In general, they must plan curriculums upon the assumption that the greater part of the students will work toward a baccalaureate degree, and it is difficult to plan good programs for students who do not intend to complete four years. I am unable to say what the precise causes of attrition at Macalester may be, although it is likely that some of them are identical with those of many colleges in a similar position. Students in a metropolitan area find it economically more satisfactory to live at home while completing preliminaries to professional or vocational studies. Many transfer after two years to the professional or vocational schools of their choice. Another class of students, and a very large class it is, enters college with no plan for completing a degree program. Social custom rather than intellectual interest is a principal motivation, and the attraction of a relatively small liberal arts college is very great for many such students. Another group is primarily interested in vocational preparation of a kind less demanding than the usual liberal arts program. It is to Macalester's credit that the general requirements have been adjusted with considerable skill to the needs of the different groups of students which are attracted to the college. Nevertheless the problem of attrition in many small liberal arts colleges is serious and one that makes more difficult the planning of well-ordered programs of both general and liberal education.

MICHIGAN STATE UNIVERSITY

Michigan Agricultural College, established by an act of the state Legislature in 1855, was the first institution of higher education in America founded for the primary purpose of providing, at the expense of the state, scientific training in the agricultural arts. It was a model of the type of college envisioned by the progenitors of the Land-Grant Act, passed by Congress and signed by President Lincoln in 1862. Upon the passage of the act, the college became the official land-grant college of the state of Michigan. The expansion of its educational services in the century since its founding is characteristic of the growth of all the land-grant institutions of higher education in the nation. As its branches of vocational instruction enlarged, its name was changed to Michigan State College; and in 1955, in recognition of its expanding graduate research activities and its extensive program of continuing education, its name was again changed to Michigan State University.

Two other institutions included in this study are land-grant institutions, the University of Minnesota and Washington State University. It is difficult to assess accurately the importance of the role which the Land-Grant Act played in higher education in America. Its purpose, to provide the means for both liberal and practical education to the citizens of each state at a minimum cost to the student, was an extension of the spirit which had motivated several of the states to provide free elementary and secondary schools. From their beginnings the land-grant colleges were designed to provide kinds of vocational education which few private colleges were prepared to offer. Because they were supported by public funds, both Federal and state, the qualifications for admission were intentionally less selective than those of most private institutions. Because they were established primarily for the benefit of the agricultural and industrial classes, the practical or vocational functions of higher education were of paramount importance, and this tradition has yielded slowly to a broader conception of the importance of liberal education. Within the last quarter of a century, however, the social structure of these institu-

169

tions has greatly changed, and with the change there have been important administrative and curricular changes which indicate that a new conception of the importance of a liberal education for the engineer, the farmer, and the housewife has gained approval. The expression of this new conception is frequently found in new curricular requirements which the institutions refer to as their "programs of general education."

The evidence of social change is reflected in the tremendous growth of the student bodies and the shift in the relative numerical strength of the several "schools" or "colleges" which constitute the separate administrative units of the institutions. The growth of the student body of Michigan State is a dramatic example of the expansion of the land-grant colleges. From the seventy-eight students which constituted its first class, it grew in 100 years to an enrollment in 1958–1959 of nearly twenty thousand students. Of these a little over fifteen thousand are full- or part-time undergraduates in residence. The most rapid period of growth has occurred since the close of World War II. Although it is no discredit in any way to the importance of their graduate services, Michigan State and the majority of the land-grant colleges are still predominantly undergraduate institutions. The undergraduates at Michigan State were distributed in 1958–1959 among the following colleges:

The College of Agriculture	1,214 students
The College of Business and Public Service	3,760 students
The College of Communication Arts	670 students
The College of Education	4,026 students
The College of Engineering	1,813 students
The College of Home Economics	747 students
The College of Science and Arts	3,296 students
The College of Veterinary Medicine	424 students

The present numerical superiority of enrollments in the Colleges of Education, Business, and Science and Arts is characteristic of the land-grant colleges, whether maintained as an integral part of a state university (e.g., the University of Minnesota, the University of Illinois, the University of Wisconsin) or as separate institutions (e.g., Michigan State University, Purdue University, Washington State University). The land-grant colleges are no longer "cow colleges," and the variety of their undergraduate educational services often exceeds that of large private universities.

In most state universities and in some private universities the various "colleges" exercise considerable independence in formulating the general curricular requirements in their courses of study leading to a baccalaureate degree; and it is not uncommon to find as many standards of general education as there are separate colleges. In a bold attempt to eliminate some of the inconsistencies and inequities resulting from variations in the common or general requirements for a degree, Michigan State undertook in 1944 an extensive administrative and curricular reform which has had few parallels among the large state colleges and universities of the nation. The Basic College, which was then established as the principal educational unit responsible for developing and administering a uniform program of general education, has been widely publicized. In 1960 the name was officially changed to University College. Descriptions of it should clearly distinguish the principle of administrative organization from the curricular structure, since the former is capable of supporting a great variety of curricular patterns.[17]

The unique feature of the administrative structure of University College is its autonomy. Its functions are no less specific than those of any other college in the university. The Dean of University College is the chief administrative officer. Appointments to the faculty and promotions may be made without consultation with the faculties of other colleges. All entering students, except such transfer students as may show evidence of having previously satisfied the equivalent of the University College curriculum, are automatically members of University College. They may be (and most are) simultaneously enrolled in another college; but they remain members of University College until they have completed all the requirements of the general education program. Normally these requirements are completed by the end of the sophomore year, although the curriculum does not demand all the student's time during the first two years. The University College curriculum is subject to the approval of the faculty of the

[17] Curricular experiments with general courses began at Michigan State in 1936 with the development of a general course in the biological sciences. In the following two years three additional general courses were introduced: physical science, the history of Western civilization, and a course in the arts. In 1942 the faculty gave approval to a plan for the creation of a two-year general college, designed for students who intended to terminate their college studies after two years. The curriculum for this division included both general and vocational courses. The General College was replaced by the Basic College.

entire university, which may increase or decrease the number and variety of the offerings; but the internal organization of courses is the responsibility of the faculty of the college.[18]

The curriculum of University College at present consists of (1) four 1-year courses required of all students, and (2) introductory courses in various subject matters taught by the staff members of various colleges, which are prerequisites to courses of study in degree programs or useful to students who do not plan to take a degree. In addition to the regular curriculum, the college is responsible for instruction in five 1-term courses called "Improvement Courses." One of these is a course in the English language especially designed for foreign students. Other courses are offered for students whose command of reading, writing, speech, and arithmetic is inadequate to the demands of regular college courses. The office of evaluation services is also under the direction of the college. This office is responsible for the evaluation of the academic progress of students and assists in the identification of student personnel problems.

Admission to the university is open to graduates of accredited high schools whose records meet the "college-recommending mark" as designated by Michigan high schools. Applicants must have completed 15 units of high school work of which not less than 3 must be in English. Of the total, 7 units (or 6, if the student presents four years of English) may be distributed among three of the following fields: foreign languages, mathematics, natural science, and social science. An additional 3 units may be presented from these fields or, according to the catalogue of the university, "from agriculture, home economics, commercial, industrial, art, music and similar subjects." The remaining 2 units may be offered from "many other subjects accepted by the high school toward graduation." In most of the colleges of the university certain degree programs specify that students must have had from 2 to 3 units of high school mathematics. Neither the College

[18] The administrative plan of University College and the definition of its educational functions were undoubtedly influenced by the plan introduced by the University of Chicago in 1931, when the College of the University of Chicago was specifically designated the autonomous ruling body responsible for the development and instruction of the university's program of general education. The General College of the University of Minnesota, established at about the same time as the College of the University of Chicago, is also an autonomous division of the university. The functions of this unit were influential in the development of the short-lived General College at Michigan State (1942–1944).

of Education nor the College of Communication Arts makes any specific requirement in preparatory mathematics, and only the degree programs in the sciences in the College of Science and Arts list two years of high school mathematics as a prerequisite. Foreign language is not a prerequisite for admission to any degree program, although several programs require two or more years of a language in fulfilling graduation requirements.

The official statement of admission policies contains the following notice:

> Under "The Michigan Secondary School–College Agreement," Michigan State University disregards the pattern of subjects pursued in considering for admission the graduates of selected accredited high schools, *provided* they are recommended by the school from among the *more able* students in the graduating classes. A lack of preparatory courses required for technical and professional curricula will not prevent a student from gaining admission to Michigan State University. If preparatory courses are needed, M.S.U. will teach them under an accelerated program without college credit. Thus in certain cases, it will take additional time to complete the requirements for the Bachelor's degree.

While this provision gives assurance that a competent student will suffer no irreparable disadvantage through his own or his school's failure to secure the proper prerequisite training, it offers further compelling evidence of the poor articulation of school and college curricular planning. Given the conditions which generally govern admission to most land-grant colleges, it is understandable that Michigan State should provide for the inadequacies in preparatory studies. But the propriety of the action does not obscure the absurdity of the fact that a great university is obliged to offer courses in arithmetic and elementary algebra to some of its students.

The curriculum of the Basic College adopted in 1944 consisted of seven general courses, in five of which all students were required to pass comprehensive examinations. The seven courses, each a year in length, were: (1) Written and Spoken English, (2) Introduction to the Biological Sciences, (3) Introduction to the Physical Sciences and Mathematics, (4) Introduction to the Social Sciences, (5) a "functional" course entitled "Effective Living," (6) History of Western Civilization, and (7) Literature and Fine Arts. In addition to the English course required of all students, the curriculum offered two courses each in the natural sciences, the social sciences, and the humanities. Students were required to take one of the two courses in each area; and for a fifth course, they were permitted to elect the remaining course in any one of the three areas.

In 1952 single end-of-year comprehensive examinations over the five courses were abandoned in favor of a system which combined term comprehensives with the instructor's personal evaluation of his students. In 1953 the number of general courses was reduced to four, the courses which presently form the basic program of general education. The course in Literature and Fine Arts was transferred to the College of Science and Arts where it became an elective.[19] The course called "Effective Living" was abandoned altogether, and the two natural science courses were revised to form a single one-year introduction to the natural sciences. The English course has undergone important revisions. After a period of some years in which it was known as "Communication Skills," it was recently reorganized and renamed "American Thought and Language."

The organizing principles of the general courses are not unlike those of many colleges. The natural science and the social science courses are currently organized in terms of problems designed to demonstrate selected basic concepts and methods of their respective fields. In the natural sciences, problems concerned with reproductive processes and cell theory are employed to demonstrate the empirical methods of the sciences, and conceptual schemes are examined through a study of genetic theories. The course continues with a study of problems in geological process and evolution. The year's work concludes with problems dealing more specifically with the role of theory in the physical and chemical concepts of matter and the historical development of atomic-molecular theory from early concepts to the present.

The social science course begins with a study of theories of social behavior and the adjustment of the individual to social and cultural groups. This is followed by an analysis of the economic and non-economic needs of man and methods of satisfying these needs. The

[19] The course in Literature and Fine Arts, which undertook an integration of literature, visual arts, and music, organized in terms of formal principles, has since been abandoned as an integrated course under interdepartmental control, and has been replaced by three parallel departmental courses.

course concludes with the study of the regulation of human behavior through social and political controls.

The humanities course, constructed in a historical framework, introduces the student to his cultural heritage through the study of the development of man's institutions—social, political, and religious —and of a selection of great works in literature and art.

The course in composition which is now called "American Thought and Language" has been organized around a selection of documents representative of several themes or issues which have played important roles in the development of American society and government. Both reading and writing skills are developed through the analysis of problems found in the selected documents. Attention is given to ideas as well as to the uses of language which are not only effective in themselves but representative of "the resources of the American language," according to a recent statement about the course. Students who fail to pass the proficiency examination in preparatory English are not admitted to this course until they have taken the appropriate improvement course.

Instruction in these four courses is conducted in small discussion sections or by means of a combination of large group lecture, laboratory, and small discussion sections. Under these conditions of instruction the staff of University College is necessarily large. The number of instructors required to staff the several courses ranges from about thirty-five in humanities to over sixty in communication skills. There is little doubt that the autonomy of the faculty of University College, as well as the prospects of promotion and tenure, is a powerful administrative instrument in maintaining stability in the staffs.

With the reduction of the number of comprehensive courses in the curriculum from seven to four, the requirements of University College which are common to all students amount to one-fourth of the entire undergraduate program. The amount of free elective time available for studies outside a student's field of concentration varies considerably among the different departmental programs. Guidance in the use of elective time is the responsibility of departmental or divisional counselors.

In reflecting upon the program of University College, two problems stand out whose significance in the further development of general education exceeds all others. The first is not peculiar to Michigan

State University. It occurs in every university of the country that is now admitting freshman classes which number in the thousands. In aptitude, previous academic experience, individual interests, and capacities for self-discipline, the ranges of difference will inevitably be great. The task of providing adequate instruction is staggering and one that may easily have more serious consequences for general education than for specialized and professional education. The second problem is the attainment of a satisfactory conception of general education that will permit of sufficient flexibility to adjust to the wide variety of backgrounds and aptitudes without loss of curricular integrity. Michigan State's University College program admits of little flexibility; and the skeptical will say that one course in science or humanities cannot possibly be adapted to the needs of 4,000 freshmen. This depends upon how a course is defined and upon the provisions made for varying methods of instruction. It may well be that there is not sufficient variety either in content or instructional methods in University College courses. It does not follow, however, that the alternatives most commonly proposed or employed achieve better results. The optional-course distributional plan which permits students to elect any one of several introductory courses in a science may offer a less comprehensive view of the nature and significance of science and its methods than the general course, and it is not certain that in overcrowded institutions, where it is difficult to find enough well-qualified teachers, the instruction will be superior. The problem of flexibility in general curriculums has been sadly neglected, and this, together with the problems which attend the large enrollments in our universities, will be reviewed in the final section.

MILLS COLLEGE

A seminary for young women, founded in 1852 in Benicia, California, was the parent institution from which Mills College grew. The seminary was moved to Oakland during the administration of Dr. Cyrus Mills, one of its early leaders in whose honor the college bears its present name. In 1871 the institution introduced its first collegiate courses, and in 1911 all secondary instruction was discontinued. In 1960 the college enrolled slightly over seven hundred students. Although the majority of students come from the Pacific Coast states, the college asserts the percentage of its student body which comes from Eastern and Middle Western states is larger than that of any other college in California.

Applicants for admission must be graduates of accredited high schools; they must have 16 units of high school studies, of which 12 must be in academic subjects. The college states that the distribution of the academic units may vary "according to the program of studies available in each school and to the particular needs and interests of each student." In the catalogue of the college for 1961, however, a new statement emphasizes a desirable distribution: "A recommended secondary school program would include four years of English, two of history, and two to four years of foreign language. If two years of foreign language are included in the program, they may be most profitably taken in the last two years of secondary school. Also recommended are three years of mathematics, including trigonometry, if available, and two years of science, one physical and one biological." Short of a specific requirement for distribution, this represents the most comprehensive and at the same time the most evenly balanced suggestion for a program of high school studies among our group of eighteen institutions. It is the only recommendation I have seen which advises that, if two years of language be taken, instruction should be reserved until the last two years of secondary school. Altogether the recommendation marks a significant step toward achieving a more effective continuity in studies from school to college. Students must also take the College Entrance Examination Board aptitude test

177

and three achievement tests, one of which must be the English composition test.

At the time that this study began, the curricular and administrative organization of the college represented in principal details the objectives of major reforms adopted in 1943. In 1959 the college announced plans for a comprehensive revision of curricular policies and administrative structure. The first stages of these plans became effective in 1960; other changes are anticipated. Changes already effective, however, reveal important curricular revisions and, by virtue of these, equally important changes in the conception of the function of a liberal arts college.

Under its new plan Mills offers only the Bachelor of Arts degree to its undergraduates. Prior to the changes, the college offered both the Bachelor of Arts and the Bachelor of Science degrees. (It continues to offer the Master of Arts in some departmental fields, as well as a Master of Fine Arts and a Master of Education.) The Bachelor of Science degree was granted to students who completed certain programs having specific vocational objectives. The discontinuation of these programs in the new plan accounts for dropping the B.S. degree.

Incidentally, it may be remarked that there is no consistent policy among American colleges governing the baccalaureate degree, a fact which is well illustrated by the variety of policies employed by the colleges in this study. Some grant only the Bachelor of Arts degree regardless of the academic program pursued. Others award both the B.A. and the B.S., but they reserve the B.S. for students completing concentration in the sciences and occasionally the social sciences. In some, the B.S. is granted only to those graduates whose programs meet all preprofessional requirements in any field of the natural sciences. Still others grant the B.S. for completing vocational programs, as Mills formerly did and as Berea continues to do. Bachelors of Fine Arts, Music, and Physical Education usually signify a vocational or preprofessional course of study.

The vocational programs which have been discontinued and for which the B.S. degree was formerly granted held an important place in the curriculum and in the concept of the proper function of a liberal arts college for women. The extent of its importance is indicated in the curricular and administrative organization of the old program of the college. This is apparent in a comparison of the two programs. In both, the faculty and the curriculum are organized on a divisional basis, with departmental subdivisions. Under the old plan there were four divisions known as "schools." They were: the School of Fine Arts, the School of Home and Community Services, the School of Humanities, and the School of Natural Sciences. Under the new plan there are also four divisions; but the division or School of Home and Community Services has been abolished, some of its departments and degree programs eliminated, and others assigned to other divisions. The four new divisions are: fine arts, letters, natural science and mathematics, and social sciences. The division of social sciences is not divided into departments. There is actually no change in the divisions of fine arts and the natural sciences. The other changes are indicative of important conceptual changes.

The School of Home and Community Services included the department of education; of health, physical education, and recreation; of home economics; a preprofessional curriculum in occupational therapy; and vocational curriculums in business, merchandising, personnel work, and secretarial studies. The first two departments are retained but are now unassigned to a division since they have interdivisional staffs. The dropping of the remaining department and all the vocational programs signifies a changed idea of the relation of vocational concentration of the types thus represented to the aims of liberal education. The catalogue of the college for the year 1958–1959 explained the former divisional structure by outlining briefly the development of the concept of the liberal arts, which it said "have traditionally consisted of Humanities and Natural Sciences," categories which grew out of the medieval distinction between the trivium and quadrivium. The statement indicated an apparent identification of liberal education and the liberal arts, for it continued with the observation that "with the waning in modern times of the aristocratic prejudice against manual work, a third group of studies has been added to liberal education, the Fine Arts." The theoretical basis for three of the schools was derived from this account of the growth of the liberal arts, an account which ignored the fact that music at least was traditionally a part of the quadrivium. The basis for the fourth of the schools was not so explicitly represented as a part of the growth of the idea of liberal education. Instead the catalogue statement asserted that "a fourth division, Home and Community Services, has been set up in recognition of the desire of the modern young woman for a professional training *built upon* (italics mine) the sound basis of a liberal education." It is this last sentence which is most significant, since it provokes questions about the extent of the "sound basis of a liberal education" which the young women who pursued any of the B.S. programs would receive. The abandonment of these programs indicates that the college has decided that, however desirable it may be for all young women to have a good liberal education, it is not the business of a college such as Mills, primarily concerned with liberal education, to engage in programs which offer such high concentration in purely vocational studies.

The general requirements for B.A. students have been and still are satisfied by the election of courses from a limited number of options in each major field. Except for a course in English (composition and literature), only one course is a common requirement, a course entitled "Introduction to Values in American Life." It is interesting that the course bears the subtitle "Humanities 1 a–b." In the former divisional structure, which united the subject matters customarily regarded as social sciences with English and the foreign languages, all disciplines concerned with human institutions were regarded as the humanities and as distinct from those concerned with the phenomena of nature. Upon this theory it is easy to understand why the course whose content is described by the title "Values in American Life" might incorporate problems concerned with both the structure of American institutions and the characteristic forms and qualities of American literature. The course still bears the categorical title, "Humanities 1 a–b," but it is classified under the division of the social sciences in the new program. The history of the course, as well as other changes in the new organization, illustrates once again the arbitrary character of all classifications of knowledge. Since this is inevitable, the need for making clear, especially to young students, the various principles which govern the classifications is important. It is evident that little attention has been given to the matter by most colleges.

To the student of the idea of general education a comparison of two statements about the basic or common degree requirements has considerable significance. In the catalogue for 1958–1959 the following paragraph appeared under the heading of "Degree Requirements": "Mills has reduced its definite requirements to a few subjects which it regards as essential tools of learning, and included selected introductory courses in the major divisions of learning for the purpose of broadening the student's intellectual interests and developing an understanding of the interrelation of ideas and knowledge."

In the catalogue for 1961 the introductory statement on college objectives asserts:

> On the principle that a broadening of intellectual interests and an understanding of the interrelation of ideas can best be achieved when each student has the widest possible opportunity to choose among courses in the college, and on the theory that "distribution requirements," when summed up by a series of selected introductory courses, appear a hindrance to education rather than a contribution to it, Mills prefers to state its requirements in addition to those in the major field of concentration in terms of "college objectives," and when practicable to leave the attainment of those objectives to the student herself, in consultation with her major adviser. For these reasons, the list of college objectives is couched in general terms to emphasize the flexibility that is possible.

Readers will not overlook the phrase "broadening of intellectual interests" in both statements as well as the reference to the desirable understanding of "the interrelation of ideas." These phrases, like "broad foundation of knowledge," used in describing the aims of general education, have become clichés. What is interesting about the two statements is that the latter (1961) is a more accurate description of the actual curricular policy of Mills even as it was represented in the curriculum in force in 1958–1959. For in fact there is as yet no important difference in the specific nature of the general requirements. They are, as they have been, based on a fairly free optional-course distributional plan, which requires English (composition and literature) one year; a foreign language (with a proficiency equivalent to that attained by two years of college work); one-year courses in the fine arts, the natural sciences, and the social sciences; a one-year course in health education; and two hours of physical education throughout four years. In the fine arts, students may choose from an extensive list of courses which embraces art history, practical courses in art (drawing and design), music history, dance, and speech and drama (oral interpretation of literature). More limited options are offered in the natural sciences. At present the Introduction to Values in American Life is the one course meeting the social science requirement. Whether it will survive the rejection of the principle of "selected introductory courses" remains to be seen. It should be recorded here that formerly the candidates for the B.S. degree (i.e., students in vocational programs) were required to complete only the English course, the Values in American Life, and the health and physical education courses.

The specified pattern of distributional requirements is supplemented by an additional provision that a total of sixty hours or one-half of the entire requirement for graduation shall be in subjects outside the major sequence. There is no requirement for a balanced distribution of courses other than in that part already described; choices are the responsibility of the student guided only by her adviser. The direction which Mills is taking in its educational philosophy is away from the dominant trend that has characterized a full generation in the history of American colleges. If the recommended pattern of distribution of high school studies is followed by most of the students, Mills will undoubtedly be able to allow the degree of flexibility in the part of the curriculum which must achieve the "broadening of intellectual interests" with more security than will otherwise be possible. Whether the college will succeed in securing such a desirable balance is an open question.

In an official description of the curriculum, prepared in 1956, a faculty committee said:

> The existing plan for general education at Mills has the defect of its virtues. The small number of required courses and the wide range of choices in several of the required areas, while providing desirable flexibility in the program of individual students, reduces the opportunity for providing a common intellectual experience for the student body as a whole. The difficulty is met in part by the program of weekly assembly speeches by Mills faculty members and visitors to the campus, and by such events as the two- or three-day visits of distinguished scholars or artists to the campus, which occurs three or four times during the college year.

Whether Mills still regards the lack of opportunity for a common intellectual experience as a defect or not, it clearly accepts the risks in favor of what is regards as the greater virtue, the maximum of freedom for the student in determining what shall be for her the best design for achieving a broad range of intellectual interests.

One can scarcely avoid a comparison of the statements of principles which have guided Mills College and Goucher College in a period of curricular and administrative reforms. The two women's colleges are of almost identical size. Both appeal to much the same kind of student; and with the dropping of the vocational programs at Mills, both are committed to a plan of liberal education as their primary objective. At the very time that Goucher was moving from a policy that stated the substance of education in terms of objectives toward a policy that placed greater emphasis upon specific disciplines, Mills appeared to be moving in the direction that Goucher had abandoned. Goucher stresses the importance of concentrating many of the general requirements in the first two years as a "broad foundation" for specialization; Mills emphasizes the value of beginning work in one's major field early, even in the first year if possible, for according to the 1961 catalogue, it is "the major field that gives direction and purpose to the educational process," and by beginning work at once in "a general field of interest," even "the undecided student may have an early opportunity to gather evidence that will help her in her final decision."

THE UNIVERSITY OF MINNESOTA

The early history of the University of Minnesota is a characteristic story of the efforts of a few zealous citizens of the frontier territories and states in the middle years of the nineteenth century to provide opportunities for higher education to all who desired it. From 1851, when the territorial Legislature first set aside lands the sale of which was to finance a university, until 1868 the institution was scarcely more than a dream. By the latter date the last obstacles in the way of recognizing the university as Minnesota's land-grant college had been removed, and a healthier financial foundation had been assured. In 1869 William Watts Folwell was appointed President, and from this date the proper history of the university as a functioning institution began.

In less than a hundred years the University of Minnesota has become one of the nation's largest institutions of higher learning. Administratively it is today an exceedingly complex organization. It unites in a single body the numerous branches of a land-grant college; professional schools, such as medicine and law; a graduate school; a research center in the sciences; and the numerous continuing educational services which characterize the modern American university. Most of its activities are centered at Minneapolis, although it maintains two regional branches. In 1958–1959 the total enrollment on the Minneapolis–St. Paul campus was 24,267. Enrollments in the College of Science, Literature, and the Arts and the General College (the two undergraduate divisions with which this report is concerned) were 7,082 and 2,241, respectively. The division between men and women in both colleges was remarkably even. The combined enrollment, approaching 10,000 students, did not represent the sum of undergraduates, since many were registered in their third and fourth years in other professional and vocational divisions.

The phenomenon of the state university which enrolls from ten to fifteen thousand undergraduate students has created unique problems and those which relate to the area of general education are among the most serious. The prospect of meeting the needs of several thousand freshman students annually and of providing competent instruction is alone staggering. Adjusting subject matter and methods of instruction to the heterogeneity of aptitudes, academic backgrounds, and intellectual interests presents problems that no private college or university which enjoys greater freedom in the selection of its students experiences in equal degree. Institutions of the size of the University of Minnesota and Michigan State University constitute a fact of contemporary American life, one that will probably exist for many years to come. What these universities do to solve the problems of general and liberal education now and in the immediate future is vitally important to all higher education. In the first place, they exert a powerful influence upon national educational policies. In the second place, they and their sister institutions, the municipal colleges and universities, are now educating as many undergraduates as all the private colleges and universities of the nation, although the number of the latter is still slightly larger. In some states undergraduate enrollment in state and municipal institutions already far outnumbers that of private institutions. There is little reason to believe that the ratio will not increase. The general education of the majority of college students in the future will be determined by institutions such as Minnesota and Michigan State. Necessities created by numbers will be powerful determinants of the patterns adopted. Nor should one overlook the fact that patterns will be made in settings where the vocational colleges of the nation are most heavily concentrated.

It is interesting and useful to compare the practices of two universities such as Minnesota and Michigan State. Both are located in the North Central region of the nation. Their student bodies are drawn from similar economic and cultural backgrounds. Both are bound by the actions of their respective state legislatures to provide comparable educational services under comparable conditions. Each has vigorously proclaimed its concern for the general education of its undergraduates. Yet it would be difficult to find two more sharply different approaches to the problem of providing a general education for student bodies which currently number between fifteen and twenty thousand students annually.

The main burden of general education for the students of the University of Minnesota falls upon two undergraduate divisions, the College of Science, Literature, and the Arts and the General College.

The College of Science, Literature, and the Arts (S.L.A.) is a four-year liberal arts college which is divided administratively into a Lower and an Upper Division. It is the largest of the university's many academic divisions. The General College offers only a two-year program, although many of its students qualify for transference to other undergraduate colleges after completing one or two years of residence. In a single year the two units enroll slightly less than one-half of the entire undergraduate body. Add to this the fact that most students in other undergraduate colleges, such as agriculture, business, education, or engineering, will have previously spent all or a part of their first two years in S.L.A. or in S.L.A. courses, and one realizes the major importance of these two undergraduate divisions in the academic life of the university. Regardless of the school or college in which a student may pursue his vocational or professional studies, the foundations of general education, in so far as the university accepts responsibility, will be laid primarily in the Lower Division of S.L.A. or in the General College.

The present administrative and curricular organization of these two colleges is the product of almost uninterrupted study and experiment which began at Minnesota, as it did in so many colleges, in the decade of the 1920s. The principal goal of the experimentation was an improved general education. The General College was established in 1932 as one consequence of the conviction that the existing liberal arts curriculum was not properly adapted to the variety of intellectual capacities and backgrounds of the large body of undergraduates. At one extreme, it was felt, there were students whose progress was retarded by the uniform methods of instruction and the narrow conceptions of specialization. At the other extreme there were too many students who were unable to keep pace academically with the demands of most of the courses in the curriculum.

Out of twenty-five years of experiment the present curricular programs of S.L.A. and the General College, conceptually quite different, have attained considerable stability. The principal conceptual difference derives from the fact that the University of Minnesota is a state institution and a land-grant college; by action of the university senate, it admits all or nearly all the graduates of the accredited high schools of the state. The College of Science, Literature, and the Arts admits students with an aptitude rating of 40 or above; the rating is the average of the student's percentile ranking in his high school class and his ranking on the scholastic aptitude test administered by the college in the junior year of high school. The General College is open to any resident of Minnesota who is a graduate of an accredited high school without reference to rank or any pattern of high school studies.[20]

The program of the General College is based upon an assumption that students who cannot meet the entrance standards of the other undergraduate colleges because of low academic aptitude or inadequate preparation or because of previous failure to discover any firm intellectual interests will profit best from an organization of subject matter different from that which is customarily offered in the other undergraduate colleges. It is also based upon an assumption, founded upon experience, that a considerable number of these students will terminate their formal education after two years and that for them a terminal program formed of functional courses which strive to be complete in themselves will satisfy a need which the curricular programs of the other undergraduate colleges cannot.

The College of Science, Literature, and the Arts, on the other hand, hopes that a majority of its students will complete studies for a bachelor's degree in one of the colleges of the university, and it is prepared to offer courses which may be prerequisites for the other colleges as well as degree programs in all its own departments. The specific differences in the two programs of general education will best be understood by a detailed review of the curricular and administrative organization of each college.

The College of Science, Literature, and the Arts

The College of Science, Literature, and the Arts is the recognized liberal arts division of the university. In addition to the admission requirement concerning scholastic rank, the college requires that all

---

[20] Admission standards of the other undergraduate colleges vary, but none except those of the General College is without specific limitations based on high school ranking and distribution of studies. The Institute of Technology, which includes the College of Engineering, the Schools of Architecture, Chemistry, Mines and Metallurgy, and Physics admits only students who rank in the upper 50 per cent of their high school class. It is also very explicit in its statement of required and recommended prerequisites. The College of Agriculture, Forestry, and Home Economics admits students who rank in the upper 25 per cent of their high school class, without regard to subjects taken, or students who rank in the upper 75 per cent, providing their high school studies have been distributed in accordance with patterns prescribed by the three major departments of the college.

applicants shall present a minimum of 12 academic units earned in the last three years of high school (grades 10 to 12). Of these units, 9 must be distributed among English, social science and history, mathematics, natural science, and foreign language. The college recommends that 3 units be in English and 2 in mathematics including plane geometry. Elementary algebra taken in grade 9 may be counted as 1 of the 2 but may not count as 1 of the 12. A similar provision is made with respect to the first year of a foreign language taken in grade 9. This is a recommended distribution, and students with high scholastic ranking are not required to conform to any distributional pattern.[21]

The declared purpose of the college is to offer a liberal education. This was described in its official Bulletin for 1957–1959 as a union through proper distribution of studies and time of a general education and a "special education." The specific functions of each part of a liberal education were described in comprehensive terms. "General education," the statement said, "is that part of a liberal education which provides you with a basic acquaintance with literature, philosophy, languages, fine arts, mathematics, and the natural and social sciences." Although general education begins before one enters college and should continue throughout life, it is a particularly important part of the undergraduate program. Special education carries the student to "a deeper knowledge and competence in a chosen field"; it may prepare the student for a career or provide necessary preprofessional training. Finally by his special knowledge the student becomes "a custodian of one field of our cultural heritage." Liberal education is not the product of either general or special education alone; but "both kinds should help."

In the Bulletin for 1959–1961 the statement of purpose was drastically revised. Instead of the distinction between general and special education which form the complementary parts of a liberal education, the revised statement begins with the formulation of another basic

---

[21] The Institute of Technology is more exacting in some of its requirements. High school graduates not only must rank in the upper 50 per cent of their classes but must offer 3 units of English and 3 units of mathematics including 1½ units of algebra and 1½ units of geometry. Courses in chemistry and physics are strongly recommended, and it would probably be a bold student who did not heed the recommendation. In addition to these requirements, applicants must pass an achievement test in mathematics at the time of entrance. Three or more of the remaining units may be distributed among history and social science, other natural sciences, and foreign language.

distinction: "The College has planned its programs to offer University students both liberal and special education, looking toward the development of satisfying and useful lives." The substitution of "liberal" for "general" in this distinction is considerably more than nominal. The intention, apparently, is to stress the qualitative character of liberal education which, though different in purpose from specialized education, embraces it. In addition, the revised statement suggests a desire to remove grounds for thinking of liberal education as the *sum* of two discrete kinds of content. The revised statement of the "liberal" goals of the College is set forth in the following paragraph:

> The term "liberal education" is difficult to define. The goal of the College is to aid students toward becoming the upright and humane men and women who are the ideal of our civilization. Among the characteristics of such men and women are a vigorous and humble curiosity about the world and its peoples; a seeking mind, open to ideas attractive or repugnant, and trained in the means of gaining more knowledge about them; the power to discriminate between what is honest and good, and what is fraudulent and mean; compelling interest in the arts and concepts through which men have caught order and beauty from the world; and a sense of personal responsibility for the advancement of learning and the improvement of the human condition.

The change in relative emphasis upon *general* and *liberal* is especially interesting in view of the fact that there is almost no substantive change in the procedures by which the students fulfill the goals of liberal education. Students will continue to acquire a general education by means of the same variety of course offerings and much the same choice of courses; only the terms in which the process is described have been altered. Henceforth they will acquaint themselves "with the principal fields of general knowledge." Since these fields are "literature, the arts, and other humanistic subjects; the social sciences such as politics, economics, and history; the physical and biological sciences," it may be a little difficult for the student to understand why they are here referred to as "fields of general knowledge" while subsequently the same fields will be presented as areas of "special" knowledge.

The revised statement also places a particular emphasis upon a feature of the curriculum which, though it has always been present, has not been so specifically pointed out in previous statements of purpose. "No two Arts College students move toward their goals by routes precisely alike," says the Bulletin; and this statement applies quite as much to the "general" as to the "special" parts of the curriculum. Minnesota is committed to an optional-course distributional plan for the completion of its general requirements and in a degree that exceeds that of any other college in this study.

Only at the conclusion of the new account of purpose does the term "general education" appear. Here it is said that "certain fundamental aspects of liberal education that should be the common possession of all cultivated men and women are called general education." This is a significant change from the earlier statement which spoke of these "fundamental aspects" as achieved through "the curriculum for general education." One suspects that the intention on the part of the faculty of S.L.A. has been to deemphasize the *term* rather than the *idea* it has long stood for on the grounds that the term has suffered abuses and that in some quarters more has been claimed under the term than can justly be attained.

To achieve an effective administration of the liberal arts program, the college is divided into a Lower and an Upper Division, formerly called the "Junior and Senior Colleges." The division is more than a curricular device. The Dean of the College coordinates all activities, but immediate supervision of the two divisions is assigned to two assistant deans. The primary educational function of the Lower Division is the advancement of the students' general education, whereas that of the Upper Division is the direction of their special fields. One faculty, organized departmentally, serves both the Upper and Lower Divisions. Students do not normally advance to the Upper Division without first fulfilling the minimal requirements of the general education program.

These requirements are satisfied by means of an optional-course distributional plan which was adopted in 1957. The present plan divides subject matters into six groups: English, foreign languages, social sciences, natural sciences, humanities, and health. In its general outline it is similar to many optional-course distributional plans. There is no single course uniformly required of all students. Even the requirement in English composition is met by one of several variants. The requirement may be waived by a satisfactory score on a qualifying examination. If it is not waived, the student is placed in one of four courses, the placement being determined by an analysis of his particular needs. Students who have secondary school credit for three or more years of one foreign language are not held for additional language as a part of their general education requirements providing they pass a departmental validating test. Those who have no foreign language in high school must secure 15 credits (one year's work) in one language. Two courses in health are offered, either of which meets the 2-credit requirement in this field.

In each of the three remaining areas of general education requirements—social sciences, natural sciences, and humanities—students must earn a minimum of 15 credits by completing lower divisional courses in two or more departments. No fewer than 5 credits may be earned in one department. The number of optional courses varies considerably from department to department; but the number of departments is large, and altogether the sum and variety of courses from which students may choose is very great. I shall refer to the scope of this optional-course plan again in the account of Reed College by way of comparing extremes in the exercise of the elective privilege.

The classification of departmental subject matters is not unusual in most respects. History is accepted in either the social sciences or the humanities, and psychology in either the social sciences or the natural sciences. One unusual dual classification is mathematics, since certain courses may be counted as either natural science or humanities. The whole of the general requirements normally covers slightly less than two years' work, although the number of credit hours varies with the results of qualifying examinations in English and foreign language. Students are also permitted to reduce the course requirements by passing exemption examinations which are offered in all parts of the general program.

One of the departments of the college is the department of interdisciplinary studies, and so far as I know it has no parallel in any other college. At present it is an autonomous department which has been given the responsibility of developing and giving instruction in several sequences of general or interdisciplinary courses at both Lower and Upper Division levels in the humanities, social sciences, and natural sciences, and a course in communication skills which is one of the freshman English courses. It has also offered in the Lower Division several courses under the general title of "Family Life" and two which are called "Personal Orientation" and deal with methods of study and problems of choosing a vocation. These have recently been transferred to the department of psychology. The Lower Division courses in humanities, social science, and natural science are included in the options listed in the distributional requirements, but a student may not elect interdisciplinary courses in more than two of the three divisional fields.

In the humanities the department offers a choice of four sequences in the Lower Division: (1) The Humanities and the Modern World, (2) The European Heritage, (3) American Life, and (4) The Arts: Visual Art, Music, and Theater. The first is a four-quarter sequence; the others are three-quarter sequences. Students are not required, however, to complete all quarters in any sequence. Three sequences are offered in the natural sciences: (1) Orientation to the Natural Sciences, (2) The Physical World, and (3) General Biology. Two sequences are listed in the social sciences: (1) Introduction to the Social Sciences and (2) International Relations. In the Upper Division two or more sequences are given in each area, most of which parallel the structure of the Lower Division courses. Exceptions are a Humanities Proseminar, History of Natural Science, and a Public Affairs Forum.

So extensive a curriculum of general courses could not have been developed had not a department been created for the task. The department, established shortly after the end of World War II, developed from early experiments in general humanities courses. One of the present courses, Humanities in the Modern World, is a modification of a course begun before the war which was concerned with concepts of democracy in modern life.[22] In the four quarters of the present sequence the scope of themes has been enlarged. The sequence is organized in a historical framework which extends from the late eighteenth century to the present day. Topics include nineteenth-century ideas of liberalism, socialism, and individualism, the impact of science and evolution upon religion and morals, the influence of analytical psychology on contemporary culture, and modern political ideologies such as fascism and communism.

European Heritage, which is also a continuation of an early experiment, is a study of the major intellectual and poetic works of

---

[22] James Gray, *The University of Minnesota: 1851–1951,* The University of Minnesota Press, Minneapolis, 1951, p. 430. This volume contains a summary of curricular reforms in the period from 1932 to the end of the war as well as a brief account of the establishing of the General College.

Western literature from ancient Greece to the Reformation. In its original form the course included the modern era; it resembled many of the so-called "great books" courses.

Reflection upon the character of the themes in terms of which The Humanities and the Modern World and the sequence entitled "American Life" are organized leads once more to the question raised in the comparison of the American civilization courses at Amherst and Antioch. Upon what principles do colleges differentiate the humanities from the social sciences? A description of the subject matter of the first term of American Life in the annual Announcements states that it is concerned with "the growth of individualism and democracy (with particular reference to minorities) as recorded in American history, social thought, literature, and the arts." The third term considers "the growth of nationalism, regionalism, and internationalism in American culture and thought." A students' manual, *Description of Courses in S.L.A. Lower Division,* gives a more detailed account of objectives, topics, materials, and classroom precedure.[23] The account stresses the importance of literature and the arts as "expressions of various American attitudes." Apparently it is the materials rather than the problems to which they are addressed which are responsible for its classification as humanities. In any event the problems I have cited are typical of many college social science courses. Yet even among these it would not be difficult to name several that use the arts freely as sources which illuminate social problems.

The general education program of the College of Science, Literature, and the Arts is proof that at least one major university does not subscribe to the opinion that general or interdisciplinary courses are indispensable to a general education or that any considerable portion of the curriculum should consist of uniformly required courses. The University of Minnesota was one of the first to develop general courses experimentally, but at no time has it imposed any course as an absolute requirement on any group of students. It is popularly supposed that advocates of general education have been the foes of the elective principle. Some have been, but there is little doubt that the majority of colleges which assert openly their commitment to general education nevertheless employ some form of an optional-course dis-

[23] This manual describes the Lower Division courses given by all departments in the college and is evidence of the great elective range open to students in fulfilling distributional requirements.

tributional plan as the partial means of achieving its objectives. The College of Science, Literature, and the Arts is not only not a foe of the elective principle but it allows its students perhaps as wide a latitude in the choice of courses with which to satisfy the general education requirements as any college which uses the distributional system.

The entire curriculum of the college is planned with a view to the interests of students who intend to obtain baccalaureate degrees or even advanced professional degrees. Yet the college recognizes that a considerable number of students will withdraw before completing the requirements for any degree. In their interest a two-year program leading to the degree of Associate in Liberal Arts is offered. It is an abridgement of the general requirements plus some time for election of courses in a special field. Students must complete the requirement in English and those in any three of the following four areas: foreign language, social sciences, humanities, and natural sciences. The entire program for the degree must be completed in not more than seven academic quarters.

The General College

The reader will recall that students who do not qualify for admission to any of the other undergraduate divisions of the university are given the option of entering the General College. In the biennial *Report of the President of the University* for 1952–1954, the General College was called by its Dean, Horace T. Morse, an experiment in "the conservation of human resources." The General College was created, said Dean Morse, for the purpose of solving "two persistent University problems. One of these was the high rate of drop-out among students who registered in the four-year colleges of the University. The second was the fragmentary education students received at the freshman and sophomore level, composed as it is almost entirely of introductory courses intended as foundation for work in the junior and senior years, which almost half of the students never reach." The General College was established as a two-year college, offering the degree of Associate in Arts to all students who complete its requirements. Its major task, however, was the construction of a curriculum designed to avoid the kind of fragmentation which was thought to be characteristic of the first two years of the other undergraduate divisions, and which would at the same time be adapted to the interests and aptitudes of students who were not adequately prepared for the normal demands of the typical liberal arts program.

The General College has been from its beginning an autonomous division of the university. It has always regarded its entire curricular venture as an experiment in general education controlled by the special needs of the students it enrolls. The faculty adopted two guiding principles in formulating the curriculum. First, each course should, in so far as possible, be a complete whole and not an introduction to or prerequisite for other courses in the same field. Second, in addition to general courses in the humanities, natural sciences, and the social sciences, new courses should be developed which, according to Dean Morse, focused upon "certain common activities in present-day American society," and which "drew their content from many fields integrated into a new and meaningful pattern." In short, the curriculum of the General College was one of the first ventures in the application of instrumentalist theories of learning to an entire program of general education.

It is therefore in the means by which the General College has undertaken to aid its students in acquiring a general education that the distinctive features of its program are found. The goals, stated in highly generalized terms, do not differ significantly from those of the College of Science, Literature, and the Arts or, for that matter, from those enunciated by the majority of American colleges. One reads that among the goals of general education are the ability to "grasp and express ideas effectively"; to "participate in civic affairs as an active and informed citizen"; to understand "our natural environment and the effect of sciences on human welfare"; and, of course, to "appreciate cultural activities as a means of richer living." Finally, a general education should help the student to "discover an appropriate and satisfying life work."

It is customary to claim that a good general education aids in the discovery of a satisfactory vocation. It is also customary to distinguish general education from vocational preparation. The General College, however, does not accept the view that a planned program of courses suitable for a general education may not also provide useful vocational preparation. The Bulletin of the General College (1955–1957) discusses at some length the relationship of its program of general education to vocational training.

The question has often been raised about the relationship of general education to preparation for earning a living. Are all courses in general education merely "cultural," without any practical value? What provision is made for the career interests which motivate many students to come to college?

The General College recognizes these vocational needs and is equipped to meet them in part. Many courses in the College have vocational applications, although they are not what is technically called vocational courses. For the most part they deal with broad, general principles, an understanding of which should enable the student to grasp the significance of an area of employment, rather than with specific skills required by a particular job.

To help the student to take advantage of the vocational utility of the curriculum, the faculty has listed some of its own courses as well as those offered in other undergraduate divisions of the university which might be useful for certain kinds of positions in business, commercial art, general office work, practical nursing, retailing and selling, etc. Many of the courses regarded as integral parts of the general education curriculum have this vocational function. The college has, however, developed a few courses, not included in the general program, which deal with specific job skills, as, for example, a course for training dental assistants. The vocational functions of some of the courses in the general program are apparent in a more particular view of the curriculum.

The curriculum is divided into seven fields called "comprehensive areas." These are (1) Personal Orientation; (2) Home Life Orientation; (3) Socio-Civic Orientation; (4) General Arts; (5) Literature, Writing, and Speech; (6) Biological Sciences; and (7) Physical Sciences. Numerous courses are offered in each area. Most are one-quarter courses, but a few are designed as two- and three-quarter sequences. The operation of the curriculum is closely related to a complex system of comprehensive examinations.

A comprehensive examination covering the seven comprehensive areas is given to each student three times during his two years of residence. The first is given when the student enters the college; the second after he has completed three quarters of work; and the third after he has completed the minimal 90 credit hours which are required for the degree of Associate in Arts. The function of the first two is primarily diagnostic, although students who attain a specified percentile ranking on the second examination may, if they wish, transfer to other colleges of the university providing they can meet the normal prerequisites. The results of the first and second comprehensive examinations are used by faculty advisers to help students to plan courses of study that will overcome weaknesses and at the same time guide them in the direction of useful vocational preparation. The students must pass the examinations in five of the seven areas to qualify for the Associate in Arts degree.

Grades for individual courses are determined by the instructors, but all students must take the comprehensive examinations, regardless of grades. The examinations are prepared by the staff. They are, for the most part, objective-type examinations. They are not designed to cover specific content of particular courses in the different comprehensive areas, but are concerned with the application of general principles characteristic of the subject matters of the areas.

In four of the areas there are "core courses" which are usually the courses recommended as providing a comprehensive view of the subject matter of the area. In the area entitled "Personal Orientation" two core courses are given, Individual Orientation and Vocational Planning; in Home Life Orientation, the single core course is Marriage and Family Living. The core course in Socio-Civic Orientation is Problems of Contemporary Society. In General Arts the core is concerned with problems common to the appreciation of music, the visual arts, and literature. The other comprehensive areas do not offer a core course.

The diversity of course offerings is well illustrated by the following list which in addition to the core course comprise the offerings of the Home Life Orientation area:

> How the Living Machinery in Man Works
> Healthful Living
> Food Selection and Purchase
> Clothing Selection, Purchase, and Care
> Selecting and Furnishing a Home
> Income Management
> Problems of Business Transactions
> Problems of Investment Transactions
> Human Development
> Personal Adjustment

Within this group of courses, practical applications are made of subject matters drawn from biology, psychology, economics, and art in accord with instrumentalist doctrine. No single student will take all these courses, but his opportunities to take several of them are enlarged through the practice of listing some of them in more than one comprehensive area. Human Development and Personal Adjustment, for example, are included in the area of Personal Orientation.

The Socio-Civic Orientation area corresponds to the division of social sciences in most general education programs. The number of courses from which students may choose is the largest of the seven areas. In 1955–1957, seventeen one-quarter courses were offered in addition to the core course, Problems of Contemporary Society. They included General Geography, General Anthropology, The Far East, The Growth of American Democracy, Community Problems, Problems in Consumption Economics, and Problems in Production, Finance, and Credit.

The area of General Arts gives perhaps more emphasis to functional or vocational ends of learning than any other. Here the student has opportunity to take the courses on clothing selection and home furnishing, which he may have missed in the area of Home Life Orientation, and in addition may elect Art in Business, Introduction to Commercial Art, Photography, and Film and Drama. Two courses, Art Today and Music Today which are two- and three-quarter sequences, respectively, place greater emphasis upon the fundamental elements of form and the bases of appreciation.

In the area of Literature, Writing, and Speech, a three-quarter sequence devoted to the literature of the Western world is organized on a thematic scheme which is reminiscent of the general humanities course at Berea. Themes such as Man and God, Man and Nature, Man and His Social Environment control the selection of materials. The third quarter of the sequence is devoted entirely to American literature. The same thematic principles determine the organization. The selection of themes gives an emphasis to the social, economic, and political characteristics of American life, and in this respect is not unlike the American Life sequence offered by the department of interdisciplinary studies in S.L.A. Six courses in writing, each designed to serve a particular function, such as Business Writing, Individual (creative) Writing, and Research Writing, are given. Speech training is given a functional approach in a course on the techniques of radio broadcasting.

The courses in the natural sciences deviate less from the conventional introductory general courses in these areas than other courses in the curriculum. There are also considerably fewer course offerings. In addition to physics, chemistry, astronomy, and geology, a two-quarter sequence in applied mathematics is available.

The courses which students take from this formidable array in the seven areas depend in part upon the counsel of their advisers and in part upon personal preferences. Obviously the comprehensive examinations, which are not adapted to each student's program, must be very general. The General College, like the College of Science, Literature, and the Arts, not only permits but encourages freedom of election within its prescribed distributional fields to a degree that exceeds that of most colleges. Yet these two programs have been stoutly defended by their respective administrations as important experiments in general education since their beginnings a quarter of a century ago. Students of higher education will do well to remember this when they undertake to find a comprehensive definition of general education. Here within a single institution are two programs, alike in that both encourage great flexibility in the structure of course programs satisfying general requirements, radically different in the principles which dominate the organization of subject matters, and both, in turn, far removed in principle from the conception and practice of general education embodied in University College of Michigan State University, which of all institutions in this study most nearly resembles Minnesota in size, in the general character of its student body, and in the scope of its undergraduate functions.

THE UNIVERSITY OF NOTRE DAME

The University of Notre Dame was founded in 1842 by a small group of priests and brothers of a French religious community, the Congregation of the Holy Cross. Its purpose was to provide educational opportunities to the resident bands of Potawatomi Indians and families of French traders of the region of northern Indiana. In 1844 the Indiana State Legislature granted the institution a charter, and for many years it combined the functions of elementary and preparatory schools and a college. Until 1865 it offered only the traditional liberal arts courses. In that year science was added, and in 1869 the first department of law in an American Catholic college was opened. The growth of the university thereafter kept pace with the changing times. Before 1900 courses in civil, mechanical, and electrical engineering, pharmacy, and architecture were added; and in 1897 the curriculum was reorganized in four divisions: arts and letters, science, engineering, and law. The divisions became colleges in 1905, and a College of Commerce was opened in 1920. Later, as the program of graduate studies increased, the Graduate School was organized as a separate division of the university.

The growth of the student body has been most rapid since the end of World War I. In 1905 the enrollment was slightly over 200 students. By 1925 it had risen to 2,156, and in 1958–1959 the sum of all divisions was 6,134. Of this, 5,331 were in the four undergraduate colleges, distributed as follows: the College of Arts and Letters, 1,762; the College of Commerce, 1,480; the College of Engineering, 1,379; the College of Science, 710.

Admission to all colleges at Notre Dame is normally based upon graduation from an accredited high school and the applicant's record on the College Entrance Examination Board tests. A few students of exceptional promise who have completed three years of high school may be admitted each year. High school graduates must offer 15 units of work, distributed according to specifications established by each of the four colleges. The College of Arts and Letters requires that they shall be distributed as follows: Group I—9 units consisting of English

(3), a foreign language (2), mathematics (2—algebra and geometry), history (1), and science (1); Group II—3 units to be chosen from any of the above subjects; Group III—3 units to be selected from any courses normally accepted for high school graduation. The Colleges of Engineering and Science make much the same requirement except that they specify 10 units in Group I, the additional unit being additional mathematics, ½ unit each of algebra and trigonometry. The College of Engineering further requires that the 1 unit of science must be physics; the College of Science allows students to offer either physics or chemistry. Two units will be chosen from Group II, and the requirements for Group III are identical with those of the College of Arts and Letters.

The account which follows is concerned only with the College of Arts and Letters. The present curriculum was adopted in 1954 with a view to achieving a greater coherence in the concept of liberal education. Although the term "general education" does not occur in the official Bulletin of the college, the concept is evident in the structure of the curriculum leading to the Bachelor of Arts degree.[24] There is, however, a deliberate intention of merging the ideas of the general and the special into a concept of liberal education. Liberal education, the college says, is "the ordered growth of the intellect and of the person" and a part of this growth is dependent upon "an exercise in inquiry-in-depth appropriate to [some] field of concentration." The inquiry-in-depth is conducted against the background of a continuing study of philosophy and religion which runs through the entire four years and of a program of required general studies which occupies most of the first two years.

Because Notre Dame is a Catholic university, religion and philosophy play a central role in the curriculum. The Bulletin states that "Christian theology and philosophy are seen and studied not only as areas of knowledge profoundly important in themselves, but also as furnishing the liberally disciplined mind with certain governing principles for the unification of knowledge and life." These studies "are not just another field or fields on a plane with all others" but "they compose a wisdom that penetrates and animates the other studies."

[24] The Bachelor of Arts is the principal degree offered by the college, although a Bachelor of Music and a Bachelor of Fine Arts are also granted. Students may take a Bachelor of Arts with concentration in a science, but students who desire a Bachelor of Science will enroll in the College of Science.

The curricular structure, shown in the following outline, is based on the Announcements for 1958–1959:

First Year	Second Year
Philosophy	Philosophy
Religion	Religion
Rhetoric	Literature
Mathematics	Natural science
Foreign language	Social science
European history	American history
Physical education or ROTC	Elective (ROTC)

Comprehensive Examination

Third Year	Fourth Year
Philosophy	Philosophy
Religion	Religion
The collegiate seminar	Major sequence
Major sequence	Major sequence
Major sequence	Departmental seminar and
Elective (ROTC)	Senior essay
	Elective (ROTC)

The curriculum is uniform for all students in the first two years. In the first year, students may elect to continue a language begun in high school or may begin a new language. Placement tests determine the point at which the student should resume his continuation of a previously studied language. Rhetoric is a course in English composition. The course in mathematics introduces students to a variety of topics: problems in elementary logic; examples of axiomatic systems and number systems; geometric concepts of distance, space, curves, and surfaces; set theory and number theory. In the second year, students may choose one of four courses in science: a general course primarily designed for nonmajors in the biological sciences, a course in elementary chemistry, a course in geology, and one in physics based upon a selection of principal concepts in the science. All the courses include laboratory work as well as lectures and discussion. The other courses admit of no alternatives. The course in literature is a study of major forms in English literature. The general social science course is constructed around problems of human relations with political, sociological, and economic implications. The courses in philosophy and religion alternate by semesters. In the first year, logic is the subject of the first semester; The Sacred Scriptures in the Christian Tradition is the theme of the second semester. In the second year, the Philosophy of Nature and Practical (Christian) Theology are the themes of the courses. Students who are not Catholics may, if they wish, substitute certain courses for those in religion and theology.

The Collegiate Seminar in the third year is organized by themes. In 1956–1957 the themes were (1) Education and the Good Life, (2) The Person and Society, (3) Man and His Fate, and (4) Action and Contemplation. Readings related to the first theme included Plato's *Republic*, St. Augustine's *Confessions*, Newman's *Idea of a University*, and selections from Langer's *Philosophy in a New Key*. The second theme (The Person and Society) included extensive selections from Aristotle's *Politics*, Tawney's *Religion and the Rise of Capitalism*, Maritain's *Man and the State*, Riesman's *The Lonely Crowd*, and the whole of Joyce's novel, *Portrait of the Artist as a Young Man*. Each semester the students were required to write a major essay on a topic related to one of the themes. A series of lectures on the fine arts was given throughout the year and designed as an integral part of the course, though the lectures were given independently of the regular seminar discussions.

In outline the seminar resembles many general courses which in other colleges bear the title of "humanities." It is interesting that the term is not used in the titles or descriptions of any courses in this curriculum. This is probably attributable to a conception that in all courses relevant to a liberal education *man* is the central object of study—man in his own person, man in relation to God, and man in relation to his physical environment. The Bulletin of the College (1956–1957) states that "as it moves toward shaping the Christian intelligence, the Catholic college has a special reverence for man, his history, his culture, his total life." In short the study of the humanities becomes identical with liberal education. In its thematic structure, the Collegiate Seminar also resembles some of the "senior seminars" or colloquiums which have attained considerable success in recent years. We shall encounter examples in the curriculums of Reed College and Stanford University and in the Honors College of the University of Oregon. Like them it aims at the application of all general disciplines to problems and issues which are within the common experience of mankind.

The comprehensive examination, given at the end of the sophomore year, is a test of the student's control of skills acquired during his first two years. It is in part written and in part oral, and serves a diagnostic function, although its results are used with other criteria to determine a student's ability to continue in the last two years of the college.

Several features of this curriculum deserve particular notice. First, the common required core is greater than in most of the programs we have considered thus far. Including the Collegiate Seminar and philosophy and religion, it amounts to about 2½ years' work. Second, with the exception of the social science course, general biology, and the junior seminar, all the required courses are "departmental" and are staffed by departmental faculties. Third, only in foreign language and in science are optional courses available. Fourth, a "minor" field, so frequently a complement to the major field of concentration, is not required. Courses in a field related to the departmental major may count toward fulfillment of the "major" requirements by permission of the departmental chairman. The total time for the major, including a departmental seminar, is approximately the equivalent of one year's work, i.e., eight semester courses plus two semesters in the departmental seminar. The Senior Essay is the culmination of the student's inquiry-in-depth and bears a significance analogous to the sophomore comprehensive. Finally, the emphasis upon philosophy and religion, which is shared by the other Catholic college in this survey, is a distinctive characteristic. Such an emphasis may be assumed of Catholic institutions, but the prominence of these courses in the program underscores the modest role which they play in most general education programs. In publicly supported colleges the absence of religion and theology as formal requirements is unavoidable. In private colleges, even those with Protestant affiliations or inclinations, their place in the curriculum is often minor and, not infrequently, is optional with courses in philosophy. The lack of serious concern for the study of philosophy or a philosophic orientation of the courses which form the heart of the general course requirements is, however, a conspicuous fact in most public and private colleges.

The General Program of Liberal Education

The curriculum described in the preceding pages is the one in which the majority of students in the College of Arts and Letters are enrolled. Another curriculum, however, deserves special attention because of its intrinsic interest and because it is an example of a kind of curricular experiment which has proved successful in a few colleges within the last ten years. The General Program of Liberal Education begins with the sophomore year. Students are eligible to apply for admission upon completion of the prescribed courses of the freshman year; and if they are accepted they pursue a common course of study for three years which leads to the Bachelor of Arts degree.

A few colleges have adopted programs of general education for selected groups of students which aim at achieving coherence through a greater degree of uniformity in course requirements than is possible in the usual optional-course distributional program. Most of them have been limited to the work of the first two years and have not infringed upon concentration in a major field carried on in the last two undergraduate years. The Directed Studies Program at Yale University, the Integrated Liberal Studies Program at the University of Wisconsin, and the Sophomore Honors Program at the University of Oregon are examples. In some instances practical considerations have contributed to these experiments. Faculties which have been unwilling to adopt a uniform program such as the Yale Directed Studies Program for all students have been willing to accept them as experiments. They have not, in every instance, been planned for the more able students, though in the course of time they may have tended to attract them.

The General Program of Liberal Education at Notre Dame was introduced in 1950 and was originally designed as a four-year liberal arts curriculum. When the regular undergraduate curriculum was reorganized in 1954, the General Program was revised to its present form. From the beginning, however, it adopted a view of the liberal arts which was more traditional than the usual modern curriculum. To this end the conventional "major" had no place in the program. Both in concept and in practical operation it resembles the curriculum of St. John's College.[25]

[25] There is some similarity in purpose between the General Program of Liberal Education and the Program of Tutorial Studies in the University of Chicago, though there is almost no resemblance in the curricular structures. Students in the tutorial program at Chicago do not major in a special field. During their first two years, their program of general studies is determined in exactly the same way as that of all other students in the college. In the third year, however, instead of devoting the major portion of time to a field of concentration, they

The principal elements of the General Program are the Great Books Seminar and the "tutorials." The seminar is continuous through all three years. It has been described as a discussion between students and teachers, between students and students, and sometimes between teachers and teachers of the great issues which confront men as they are presented by the greatest teachers, the authors of the great books. As a rule two members of the faculty are assigned to each seminar. Discussion is not intended to be about any book in itself, but is "about what the book is about"; or, as one account says, the seminar is an occasion for students and teachers alike to engage in discussion with an author about a problem or issue of perennial concern. The books selected for study in the seminar cover all periods from Greek antiquity to the present. The historical scope of the chosen texts is from ancient Greece to the present in the sophomore seminar; from ancient Greece to the Renaissance in the junior year; and from the seventeenth century to the present in the senior year.

The tutorials serve a different function, for these are concerned with particular disciplines, whereas the seminar brings all basic disciplines of the liberal arts into operation. In the tutorials a close analysis of texts is required. Language, mathematics, science, literature, philosophy, and religion are the basic disciplines of the tutorials, and to some degree the study of all of these is continued in each year. Descriptions of the tutorials stress the point that these are not conventional courses. Neither lectures nor conventional textbooks are employed. Instead, great books which require the exercise of each discipline are the texts. These do not duplicate the works read in the seminar, nor are they studied for the same purposes. The structure of the entire program is shown in the following diagram.[26]

---

continue a distribution of their studies in four fields: humanities, social science, natural science, and philosophy. Limited freedom in the choice of courses in each area is permitted. Each student must write a major essay in one of the four areas. During his third year, also, he is expected to choose a problem of some magnitude which will be the major object of his studies during his final year. When the topic has been chosen and approved by the council for advanced general studies, each student is assigned to a member of the faculty who will be his Tutor and who will guide him in the writing of his Tutorial Essay, the major activity of the final year. With the advice of his Tutor, he will register for three courses especially chosen for their relation to the subject of his Tutorial Essay. A written and an oral examination based on the field of his tutorial study completes his work. There is also available time for some free electives in the last two years.

SECOND YEAR	Great Books Seminar	Philosophy of Nature and Psychology / Christian Doctrine	The Lyric / Biology	Mathematical Analysis	Foreign Language
THIRD YEAR	Great Books Seminar	Metaphysics / Ethics and the Christian Virtues	Tragedy / Elective	Physical Science	
FOURTH YEAR	Great Books Seminar	Politics / Church and Sacraments	The Novel / Elective	Logic and Language / Philosophy of Science	

[26] The diagram is an outline of the program as given in 1958–1959. A divided square indicates a semester course; where not divided, the course runs for both semesters.

207

The intention of the General Program is to restore, within the context of modern knowledge, an approximation of the meaning which was once attached to liberal education when liberal knowledge (which is not construed by the faculty of the General Program as identical with the liberal arts) was more sharply differentiated from vocational or specialized knowledge than it is today. In this respect the program is akin to the conception of liberal education which has determined the curriculum of St. John's College.

It will not pass unnoticed that the General Program contains no tutorial in history. As freshmen the students will have taken a year of European history, but the year of American history, required in the sophomore year of the regular program, is omitted and there is no equivalent. In the sophomore year, however, there is a history lecture one hour each week designed to provide background for the books being read in the seminar. A few great histories are read in the seminar (e.g., Herodotus, Thucydides, Gibbon), but the omission of history among the tutorials implies that it is not a discipline in the same sense as language, mathematics, science, and philosophy, or perhaps that skills in the exercise of science, philosophy, and the basic linguistic disciplines are prerequisites which are useful to reading of history and which have a prior claim in the curriculum. Since history as a discrete subject matter is not a part of the St. John's curriculum, there will be occasion to return to the issues which are raised by the omission later and to examine some problems pertinent to the role of history in liberal education.

THE UNIVERSITY OF OREGON

The University of Oregon, established by action of the state Legislature in 1872, opened for instruction in the liberal arts in 1876. Its growth, first as a liberal arts college and later as a university, followed the pattern of most of the state universities which were founded throughout the Middle and Far Western states during the latter half of the nineteenth century. In 1884 an evening School of Law was opened in Portland and was later moved to the Eugene campus. The Medical School, also located in Portland, was added in 1887. Between that date and 1945 other vocational and professional schools and a Graduate School increased the number of separate schools, including the College of Liberal Arts, to its present total of eleven. The list does not include schools of engineering, agriculture, and forestry, and other vocational schools which are units of the Oregon State University, the state's land-grant college located at Corvallis.

The university is not one of the large state universities. Its total enrollment in all divisions, including the Schools of Medicine and Dentistry located in Portland, was slightly over 7,000 in 1956-1957. Enrollment on the main campus at Eugene was just above 6,000, of which 797 students were in the Graduate School. The College of Liberal Arts is by far the largest unit of the university, having an enrollment of over 4,000 in 1956-1957. All students are enrolled in the College of Liberal Arts during their first two years of residence; hence the 1,100 students distributed among the other undergraduate schools were actually third- and fourth-year students. As in most state institutions of higher education, the attrition over the four undergraduate years is very high.

The university admits applicants who are residents of the state of Oregon if they have graduated from an accredited high school with an average grade of C in all studies which are accepted for a high school diploma or if they rank in the upper 60 per cent on a standard college aptitude test. Effective selection of the student body, however, takes place, as one administrative officer expressed it, more often in the classroom than in the admissions office. In this respect Oregon does not differ from the majority of state colleges and universities.

This account is concerned only with the College of Liberal Arts. Since all undergraduates except those in the School of Health and Physical Education are enrolled for at least two years in the college, we must take notice of a distinction between the general requirements applicable to those who major in the College of Liberal Arts and those who transfer to another school. Basically the curriculum is organized on the familiar distribution and concentration principle. The first two years (the Lower Division) are chiefly devoted to fulfilling distributional requirements; during this period students are required to distribute their studies among three divisions (groups) of subject matters. The last two years whether in the Upper Division of the College of Liberal Arts or in any other school are primarily years of concentration.

All undergraduates are required to take a one-year course in English composition unless all or part of the course is waived by the English department on the basis of qualifying tests. Two years of physical and health education are also common requirements. All other subject matters are classified in one of the three following groups: (1) arts and letters, (2) social science, (3) natural science. Students not majoring in the College of Liberal Arts must complete four course sequences, one in each of the three groups and a fourth in any one of the three. A sequence consists normally of three one-term units in a single subject matter extending over one academic year. Students who major in the College of Liberal Arts must complete six course sequences, two in each of the three groups. Most of the sequences are departmental courses, but in each group there are one or more general or interdisciplinary courses. The grouping of the departments is unusual only in that history, philosophy, and religion are classified exclusively with the social sciences. One course in philosophy is accepted in the humanities requirements. Many of the sequences are introductory departmental courses, required of majors in those departments. A few, including the general courses, are planned with particular concern for the nonmajor, as, for example, a course entitled "Essentials of Mathematics." In some areas only one sequence is offered; and in departments where three or more sequences are given, at least one is available only as a second sequence in the field.

The present curriculum was adopted in 1951 following the recommendations of a committee of the faculty, especially appointed for the task. Its fifty-page report was the work of three years and is exceptionally comprehensive.[27] The major changes proposed by the committee were deliberately intended to strengthen the general education requirements. The Report stated:

> In the first place, the committee feels that concentration and general education are out of balance in our present course of study. The curriculum is dominated by concentration, by the vocational or specialized function. Specialized training is strong and effective, general education relatively weak and ineffectual. The committee has no desire to attack the professional aspect of College training, nor to weaken what is strong and well done. At Oregon as elsewhere, it is in general education that reform is needed.
>
> In our own College, it seems to the committee that general education might be strengthened in two ways. The first is the simple increase in the quantity of work required in fields outside the major. Our present distribution requirements are certainly very feeble. Each student must take four courses intended to contribute to general education, but since two of these are normally elected

[27] *Report on the Curriculum,* submitted by the committee on curricular revision, College of Liberal Arts, November, 1950. Three sections of this Report merit detailed study by anyone who has a historical interest in the development of concepts of both liberal and general education. The first is entitled "Educational Functions of a Liberal College." The premises which guided the committee are set forth in detail. The committee accepted the dual functions of the modern liberal arts college, i.e., the general and the specialized functions; but it supported the premises with more detailed argument than most reports of the kind. A second section places the problems of the modern liberal arts college in the context of the historical development of the curriculum of the American college after 1865. It may be argued that the historical record rests too heavily upon the curricular innovations at Harvard under the leadership of Eliot, Lowell, and Conant and neglects other important contributions to the concept of liberal education between 1865 and 1945; but it is unusual for a curriculum committee in any college to acknowledge the importance of the history of the ideas which are central to its task. A third section, entitled "General Convictions of the Committee," deals with the curricular problems which the committee regarded as most acute at the University of Oregon. Here the committee is explicit in its declaration that the curriculum in force at the time of writing was particularly weak in the area of general education. The Report was prepared under the direction of Prof. Hoyt Trowbridge, chairman of the committee.

> in the division of the major—and hence are in actual fact a part
> of the student's program of concentration—the whole weight of
> general education may well be carried by two elementary courses.

This passage touches upon a point which is often disregarded in
the heat of discussions about general education. The notion is widely
held that the content of what we denominate professionally as "general education" is wholly distinct and separable from the content of
the students' areas of concentration. Once a course has been labeled
a "general education course" or identified as one that satisfies the
general requirements for a degree, it is regarded as outside the area
of concentration even though departments have fought strenuously
and successfully to obtain their introductory courses in the list of
options which satisfy general requirements. There is some dishonesty
—unintentional of course—in the practice of asserting that one-half
of the undergraduate years are devoted to a broad general education
and the other half to concentration if, as is usually the case, at least
one-third of the studies in the distributional requirements are also in
the area of concentration of each student. The point is that no absolute dichotomy exists between the content of general and specialized
education. By its very nature any program of general education, if it
is at all worthy of the name, must embrace knowledge which is pertinent to some special field, and the curriculum committee at Oregon
did well to call attention to this fact.

The intention of the committee to encourage a quantitative
strengthening of subject matters outside the area of concentration
was perfectly clear; and one result of its recommendations was the
increase in the requirements for majors in the College of Liberal
Arts to two sequences in each of the three group areas, with the
further provision that no two sequences could be chosen from the
same departmental field.

A second recommendation for strengthening the general education
program urged the development of new types of courses especially
planned to serve the needs of the nonmajor. Such courses, the committee pointed out, might be of a general or interdisciplinary type or
they might be departmental. The committee hoped that the faculty
would experiment with both types. It took notice of the usual criticisms of superficiality charged against general courses, but argued
that experience in some colleges had demonstrated that a degree of
rigor could be achieved in well-planned general courses equal to that

of the usual types of introductory departmental courses and it cited the accomplishments of Columbia, Chicago, Harvard, and Yale.[28]

Perhaps the most significant proposal made by the committee derived from its recognition of the ever-present problem of large institutions which cannot exercise great control over admissions. In a section titled "The Needs of Students" the Report asserted:

> The adjustment of the curriculum to the student is always difficult, but the problem is particularly acute in this country, where we are making a heroic and unprecedented attempt to educate a very large number of students, who differ widely in character and capacity. The range of ability and preparation among students, which is wide at even the most selective private colleges, is of course broader still at state universities, like Oregon, which admit any graduate of an accredited high school within the state.

The Report acknowledged that some provision for individual needs had been made through the optional courses in the group requirements, the free choice of a major field, and the provision for a number of unrestricted electives, but asserted that this is not enough:

> There is not much provision in the first two years for the special needs of the more poorly prepared students, and none at all for the most gifted. On the whole, our freshman and sophomore program rests on the assumption that students at every level of maturity and capacity may be educated in the same courses

> In a mass system of education, the gifted students, who can profit most from university work, are often those for whom least is done. The College has not done what it should, either for them or for society, unless it has given these students the best training they are capable of assimilating. The committee believes that students in the upper fifth of their class should have an opportunity to do part of their lower-division work in small classes, under expert instruction, in courses specially designed for them. They should also be allowed to meet group requirements by examination, with or without preparatory course work.

Concerning the needs of the weaker students, the Report first called attention to the high dropout rate and added:

[28] The University of Oregon had introduced a few "survey" courses as early as 1929 when this type of general course first became popular. These courses were still offered as electives when the committee submitted its report.

Yet we could do more for this group than we now do. In the opinion of the committee, the College should establish a small number of one-term special courses, designed to provide general education in the main subject-matter fields, which could be combined with standard courses (in the College and in the professional schools) in a new two-year curriculum leading to the degree of Associate in Arts. Unless excused by examinations showing equivalent competence, students in the lowest fifth would be required to take the new special courses before they were admitted to the corresponding standard courses.

The proposal for this two-year curriculum with the attendant Associate in Arts degree was not adopted by the faculty. From the other proposal, however, came the Sophomore Honors Program which is described in the University Catalog for 1958–1959 as follows:

> The University offers a "sophomore honors" program planned to provide a solid general education for freshman and sophomore students of superior ability. Honors are awarded to students who pass with distinction four comprehensive examinations, one each in the fields of literature, social science, and history and the fourth in either biological or physical science. These examinations, which are offered twice each year, in the fall and in the spring, must be taken before the student has completed 93 term hours of University work.
>
> The sophomore honors examinations are open to students in the upper 20 per cent of each entering class . . . ; with the consent of the committee in charge of the program, the examinations are also open to students who have completed 15 or more term hours of work in the University with a cumulative grade point average of 2.75 or higher.

Preparation for the honors examinations might be made through completing a series of courses especially planned for the program, one general course in each of the five subject matters covered in the examinations. It might also be made through independent study; students who pass the examinations, after independent study, receive appropriate credit toward their group requirements in the Lower Division. Students were given a statement describing the general scope of the examinations and lists of readings upon which the examinations are based. No student, however, was required to enter the honors program merely because he is eligible. The program was placed under the direction of a faculty committee, the committee on sophomore honors. A large percentage of the students eligible for honors have taken some of the courses in the program or have taken examinations independently, but only a small number of these have completed the full requirements for honors.

The five courses which comprise the curriculum of the honors program are:

1. *Literature*—an intensive study of Western literature, limited to drama, fiction, epic and lyric poetry. Three hours per week throughout the year.

2. *History*—Western civilization, organized around broad themes dealing with major movements of thought in the spheres of political, religious, and general cultural activity. A considerable part of the reading consists of primary documents, and here there is much attention to philosophic texts which are omitted from the literature course. Three hours weekly throughout the year.

3. *The Study of Society*—a "problems" course, designed to introduce students to the subject matter and methods of sociological, political, and economic dimensions of human behavior and action. Three hours a week throughout the year.

4. *Biological Science*—a selection of problems dealing with biological principles, with laboratory work. Four hours a week throughout the year.

5. *Physical Science*—an introduction to a selection of basic concepts in the physical sciences, their interrelation with one another and with other fields of knowledge, with laboratory work. Four hours a week throughout the year.

Though the administrative procedures in the Sophomore Honors Program are unusual, the purpose is similar to that of other programs which have been established in a few large universities within the last fifteen years, notably the Directed Studies Program at Yale and the Integrated Liberal Studies Program at the University of Wisconsin. Each of these has been designed as an effective program of general education for a selected group of students of more than average ability and each is by design relatively small. Instruction in each is in the hands of a staff of teachers especially chosen for their interest in the program.

For several years prior to the adoption of the present curricular requirements, the university offered a degree program called "Basic Liberal Studies." It was a four-year program intended for superior students and was described in the Catalog for 1958–1959 as a program which would "lay a substantial foundation for understanding literature, science, and the history of civilization." The description also stated that "it represents a departure from the free-elective system that has prevailed in American colleges for many years. It should be called a restricted elective program since the greater part of a student's work must be selected from a restricted list of courses." It was open only to students in the upper 20 per cent of their class. It was, in fact, a four-year general studies program. It failed, however, to attract a very large number of students and has since been discontinued. The curriculum committee took notice of this failure in its report; and while approving of the purpose of the program, the committee stated the opinion that it was too rigid and recommended several modifications, including the meeting of Lower Division requirements in part by examination in accordance with the principle proposed for the Sophomore Honors Program. In 1958 a new committee was appointed to review the basic problems to which the Sophomore Honors Program and the Basic Liberal Studies Program were addressed. The specific charge to this committee was to develop plans for the organization of a four-year college for superior students within the framework and jurisdiction of the College of Liberal Arts.

The work of this committee resulted in the recommendation for the establishment of an Honors College. The plan was approved and the college admitted its first students in the autumn of 1960. Administrative control rests with the Dean of the College of Liberal Arts, and in this respect it resembles the General Program of Liberal Education at Notre Dame. Designed to serve the interests of the ablest students of the College of Liberal Arts, it performs a special function which is the opposite of the special function of the General College at Minnesota. In its curricular organization, which departs radically from the structure of the basic program of general studies and concentration, it is an example of a new type of four-year curricular experiment that has appeared in the last few years. Monteith College of Wayne State University and the Oakland branch of Michigan State University, though not intended to serve only the ablest students, offer examples of liberal programs which are planned for special groups or have adopted principles that differ in fundamental respects from the standard liberal arts curriculum of their respective institutions.

The Honors College at Oregon offers a four-year undergraduate program and awards the Bachelor of Arts degree to its graduates. Its program provides for both "liberal and specialized training" and it is open to students in both liberal arts and professional school programs. Admission standards and degree requirements differ sharply from the standard requirements for admission to the university. Students who rank in the top 10 per cent of their high school classes are invited (though not required) to apply for admission to the College; but they must present the following distribution of high school courses: "English, four years; social science, three years; mathematics, two years; natural science, two years; foreign language, two years." Some exceptions are granted to superior students who may not have met all the above requirements. In addition to these prerequisites, the college requires all applicants to take the College Entrance Examination Board aptitude test and achievement tests in English, mathematics, and a foreign language. The foreign language test may be waived if the applicant comes from a school which does not offer language. Transfer students may apply, and their qualifications will be judged on the basis of their previous college record.

The Bachelor of Arts degree in the Honors College is awarded to students who meet the following requirements:

1. Proficiency in a foreign language equivalent to the standard achieved in a second-year college course.

2. Passing comprehensive examinations in *each* of six core areas. These are: history, literature, social science, natural sciences, philosophy, and mathematics. (Advisers may permit some liberal arts majors to omit one comprehensive area and some professional school majors to omit two areas.) Students may prepare for the examinations by taking courses in the six areas, some of which are planned for the Honors College and some of which are honors sections of courses in appropriate departments. They may also prepare for the examinations independently, a continuation of a policy adopted in the Sophomore Honors Program.

3. Two terms in the colloquium. The two colloquiums may be taken in either the junior or senior year. Like the Senior Colloquia at Stanford, several seminars are offered, and the student is required to choose a colloquium based on a theme outside the field of his concentration.

4. Completion of an honors program in the student's major field. The requirements vary with the several fields.

5. Satisfactory performance in an oral examination on the work in the major field.

6. Fulfilling all general university requirements for the bachelor's degree not covered by the foregoing requirements.

Although this brief outline does not describe all details of the Honors College program, it is sufficient to reveal a new approach to the problem of meeting the special needs of the ablest students in a large university.

Another type of degree program at Oregon falls within the larger sphere of general education. In each of the three divisional fields, provision is made for a divisional or general degree program. Thus it is possible to take a degree in General Arts and Letters, General Science, and General Social Science. The curriculum for the degree in General Arts and Letters is described as intended for students "who wish to build a program of general studies around a core of literature." The curriculum for the degree in General Science leads to either the Bachelor of Arts or Bachelor of Science and is designed for students "who wish to build a program of cultural studies around a central interest in science as an aspect of civilization, for students preparing for professional careers in science ... for whom a departmental science major may be too narrow and highly specialized, and for prospective science teachers." The curriculum for the degree in General Social Science is planned for students "who wish a broad cultural training and for prospective teachers for whom a departmental major may be too highly specialized." The number of students in these programs is small. The programs are more formalized versions of the interdepartmental major which has grown in favor in many colleges in recent years. For each of these programs some courses of an interdisciplinary nature have been developed at the Upper Division level.[29]

I have frequently referred to the uneasy role of foreign languages in general education. The recommendations of the curriculum committee on this subject are pertinent to the issue. At the time that the committee submitted its report, no language requirement was made

---

[29] The University of Chicago has experimented for several years with divisional degree programs. The General Humanities Program offers both a B.A. and an M.A. degree.

of candidates for the Bachelor of Science degree. For the Bachelor of Arts 24 credits (two years) in a single language were required without reference to any previous training. The committee examined in considerable detail the place of language in a liberal education, recognizing with regret its gradual deterioration in American education, while taking a reasonable view of the causes. The Report stated:

> Ideally, some knowledge of a foreign tongue should be required of all graduates of a liberal college. At the undergraduate level, this requirement could not be defended on instrumental grounds, as a tool of scholarship or professional training; undoubtedly there are subjects which can be profitably studied at this level without knowledge of foreign languages. For general education, however, a second language seems essential. The mere realization that there are other ways of saying things, just as vivid, efficient, and natural as our own, contributes immensely to detachment and breadth of view, to the weakening of intolerance and parochialism. The nature of language, surely the greatest of human inventions, can only be dimly and superficially understood without the control provided by some knowledge of another tongue. And half the beauty and power of our own speech is lost, unseen and unusable, to those who know no other language.

This eloquent defense of the study of a foreign language as an essential part of a general education is followed by another statement, as honest as this is moving: "But it seems impossible, under present conditions in this state university, to require such knowledge of all our students. The causes of the decay of language study, as we have said, lie deep in our national culture. The College may call attention to the loss entailed, but to change the situation is beyond our power."

The committee therefore recommended that the existing distinction between the requirements for the Bachelor of Science and the Bachelor of Arts degrees be retained. But it added a recommendation, which was adopted, that the language requirement for the Bachelor of Arts degree should be a qualitative requirement, the level of attainment to be equal to that expected of students who had completed two years of study in a single language. The practical effect of the change for most students would be slight, but the intention of the committee was to place emphasis upon competence and to encourage students to begin the study of language before entering college. The final comment of the committee is pertinent: "The secondary schools could do much for general education and for advanced professional study if they would urge students intending to go on to college to learn a second language and learn it early." The recent action of the university in creating the Honors College is an important first step in the direction of restoring foreign languages to their proper place in general education, if only for a limited group of students.

REED COLLEGE

Reed College, founded in 1911, is a comparatively small coeducational liberal arts college. Its enrollment in 1960–1961 was slightly over seven hundred students, of which 61 per cent were men. Throughout its history Reed has initiated many experiments in administrative organization, curriculum, and student-faculty cooperative enterprises. I have already referred to its early experiments with general courses and to the administrative and curricular reforms adopted in 1921 under the direction of President Richard Scholz.[30] The college has long attached great importance to small classes, close ties between students and faculty, and the encouragement of individual initiative and independent study. Formal grades are withheld until graduation, but students are regularly informed of their progress and of their individual strengths and weaknesses.

Although Reed's students do not share with the faculty and administration a responsibility for the formulation of educational policies and direction of campus life in a degree equal to that of Antioch's students, they are granted opportunities which exceed those of most small liberal arts colleges. The student council appoints an educational policies committee of ten students which is expected to study the policies of Reed and other colleges and to confer with the members of the faculty committee on educational policy. The student council itself has great responsibility in the management of student affairs, student finances, and the handling of disciplinary matters. Like Antioch, Reed considers these responsibilities an important part of general education.

Two-thirds of Reed's students are from West Coast states, with about one-tenth from Portland. Another one-third come from widely distributed sections of the nation. Although there is no specified distribution of high school studies as prerequisites for admission, students are strongly encouraged to prepare themselves in the traditional academic courses. Applicants are required to take the College Entrance Examination Board aptitude tests and three achievement

[30] Part 1, pp. 80–82.

tests. For the latter English, social science, and intermediate mathematics are recommended.

The administrative organization of the faculty is divisional rather than departmental. All subject matters are allocated to one of four divisions:

> Letters and arts
> (English, French, German, Russian, Greek, Latin, art, music, theater)
>
> History and social science
> (history, economics, politics, sociology, and anthropology)
>
> Mathematics and natural science
> (mathematics, biology, chemistry, and physics)
>
> Philosophy, psychology, and education
> (Religion and physical education are included in this division.)

The divisional organization is designed to circumvent tendencies toward too narrow specialization. A student's major field is usually divisional in scope, particularly in the first two divisions named above; and his work is supervised by his divisional faculty as well as by a professor in his chosen field. The college offers one undergraduate degree, the Bachelor of Arts. It also offers the Master of Arts in Teaching, as many small colleges now do.

The curriculum for the bachelor's degree is a carefully restricted form of concentration and distribution. As they have been since 1921, the first two years are primarily devoted to courses which form the core requirements of general education, and the last two years principally to work in a major field. The requirements of the freshman and sophomore years, as they are given in the Catalog for 1960–1961, are shown in the following tabular view:

> Humanities 11 or 12
> Foreign language
> Physical education through the first two years
> Three year-hours from Group A
> Three year-hours from Group B
> Six year-hours from Group C
> 　　(Note: a year-hour equals two semester hours.)

Group A—literature, philosophy, and the arts: a minimum of three year-hours, which may be selected from the following: History of Art, Introduction to Music, History of the Theater, Problems in Philosophy,

Problems in Religious Thought, Humanities 21 or 22 (a continuation of Humanities 11–12). In some instances more advanced courses in each area may be substituted.

Group B—history, psychology, and the social sciences: a minimum of three year-hours, which may be selected from Political Science (national and international political institutions and problems), Introduction to Sociology and Anthropology, General Psychology, and Humanities 21 or 22 if not used in Group A. Advanced courses in these areas and in history may be substituted in some cases.

Group C—mathematics and natural science: a minimum of six year-hours to be selected from *two* of the following three groups: mathematics, biology, and physical sciences. By way of explanation it is important to describe the provisions in each of these fields. Two courses in mathematics are offered, one of which is specifically designed for students who do not have a professional need for higher mathematics; the other is preprofessional. The general introductory course in biology is divided into a pre-professional course and a "general" variant. The latter differs from the first only in that laboratory time is reduced. Introductory courses in chemistry and physics are part of the offerings in this group; but a general course in physical science (problems in physics, chemistry, and astronomy) is also given for nonmajors who may prefer it. Qualified students may take advanced courses instead of the introductory courses in any field.

Humanities 11 (or 12) is the only course required of all students. The only difference between the two versions is that Humanities 12 is an abridged version for science majors. Humanities 11 grants seven year-hour credits and the other only four. In an effort to secure more flexibility in the programs of science majors, Humanities 12 will be eliminated beginning in 1961–1962 and Humanities 11 will be reduced to six year-hours. It will remain the one uniformly required course in the curriculum. Other changes are contributing to the effort to secure less rigidity in the science program. It has been said that students were forced to choose their major in this area almost as soon as they entered college.

The foreign language requirement may be met by a proficiency test, but no student may graduate without the completion of six semester hours in the second year of a language, or by demonstration of an equivalent competence through an examination. Students may be admitted to Reed who have had no previous study of foreign language.

The present group distributional plan is a very recent revision. Until two years ago, subject matters were divided into two groups, the natural sciences (which included mathematics and psychology) and another group which included a very restricted list of courses in the social sciences, philosophy, and the second year of the humanities sequence. The addition of the third group enlarges the scope of the general requirements by making possible a choice of courses in the fine arts, religion, and the theater. The change also permits advanced students to choose more advanced courses.

Because Humanities 11 is the only required course in the program and because it engages so large a proportion of the freshman student's time, it deserves particular attention. It is a historically oriented course and is a lineal descendent of the complex group of required courses in history, literature, the social sciences, and the arts which was introduced in 1921. The historical scope of the course extends from Homeric Greece to the mid-eighteenth century. It is organized topically; the topics deal with major political, intellectual, and artistic movements in Greek, Roman, medieval, Renaissance, and early modern European history. The course is conducted through a combination of lectures, group discussions, and individual conferences. The required readings for Humanities 11 are very extensive; they consist of both primary and secondary source materials and include representative works of poetry, fiction, drama, and philosophy. The historical development of the graphic arts and architecture is also traced from the classical era of Greece to the development of eighteenth-century baroque art. Students are required to write both long and short themes throughout the course; and these are used, through individual conferences, as materials for training in writing. Since the required core of studies contains no formal course in English composition, this course assumes the major part of the task of instruction in writing disciplines.[31]

In 1921 two themes controlled the organization of the curriculum of the first two years. The theme of the first year was Man's Social and Biological Heritage. Of the sixteen course hours required in the first year, seven were devoted to the history and literature of Europe from ancient Greece to the middle of the eighteenth century, supplemented by optional courses in the arts, philosophy, and social

---

[31] The course and its second-year companion, Humanities 21, are described in detail in an article by R. F. Arragon, "The Humanities Program at Reed College," in Earl J. McGrath (ed.), *The Humanities in General Education,* W. C. Brown Co., Dubuque, Iowa, 1949.

institutions of the times. Three hours were given to biology, which was centered on the theme of human evolution. The theme of the second year was Contemporary Civilization, and not less than 9½ course hours were directed to this theme through the study of the social sciences and the continuation of the history-literature course which brought the historical narrative to the contemporary period. The six year-hours hereafter to be devoted to Humanities 11 are nearly the same amount of time formerly credited to the study of Western cultural history and world literature; thus the importance which Reed has attached to this subject matter as a necessary part of a general education has apparently not changed in the course of nearly thirty years. The emphasis given to it recalls Woodrow Wilson's proposal that the study of our cultural heritage as reflected in our institutions and our intellectual and artistic achievements should be the one uniform requirement of all students seeking a liberal education.[32] Although Humanities 21 and 22 are no longer required as a part of the sophomore year, the courses which form Groups A and B support the conclusion that the study of contemporary civilization continues to be a principal concern in the core program.

Perhaps the most noteworthy detail of Reed's optional-course distributional plan is the remarkably small number of courses in Groups A, B, and C. Up to this point, I have given little attention to the differences among the several core programs which employ the optional-course principle. The extremes in differences are sufficiently great to justify thoughtful attention; and they are well illustrated in the programs of Reed and the College of Science, Literature, and the Arts of the University of Minnesota. In the latter college, it will be recalled, students must earn 15 course credits in each of three divisions: social sciences, humanities, and natural sciences. These are in addition to the requirement in English composition, foreign language, and health education. The 45 credits may be obtained by satisfactory work in at least two departmental fields in each division. The total number of departments in the three divisions is well over twenty. Since most departments offer optional courses, the sum of courses from which students may choose in fulfilling their distributional requirements is considerably in excess of a hundred. In comparison with so wide a range of options, the Reed program, which limits the entire number of options in all groups to less than fifty courses

[32] See Part 1, pp. 45–46.

including variant forms of some courses, seems closer in spirit to the curriculums of colleges which are uniformly required of all students. All the courses in the Reed program normally taken in the first and second years are one-year courses, and this points to another important difference. At Minnesota courses are defined as units of work extending over one term, i.e., one-third of the academic year. Although many courses are related to form a one-year sequence, it is sometimes possible to elect the first term without obligation to continue, and there are numerous one-term courses which form no part of a sequence.

The differences are not attributable to the size of the institutions. No small college can offer the great variety of courses which make up the sum of the distributional program at Minnesota, but there has been ample evidence in this study that small colleges similar in kind and size to Reed do offer a greater variety of options than Reed, and some of them offer options within a single departmental field. A matter of principle is involved here which concerns the long-standing issue of breadth of learning in relation to depth. The Reed policy is a clear commitment to depth within a limited subject matter; the Minnesota policy does not exclude an opportunity for an equivalent depth, but it permits a much greater diversity of subjects. A principal defense of the optional-course plan has been the argument that it is better for the student to explore one subject matter in depth than to expend the same amount of time in a course which seeks to integrate two or more related subjects. Whether the argument is sound is debatable; but it appears that some optional-course plans offer no certain guarantee of study-in-depth.

The presuppositions made concerning lack of depth in general courses may also be reviewed in the light of four general courses in Reed's program. In addition to the humanities courses there are two others which are optional, Biology 11 and Natural Science 11.[33] By quantitative standards it would be difficult to support the charge that study-in-depth is denied in any of these courses. The six year-hours given to Humanities 11 is nearly matched by the class hours (though not credit hours) given to the two science courses. Biology

---

[33] General or integrated courses in biological science have now become so commonplace that many teachers have forgotten or do not know that twenty-five years ago they were a rarity and that the usual distributional pattern provided options in botany, zoology, and sometimes physiology.

11 is offered in two forms, one for science majors and one for non-majors. Biology 11 S (for majors) meets for three lecture hours per week and two 3-hour laboratory periods. Biology 11 L (for non-majors) differs in that only one 3-hour laboratory period, in addition to the lectures, is required.

It is decidedly worth considering whether, with so much time available, a great deal in the way of depth may not be achieved in these courses. Breadth and depth are always relative terms, and in fact, they can hardly be said to be true opposites. Broad might more accurately be opposed to narrow, and deep to shallow. Discussions concerning the relative breadth and depth of general and departmental courses have frequently been confused, because they have erroneously assumed a single referent as a standard of measurement, whereas more than one standard usually exists. Seven weekly class hours devoted to the general course in physical sciences cannot offer depth in chemistry equal to that of introductory chemistry, but it is possible that within a year's time the course (Natural Science 11) may, by virtue of its greater breadth of scientific problems and methods, yield a deeper knowledge of the scope and meaning of the physical sciences than Chemistry 11. For the student who will not major in science and who may take no other course in science the kind of depth achieved by the general course may be very important.

There are no general courses in the social sciences comparable to those in humanities and the natural sciences. This is policy of long standing on the part of the social science divisional faculty. It will also be noticed that it is possible for students not majoring in this division to omit any of the formal courses in the social sciences in Group A by electing Humanities 21 or 22. It is also possible to omit either a physical science or biological science option by taking Mathematics 11.

The account of the general education program at Reed will not be complete without reference to the Senior Symposium. The symposium is an elective open to seniors with the consent of the instructional staff. It is an interdivisional seminar in which members of the staffs of the four divisions participate. Students meet in sections of twelve members each with two or three faculty representatives from different divisions. The Senior Symposium was introduced in 1951 and is similar in its broad objectives to many courses which have become popular in the last fifteen years. In several colleges such a course is required. Without exception these courses, under a variety of names and with widely differing content, have arisen from a conviction that some means must be found to bring students at the close of their undergraduate years into an effective relationship with problems of value which transcend all departmental lines of concentration.[34]

The following account of Reed's Senior Symposium is given in the Catalog for 1958–1959:

> Using significant works written in the past 50 years by such men as Whitehead, Dewey, Bergson, and Niebuhr as a basis of discussion, the course considers interpretation of current social, economic and political issues; the problem of the relation of science to society; and the nature of science and the limits of knowledge. The last and largest part of the course concerns itself with a basic diagnosis of our age made in terms of differing fundamental points of view.

In a report on the progress of the course after three years of experience with it the staff said:

> We have come to see that the weakness of the thinking of many Reed seniors outside of their specialization is not so much the absence of any community of ideas as its vagueness. We sense an apathy concerning the decisions faced by the individual and by society and a need for the rational definition of the grounds upon which such decisions and significant communication among the members of society would rest. What is needed is the discovery by the students of the areas of agreement and disagreement among them and the reasons therefor. What is needed even more is a sharpening of the students' perception of the importance of moral choice and the consequences of moral indecisiveness.

Conducted as a seminar with weekly discussions, the problems derive from an extensive list of important works, most of which have been written within the present century. A single text is the point

[34] A few institutions which have introduced such courses are Colgate University, Dartmouth College, Denison University, Knox College, Northwestern University, Oberlin College, Purdue University, Sarah Lawrence College, Stanford University. See Hugh Stickler, "Senior Courses in General Education," *Journal of Higher Education*, vol. 25, March, 1954, p. 146. The required Junior Seminar at Notre Dame is similar in function.

of departure for each class session. The readings for the year 1955–1956 began with Arthur Miller's *Death of a Salesman* which was followed by David Riesman's *The Lonely Crowd*. During the year some of the authors read were: Eric Fromm, Karl Mannheim, Aldous Huxley, Sigmund Freud, Reinhold Niebuhr, Feodor Dostoievsky, Sören Kierkegaard, Albert Camus, Bertrand Russell, Francis Bacon, Max Planck, A. N. Whitehead, Franz Kafka, John Dewey, Herman Melville, and Julian Huxley. One criterion in the selection of works was to bring different approaches and points of view to bear on a problem. Another, evident from the several novels and dramas which appear in the readings, was to view a problem in terms of the drama of the human individual as well as in terms of the different dialectical approaches of philosophers and scientists.

Like the majority of senior seminars, the Senior Symposium emphasizes the contemporary world. It is less rigidly schematized than some, and it relies chiefly on the techniques of small discussion groups. Organizational principles and instructional methods differ greatly in these experiments, a consideration to which we shall return in the account of the curriculum of Stanford University.

ST. JOHN'S COLLEGE IN ANNAPOLIS

In 1784 the Maryland General Assembly granted a charter for St. John's College. The college was soon merged with King William's School, founded by Royal Charter in 1696. St. John's is the oldest college represented in this study; and as almost everyone knows, it is the only one to which the adjective "unique" can be applied in literal truth with regard to its conception of the meaning of liberal education. It is a small college, by far the smallest in this group. In 1960–1961 its enrollment was approximately 277, and its present policy is to remain a small college.

Until 1937 the history of the college's educational policies did not differ greatly from that of the majority of small liberal arts colleges in America. As late as the mid-nineteenth century it retained the standard classical curriculum of the times. Its curriculum gradually expanded, but it did not offer optional courses of study as soon as some colleges. In 1886, however, four courses of study were introduced: a Classical Course leading to the Bachelor of Arts degree, a Latin-Scientific Course leading to the Bachelor of Letters, a Scientific Course with the Bachelor of Science degree, and a Mechanical Engineering Course for which an appropriate degree was awarded. In 1923 the college adopted an open elective system which continued until the complete reorganization in 1937.

That reorganization, under the leadership of Stringfellow Barr and Scott Buchanan, is described by the college as the restoration of the traditional program of the liberal arts. This did not signify a literal return to the courses which formed the conventional curriculum of American colleges at the beginning of the nineteenth century or to the pedagogical methods characteristic of that era. The aim was to achieve "a modern equivalent of the traditional curriculum of the *trivium* and *quadrivium*, which had once so effectively developed the mental powers of a man." [35] Actually the modern equivalent is, in

---

[35] "A Report on a Project of Self-study," *Bulletin of St. John's College in Annapolis,* vol. 7, no. 2, April, 1955, p. v. The self-study project is one of several made by American colleges between 1952 and 1954 which were supported by grants from the Fund for the Advancement of Education.

materials and methods, quite different from the liberal arts curriculum which was standard fare in 1800. The new administration sought to recover what it believed to be the essence of an educational idea which reached much further back in time. It had no intention of ignoring either the great changes in the sum and substance of learning which had taken place since the demise of the classical tradition or the consequences of changes in the functions and practices of preparatory schools.

The only program in this study which resembles St. John's conceptually is the General Program of Liberal Education at Notre Dame University which, as we have seen, is an alternative for a selected group of students to the regular course of study in the College of Arts and Letters. Both programs reject the dualistic concept of liberal education which has dominated the philosophy and practice of American colleges for the last half century. The basis of rejection at St. John's is stated in two introductory paragraphs in the Catalogue for 1958–1960 which bear the title "The Goal of Liberal Education":

> That young people are in need of education is a generally accepted proposition. But there is no agreement as to what education means, what its goals are and what its methods should be. It can be said, however, that two ideas of education prevail universally. Children and adolescents have to learn, and do learn, the habits and customs of the society to which they belong and into which they grow; they have to assimilate, and do assimilate, the religious, moral and political traditions of their elders. On the other hand, young men and women have to prepare themselves for their later lives and the specific tasks they will shoulder by choice or necessity; they have to acquire, in addition to a minimal literacy, expertness in certain fields, mechanical skills for example, trade experience, knowledge of a definite kind.

> Do these two ideas of education define the goal of education sufficiently well? They do not. For all depends upon the spirit in which those traditions are kept and on the understanding that underlies those various skills, experiences and knowledges. All customs, all arts and sciences, however particular, embody principles of a general nature. To be aware of these principles means to be able to look beyond the immediate, the accepted and the necessary. The acquisition of such ability is the goal of a liberal education. In a free society this goal can never be dispensed with.

For in deliberating about a course of action, in deciding what the welfare of an individual and what the common good require, one has to distinguish between the expedient and the just, the apparent and the true, the contingent and the essential; one has to have acquired, in other words, a minimum of critical intelligence and an awareness of principles that govern our behavior and our understanding.

The cultivation of awareness of those general principles which are embodied in "all customs, all arts and sciences" is, according to St. John's view, the traditional goal of liberal education because it is the very foundation of a free society. Furthermore the college holds that in the absence of this awareness no specialized form of education, however exacting, can give assurance of freedom to either the individual or society. The exclusion of specialization from the St. John's curriculum follows not from notions of its irrelevance to the total educational process but from convictions about the prior and over-ruling importance of a knowledge of these general principles.

In subsequent paragraphs the catalogue asserts that this goal of liberal education was the source of the original impulse of all institutions of higher learning; historical circumstances, however, united to produce a confusion between the *idea* of liberal education and the *ideal* of scholarship. Knowledge advances through scholarship, and scholarship defines the subjects taught in schools and colleges. But scholarship implies specialization in minute detail. "Applied to the enterprise of liberal education, to the process of learning, scholarship ... seems to entail a fractioning of the students' attention, a multiplication of special disciplines." This contradicts the purposes of liberal education, and as a consequence "either the education of the students or their scholarship or both are in danger of suffering injury." The circumstances of the nineteenth century encouraged pursuit of the ideal of scholarship and with it the multiplication of subject matters and the demands of vocationalism. The result for the colleges has been that "the ideal of scholarship degenerated into an empty form; curricula were conceived with reference to the requirements of graduate professional and vocational schools or to the conditions of employment in the contemporary world. Colleges became timidly and fanatically preparatory."

This summary of the conception of liberal education at St. John's will help us to grasp the rationale of its curriculum, its administrative organization, and its instructional procedures. Furthermore the goals of liberal education defended by St. John's resemble closely the goals which most colleges proclaim to be those of general education. Colleges which assert a desire to cultivate "an understanding of our cultural heritage," "an understanding and acceptance of our responsibilities as citizens," and "habits of clear and logical thinking" will not take exception to the following statement: "The liberal arts enable men to win knowledge of the world around them and knowledge of themselves in this world. Under their guidance men can free themselves from the wantonness of prejudice and the narrowness of beaten paths. Under their discipline men can acquire the habit of listening to reason."

St. John's acknowledges the identity of interest between its conception of liberal education and the commonly proclaimed goals of general education. The differences in view lie chiefly in the realm of means; for St. John's holds that by compromising these goals with the aims of specialization, most colleges have not given adequate attention to "the principles of a general nature that underlie all customs, all arts and sciences." In other words it is "the *spirit* [italics mine] in which the customs and traditions [in religion, morals, and politics] are kept" which is lacking in the conventional modern college programs of general education.

St. John's concedes that the recovery of the true meaning of the liberal arts "involved a new approach to the vast tradition of Western thought" and it believes that it has found the approach through the intensive study of "the great books of that tradition" which, it says, "is built on the practice of the liberal arts."

> In a way this tradition of ours is not in the books, it is rather the heritage by which we live, the spirit which permeates our thinking and speaking, our attitudes and concerns. This heritage, however, can wither away. It is necessary, then, and on more than one occasion, to go back to its sources and to reflect on what they have to say. This is the way in which education can become a deliberate and planned undertaking. And it is at this point that specialized scholarly pursuits might well interfere with the overall educational goal.

The college has avoided the classifications of subject matters, such as humanities, social sciences, natural sciences, arts and letters, life sciences, etc., which are the trademarks of modern curricular organization. Instead its program is organized in six divisions: the Seminar, the Language Tutorial, the Mathematics Tutorial, the Music Tutorial, the Laboratory, and the Formal Lecture. These divisions are not subject matters in the usual sense of the term. Each constitutes a distinct kind of intellectual activity. The tutorials are intended to provide intensive training in the traditional liberal arts which are concerned with modes of symbolic expression. Language, mathematics, and music are not separate departments of learning according to St. John's: "The human mind does not function by departments. It functions as a whole or else it is mutilated; .... Man would not think as he does if he did not speak *and* count *and* sing. None of the three activities can be adequately understood without taking into account the other two."

Similarly the Laboratory constitutes a continuous exercise in the methods and techniques of scientific inquiry. The Seminar, which finds its materials in the ideas represented in the great works of the Western tradition, is supported by the work of the tutorials and the Laboratory; but it opposes classification either of books or problems specifically as science, philosophy, or the arts; it asserts that the methods of aesthetic, scientific, and philosophic inquiry converge in the problems encountered in these works. The Formal Lecture is a kind of counterpart to the Seminar. Here the students listen once a week to eminent scholars and artists who unfold ideas pertaining to their scholarly and artistic pursuits. Each lecture is supplemented by an open forum upon the ideas presented.

The following tabular view is a greatly condensed representation of the curriculum.

First Year	Second Year	Third Year	Fourth Year
Seminar	Seminar	Seminar	Seminar
Language Tutorial	Language Tutorial	Language Tutorial	Language Tutorial
Greek	Greek	German *	French
English	English		
Mathematics Tutorial	Mathematics Tutorial	Mathematics Tutorial	Mathematics Tutorial
Music Tutorial	Music Tutorial (first semester)		

FIRST YEAR	SECOND YEAR	THIRD YEAR	FOURTH YEAR
Laboratory Biology (first semester) Theory of Measurement (second semester)	Laboratory Chemistry (first semester) Optics (second semester)	Laboratory Biology Mechanics	Laboratory Electromagnetism Laboratory Projects
			Thesis Writing
Formal Lecture	Formal Lecture	Formal Lecture	Formal Lecture

* Recently the German Tutorial has been replaced by two years of French Tutorial. This action is tentative, however.

Although the list of books read in the Seminar is subject to change from year to year, a substantial number is consistently retained. The works are read in chronological order, but they are not studied within the context of Western history or as documents in cultural history. In the first year the works range from Homer to Lucretius; in the second year from Virgil to Shakespeare and Bach. The Seminar includes a selection of great musical works. The second year concludes with a study and discussion of Gregorian chants and a representative work by Bach—the *St. Matthew Passion*. The third year extends from Rabelais to de Tocqueville, Mozart, and Beethoven; and the fourth year from Jane Austen to Freud, Schumpeter, and Stravinsky.

The Seminar meets in two-hour sessions twice each week. Each section of the Seminar has about twenty students and two or three tutors. All members of the faculty are tutors. The college makes no distinctions in its faculty by rank. Procedure is by discussion, but no restrictions are imposed upon the manner or point of view by which the several sections of the Seminar are conducted.

The full list of works read in the Seminar is formidable; yet with the exception of those which are primarily scientific, there are few titles which are not found among the reading lists of general humanities and social science courses in scores of colleges, and a few general courses in natural science have introduced several of the scientific texts. The Catalogue for 1958–1960 contains a classification of the works by conventional subject-matter groupings: literature, philosophy and theology, history and social science, mathematics, and natural science. In each year works from each of these fields are read, although this principle of classification is not employed in the organization of the Seminar. In literature the readings range from Homer in the first year to Thomas Mann in the fourth year; in philosophy from Plato to Poincaré. History and social science texts extend from Herodotus to Hegel and a selection of documents from American history; mathematics from Euclid to Dedekind. In the natural sciences the list begins with Hippocrates and concludes with Freud and Einstein.

The extent of the readings should dispel any notion that St. John's regards the great books as only those which belong to the distant past. Both in the Seminar and in the tutorials the readings include the contemporary with the past; and according to the faculty, it is the implications for contemporary life which give any work a place among the great books. In the senior year the Seminar stresses the modern era, and as discussions turn to more recent times the Seminar is supplemented by special lectures and tutorials.

In the account of the General Program of Liberal Education at Notre Dame, I remarked upon the omission of history as a special discipline. The role of history at St. John's is similar. Not only does the Seminar refuse to treat the readings as documents in cultural history, but the tutorials, too, refuse to accord history a special place. The theory upon which this policy rests is that historical reconstructions conceal philosophies about the organic unity of the past which at best are partial and at worst seductive and misleading. Moreover texts read primarily as signs of a particular cultural ethos tend to lose much of their contemporary significance. This attitude is essentially a denial of the value of history as an "integrating" discipline and, consequently, is opposed to a view shared by many general courses in humanities and social science. St. John's does not exclude historical works from among the great intellectual achievements of mankind nor does it deny the importance of knowing the historical order of the affairs of men. Thucydides, Tacitus, Gibbon, and de Tocqueville, among others, have a place in the Seminar. Nor is it without significance that the progression in the readings of the Seminar and the tutorials is chronologically ordered. Although this attitude toward history as a discipline will not be shared by most colleges, it may serve as a useful warning against the pitfalls which attend some of the oversimplified classifications and interpretations made in general cultural history courses based on premises often left unexamined.

The habits of reading and discussion which the Seminar encourages during the four years can only be the product of a kind of concentration which is generally disregarded in discussions of the relationship of concentration to liberal education. As we have seen, it is commonly agreed that concentration or study-in-depth is an important element in liberal education. The importance of concentration has never been denied, and the classical curriculum achieved or sought to achieve it through the study of classical languages and literature supported by the study of grammar, logic, and rhetoric. Since President Eliot's day, colleges have gradually accepted the idea that the values of concentration might be better achieved if students were allowed more latitude in the choice of the subject of concentration. President Lowell undertook to separate the ends of concentration from those of vocationalism or specialization and firmly maintained that the sole purpose of concentration was the strengthening of the "mental fibre" of the student. The separation seems not to have been so sharply drawn by President Eliot, and certainly it has not been made by most modern educators for whom the terms "concentration" and "vocational specialization" are practically synonymous. The St. John's Seminar, supported by the intensive training of the tutorials, is a commitment to a concept of concentration quite disjoined from the commonly accepted idea of specialization. So too is the General Program of Liberal Education at Notre Dame. There are other indications that ideas about the relation of concentration to both general and liberal education are changing. The identification of the idea of general education solely with a superficial survey of knowledge seems to be yielding as area-study programs, interdivisional and interdepartmental majors, four-year degree programs in general studies, and such innovations as the Program of Tutorial Studies at the University of Chicago increase in numbers. All such programs demand concentration, but of a substantive kind that differs from the traditional forms of departmental concentration.

Where the work of the Seminar is extensive and discursive, the work of the tutorials is intensive and analytical. The Language Tutorial and the Mathematics Tutorial meet five hours weekly throughout four years and the scope of their subject matter has no parallel in the general requirements of any other American college. The scope of the Language Tutorial is not in the degree of mastery sought in any single language; however, no other liberal arts college asks that all its students shall achieve a reading knowledge of two languages and a reasonable familiarity with a third. The college recommends, moreover, that its students have not less than two years of study in one language in secondary school. The objectives of the Language Tutorial are not, however, identical with those usually cited by colleges which include a knowledge of a foreign language among their general requirements.

> The primary purpose of the language tutorials is thus not the mastery of any foreign languages. By studying them, however, and by translating them into English, by comparing them with each other and with English, the student learns something of the nature of language in general and of his own in particular. During the four years, then, he is studying language as such, the discourse of reason, and through the medium of foreign tongues, his own native English.

Whether these goals can be as effectively achieved through four years of continuous study of a single language may be debated, but in so far as general education is concerned the debate is wholly academic since no American college imposes or is soon likely to impose such a general requirement. The choice of languages studied in the tutorial is more or less arbitrary. Although the books read in the Seminar are studied in English translations, the original tongues of the majority of the non-English works has had considerable influence on the choice of Greek, German, and French. The college admits that other languages would serve most of the purposes equally well.

The Mathematics Tutorial is designed to restore "the language of numbers and figures" to an eminence in liberal education which St. John's believes that it once had but which has been surrendered to the exigencies of vocationalism. The college expects that students shall have had 1½ years of algebra and 1 year of geometry in high school, but the expectation does not preclude further study of either algebra or geometry. The basic texts of the tutorial are, with few exceptions, classical works in mathematics from Euclid to Lobachevski, Dedekind, and Cantor; and the chronological order of the content over the four years presents a kind of disciplinary history of mathematical thought from Euclidian geometry through a study of number theory, trigonometry, algebra, analytical geometry, calculus, and differential equations to non-Euclidian geometry and transfinite numbers. The college claims no immediate interest in training professional mathematicians but rather in having students learn mathematics as a mode of human understanding and in having them learn "what is meant by accuracy, rigor and elegance in thinking." The college believes that the decay of mathematics as a part of the liberal educa- tion of all students is peculiarly distressing in view of the conditions of modern life, and it repudiates the notion that students require a special competence to succeed in all save the most elementary mathe- matics. It holds the decline of mathematics as an essential liberal discipline to be due to poor techniques in teaching, which in turn are attributable to "a misunderstanding of the fundamental nature and intention of mathematics."

The Music Tutorial was added to the St. John's curriculum in 1950. The tutorial meets twice weekly through the freshman year and the first semester of the sophomore year. Music is regarded as another mode of symbolic expression and it is accorded a place in the cur- riculum quite different from that given to it in most liberal arts programs. The college asserts the intention of restoring music to a place which it once held among the liberal arts, but which it considers to have been sacrificed as the motives for teaching music shifted to a concern with the development of the emotions. As one surveys the role of music in liberal education today, particularly in the narrow area now defined as general education, one is inclined to think that it is the nearly total neglect of music rather than a shift in the concep- tion of function that is the chief characteristic of modern practice.

Several colleges, however, have found a place for music even within the sphere of general education, some of which are represented in this study. Moreover some of them agree with St. John's that music ought not to be understood as "essentially an outpouring of emotions," and in practice they agree with St. John's that the foundation of musical education ought to be the study of the properties of tone and its organizations, topics which form the substance of the Music Tu- torial. There would, nevertheless, be objections to some statements of theory concerning the function of music in liberal education, a view which seems to separate without warrant the intellectual and emotional aspects of musical experience. Appreciation is a much abused word, but it is one that is difficult to avoid in the discussion of music in relation to education. The colleges to which I refer con- sider the appreciation of music a part of general education, but they make no distinction between music, visual art, and poetry in this respect. Moreover, by the organization and instructional methods of their courses, one might judge that they would not accept the St.

John's view that the "balance which the study of music should be charged to maintain" lies wholly within the intellectual life itself. Enjoyment of the arts is a legitimate end of liberal education; and, they will argue, enjoyment does involve emotional participation in the experience of works of art.

The key to the difference between the two attitudes toward music seems to lie in a distinction which St. John's makes between music and the fine arts. Music is a liberal art, not a fine art. Painting, sculpture, and architecture are fine arts. St. John's makes no provision for the study of the visual arts in a tutorial or in the Seminar. The policy is stated in the Catalogue:

> While St. John's has included music in the curriculum, it leaves the fine arts to extracurricular activity. The relation of the fine arts to the liberal arts is not sufficiently clarified by the current interpretation of the fine arts as an integral part of the humanities or as a conspicuous manifestation of culture. This interpretation permits them, at best, to become the subject matter of certain historical, psychological, and philosophical disciplines, but does not contribute to the development of genuine artistic skills.

It will not be denied that the study of music, the visual arts, and poetry have often suffered from the kinds of reductions of a historical, psychological, or philosophical kind to which the statement refers. On the other hand, some teachers believe that there are concepts of the arts which do not necessarily lead to such reductions. Their view is supported by respectable aesthetic theory. What tone is as a medium to music, color is to painting; and the organization of the properties of color are coordinate with the organization of the properties of tone. Thus color is "language" quite as much as tone. The end of instruction is, they think, to enable students to participate as fully as possible in the experience or "expressiveness" which is unique to each work of art in each medium. The qualities of expression vary from work to work. Informed judgment, which is appreciation fully developed, is a proper goal of liberal education and one that is equally desirable in the visual arts and music. This, I believe, is the kind of response we might expect from some teachers who are no less interested than St. John's in securing for music a better place than it now holds in most general education programs.

I must add that St. John's maintains a studio where students interested in drawing, painting, and sculpture may secure guidance under the supervision of an artist in residence. This, however, is done in several other colleges, not primarily with the idea of cultivating the visual arts either as a vocation or as an avocation, but in order to enable students to learn through practice something of the problems of visual organization and perception. Some colleges would regard this activity as coordinate with the choral activity which St. John's includes as part of the Music Tutorial.

The revolution in science and technology in the nineteenth century was a principal reason for the decline and fall of the traditional liberal arts curriculum. St. John's maintains that the "reconciliation between the sciences and the rest of our intellectual tradition" is one of the more serious duties of modern education, yet it believes that colleges have thus far failed to provide "the conditions and techniques for the liberalizing and humanizing of science." Its faculty does not claim to have found the perfect solution to what it believes to be one of the most serious problems confronting modern education; but through the Laboratory it has undertaken to provide a continuing experience for four years in the investigation of the ways in which men have defined and explored scientific problems and in the exercise of methods for the testing of scientific hypotheses. In each year students are required to study a selection of scientific papers and to trace "a scientific discipline to its roots in principle, assumption, and observation." The tabular view of the curriculum on pages 234–235 shows the division of scientific subject matters by semesters throughout the four years. In terms of class hours given to laboratory exercises, lectures, discussions, and conferences, the time allotted to the natural sciences, exclusive of mathematics, exceeds the general requirements imposed by any other college in this report. The two semesters of biology are devoted to exercises in anatomy and physiology, invertebrate zoology, histology, embryology, and genetics. The principal activities in the physical sciences are the study of theories of measurement, optics, mechanics, electromagnetism, and an introduction to atomic theory, in addition to one semester devoted exclusively to chemistry. The combined physics and chemistry exercises form about three-fourths of the total science requirement.

To some teachers this program will seem too ambitious for the nonspecialist. If this is a fault, it scarcely seems more serious than the reduction of the nonspecialist's experience in natural science to a single one-year course. What emerges, as one reviews the differences in curricular approaches and the time granted to the general education of students in science, is a conviction that the colleges have scarcely begun to formulate adequate conceptions of the kind of training and knowledge which the liberally educated nonspecialist needs in the modern world.

I shall risk the opinion that teachers of science share a great responsibility for present inadequacies, despite the increasing emphasis upon science in secondary schools, much of which is addressed to preprofessional and vocational interests. As a whole, college teachers of science have been so greatly involved in professional and preprofessional training that they have not given sufficient thought to the needs of the nonspecialist students. The task of meeting the needs of the nonspecialist is one which only the scientists can perform, and there is a possibility that if they fail to perform the task, they may transform science into a new mythology for the layman who will leave its mysteries entirely in the hands of a select priesthood.

Estimates of students' progress at St. John's are based upon a system of examinations, oral and written, and annual essays. The latter culminate in the Senior Thesis. Half-hour oral examinations conducted by the leaders of the Seminars are given at the end of each semester; the examinations are followed by a critical review of each student's work, made by the tutors to the Seminar leader in the presence of the student. Each year the student must write an essay upon a topic suggested by works read in the Seminar, tutorials, laboratory, and the formal lectures. At the end of the second year a series of comprehensive examinations called the "preliminary enabling examination" constitutes a part of the diagnostic measure of the student's competence to continue his studies for the bachelor's degree. In addition to the oral examination of essays, written examinations of three hours each are given in language, mathematics, the theoretical elements of the Laboratory, and the operational or technical procedures of the Laboratory. At the beginning of the senior year an enabling oral examination is given, based upon a selection of readings from the Seminar list and upon one work chosen by the student which has particular significance for his Senior Thesis. The subject of the thesis must be approved by the faculty, and when the thesis is completed it must be defended by the student in a public oral examination. Before graduation each student must demonstrate by examination a reading knowledge of two of the foreign languages studied during the four years.

Members of the faculty are not differentiated either by rank or by fields of special competence. This does not mean that an appointment to the faculty is not determined by qualifications in special fields; but consistent with its views about the liberal education of students, the college holds to the ideal of appointing what it considers liberally educated men to its faculty, which implies a broader range of intellectual interests than is commonly expected of the faculty members of most colleges. The ideal that each tutor should be competent to instruct in any tutorial as well as in the Seminar is not always realized, but a part of the experience of each tutor is the extension of his qualifications through participation in various parts of the curriculum even though at first his participation may be as an observer or an apprentice teacher.

In our age of specialization this aspect of St. John's educational philosophy and administrative policy has excited much adverse criticism. Specialists are often timid about invading fields outside their own, even those which have close disciplinary ties. Some are affronted when novices dare to invade their domain. These attitudes have affected adversely many so-called "interdisciplinary courses." They are, however, yielding with the increase of interdepartmental degree programs, divisional committee programs, and the successes of the more carefully planned general courses. The faculty of St. John's would say that they had no general or interdisciplinary course in their curriculum, although many colleges could consider the Seminar truly interdisciplinary. And indeed it is little different from many general humanities courses or senior seminars either in materials or in instructional methods. The great difference is that it continues for four years instead of one or two and that it is the focal point of the whole curriculum. Aside from the Seminar, however, no course remotely resembles the usual general courses, except possibly the Laboratory. St. John's is skeptical of modern tendencies to integrate subject matters which have no natural affinities. On the whole the official view of integration is that it is best achieved in a community where the students are engaged in a common intellectual enterprise and have therefore a common matter of discourse, and in an environment in which teachers and students alike are concerned with the same subject matters and problems. Hence, one can see the importance of extending the tutors' familiarity with the entire curriculum.

SAINT XAVIER COLLEGE

In 1847 the Saint Francis Xavier Academy for Females was chartered by the Illinois State Legislature; it was the first institution for the higher education of women in the city of Chicago. Now officially titled the Saint Xavier College, the institution has enjoyed a continuous history since its founding under the direction of the Sisters of Mercy. From its beginning it included elementary, secondary, and collegiate instruction; and in recent years the attention which it has given to an improved and continuing liberal arts curriculum embracing these three divisions of education has attracted widespread interest. In 1958–1959 it enrolled about seven hundred young women in its collegiate division.

In 1935 Saint Xavier introduced extensive curricular reforms, stimulated by the contemporary concern for an improved general education. Modifications of that curriculum have since been frequent, and the most recent have come about through the labors of a faculty committee on self-study in 1952 supported by aid from the Fund for the Advancement of Education.[36] A principal consideration in the study was the examination of the continuing nature of the process of liberal education from the elementary school through college. In the application of the principles evoked in the study, the college has worked closely with the elementary and secondary schools conducted under the administration of the Sisters of Mercy in the city of Chicago.

The college accepted the premise that liberal education is the shared responsibility of the whole educational system and took it to be a fact that the various branches of the system have operated in modern times altogether too much in isolation from one another to the detriment of the students, the schools, and the colleges. Within the context of what it defines as the educational commitments of an institution supported by the Catholic church, Saint Xavier has sought to achieve an effective program of liberal education from the lower

---

[36] The title of the published report of the committee is *The Saint Xavier College Self Study: The Liberal Education of the Christian Person.* I have referred to it in the text as the self-study report.

244

school through the college. The policy, however, is not so rigidly formulated as to restrict admission to the college to students who have passed through its own elementary and secondary branches or other schools conducted by the Sisters of Mercy. The college accepts transfer students from other colleges as well as high school graduates from other schools, private and public. It does, however, use its own elementary and high schools as laboratories for experimental work in curricular organization and as a training center for teachers.

Formal requirements for admission to the college do not differ greatly from those of many colleges. Normally applicants will be graduates of accredited high schools who are expected to have completed 15 units of high school studies. Students are advised to include English (3 units), a foreign language (2 units), mathematics (2 units), natural and social science (4 units). Other credits may be distributed among any courses acceptable for high school graduation. The distributional pattern is strictly a recommendation however; the Announcements state that "the quality of a prospective student's work and ... her general promise and seriousness of purpose" are of greater importance than an audit of specifically required subject matters. All applicants are required to take the College Entrance Examination Board aptitude tests. The formal requirements for admission are necessarily related to and, in a sense, subordinate to the student's desire to commit herself to Saint Xavier's conception of liberal education.

For this reason the official Announcements are explicit in setting forth the theoretical foundations of the administrative and curricular structure of the college. The structure is divisional and the curriculum is organized under the following four divisions:

> The divisions of the liberal arts and the humanities
> The division of natural science
> The division of the social sciences
> The division of philosophy and theology

The *rationale* of this division has been described as follows: The division of the liberal arts and humanities is concerned with those disciplines whose chief objective is to provide the *instruments* of research and expression, rather than the substance of truth itself. These include logic and the linguistic arts, together with the fine arts which use nonverbal media of expression, and mathematics. The work of this division is concerned both with these arts themselves and with the great works which are examples of their employment.

The other divisions have as their primary consideration the substance of truth rather than the forms of its expression, but they necessarily presuppose that both students and faculty make use of the liberal arts. The division of natural science is concerned with the world of nature and man as these are the products of natural forces. The division of the social sciences deals with human life and institutions as they are the product of man's own historical choice and effort. The division of philosophy and theology contrasts with all the other divisions in that it considers the topics treated by all of them but "in relation to the ultimate problems accessible to reason and to faith."

The study of the subject matters appropriate to each of these divisions is asserted to be the means of acquiring the intellectual habits of *wisdom, understanding, science, practical wisdom,* and *art,* and the "configuration" of these habits is the ideal of liberal education. All divisions of knowledge are comprehended in all levels of education, and all stages of education contribute to the formation of the several habits. The problems of education therefore are concerned with determining "modes of attack, emphasis, detail, kinds of intelligibility, and order and balance among the parts" at each level of education. By seeing the process of a whole and by taking account of differences in modes of attack or kinds of intelligibility sought, the school and the college can guide the student progressively through the common content of a liberal education. The principles by which the proper attack, emphasis, detail, etc., can best be attained lie in conceptions of the *liberal arts, general education, wisdom,* and *advanced and specialized studies.* "A balanced organization of the materials of education in accordance with these principles comprises the substance of a liberal education."

Since these terms are employed with connotations which are in some respects unconventional in educational usage, further explication is needed. Obviously general education is distinguished from liberal education in a part-whole relationship, which is a commonplace. General education, however, is used in a more restricted sense than is usual. The distinction between the liberal arts and general education is historically a departure from common usage which has regarded the liberal arts as an essential element of general education. The distinction is primarily concerned with functions. The liberal arts—language, mathematics, and the fine arts—are the *instruments* of learning. General education supplies the *content* of learning in a comprehensive view of the achievements of the arts and sciences. The liberal arts are defined as the sciences which establish "the intellectual emancipation of their possessor" and which provide "the intellectual charter for independent study in any field." General education is "the attainment of a level of competence in the major fields of knowledge (rather than the specific sciences) below the level of a scientific habit of mind." Through general education one acquires "a background of experience and information that is needed for higher and more scientific study in a given discipline." It offers "a sketch of the fields of knowledge." This conception stresses the preparatory values of general education and excludes the possibility of any kind of study-in-depth.

This, however, is only one aspect of the conception. The college also emphasizes the importance of the capacity for judgment as a mark of the generally educated person. Judgment in matters of practical action and of the quality of products of the arts falls within the sphere of general education; and the student who has a good general education should be able to read and judge a poem and "to judge the internal parts of an exposition or an argument and determine which parts are satisfactory and which are not and whether the whole hangs together properly." Some critics will say that such competence demands more than a sketch of knowledge. Furthermore they will say that it cannot be achieved apart from the exercise of the liberal arts and a kind of philosophic wisdom. Saint Xavier acknowledges that there is considerable overlap in the areas of the liberal arts and general education. At the same time the classification of subject matters which form the common requirements of Saint Xavier's program seems to confuse the problem since the fine arts and humane letters are classified with the liberal arts, and the natural sciences and social sciences form the area of general education.

The separate and specific function of the principle of *wisdom* in the ordering of the curriculum points to the Catholic philosophy of the college. It points to the sciences of philosophy (metaphysics) and theology, which are treated as the integrating sciences whose function is to establish the relationships and principles of order among all parts of knowledge. As such the study of these sciences is continuous throughout the program.

The liberal arts, general education, and philosophy and theology define the areas of knowledge which should be shared by all liberally educated persons. None of these, however, supplies the kind of knowledge which is productive of *habits* of precision. These come only from specialized study. The case for specialized study in the Saint Xavier program does not rest upon utilitarian grounds, i.e., the need to earn a living. It derives from "the uniqueness of each student, her God-given leanings in some direction" which must be developed for the realization of self and for the acquiring of a sensitivity to "profundity in intellectual matters." In the chronological order of learning, advanced and specialized studies must rest upon the foundation of the liberal arts and general education; but they are not the logical end of education. The college recognizes that specialization tends to fragmentize knowledge and holds that liberal education is achieved only when the student understands the principles which give order and unity to all learning, hence the significance of philosophy and theology as the crowning sciences in liberal education.

Within this conceptual framework Saint Xavier has organized its curriculum. The program is divided into two parts: the College Requirements which are uniformly required of all students and Advanced and Specialized Studies. The College Requirements are subdivided into three areas: (1) liberal arts and humane letters, (2) general education, and (3) philosophy and theology. The sum of the College Requirements is quantitatively a little more than one-half of the full requirements for a bachelor's degree. The unusual classification of subject matters in the College Requirements is shown in the following outline:

Liberal Arts
  Arts
    Critical Analysis   8 semester hours
    Speech   2 semester hours
    Second Language (foreign language)   6 semester hours
    Humanities (music, art)   4 semester hours
    Mathematics   6 semester hours
  Humane Letters
    Interpretation of Poetic Texts   4 semester hours
    Interpretation of Rhetorical and Historical Texts   2 semester hours
    Interpretation of Philosophic and Scientific Texts   2 semester hours

                                       34 semester hours

General Education
Introduction to Natural Science

Fundamental Science of Nature	3 semester hours
Principles and Methods in Physical Science	3 semester hours
Principles and Methods in Biology	3 semester hours
Principles and Methods in Psychology	3 semester hours
Introduction to the Sciences of Human Action	6 semester hours
Choice of Political, Economic, or Sociological Theory, or Historiography	3 semester hours
	21 semester hours

Philosophy and Theology
Metaphysics

Ontology and the Theory of Cognition	3 semester hours
Classification and Hierarchy of the Arts and Sciences	3 semester hours
Senior Seminar (noncredit) A weekly colloquium based on the program of advanced and specialized studies considered from a philosophical standpoint	
Theology	18 semester hours
	24 semester hours

The most striking departure from conventional classification in this curriculum is the limitation of general education to the natural and social sciences. The humanities are grouped with the liberal arts, and even here the distinction drawn between literature and the fine arts is unconventional. The classification of mathematics with the liberal arts is not surprising in view of the general philosophy of the sciences which underlies the curriculum, but I know of no other college in which a student who majors in mathematics would do so in the division of liberal arts and humanities.

Critical Analysis is a one-year course in grammar, logic, and rhetoric, with reference to the English language, and is essentially a course in the training of writing skills. Students may elect one of three mathematics courses in satisfaction of the mathematics requirement. One is planned for prospective elementary school teachers, one for students with no special or professional interest in mathematics, and one for those who may wish to specialize in the field or have preprofessional needs. The three courses in interpretation of literary texts are similar to some general courses in humanities offered in other colleges which concentrate on the study of the great books of the Western tradition.

The general courses in natural science and the social sciences observe patterns that stress the philosophical foundations of the sciences. It will be noticed that students are given options in meeting the requirement for a third semester of social science. The only course that is unusual in this list is historiography. The natural science courses have been influenced by one of the general courses at Harvard, and by the general science programs developed at St. John's and the University of Chicago.

The courses in philosophy and theology extend throughout the four years, as they do in both programs at Notre Dame. There is considerable difference, however, in their content. The studies in theology are based on the *Summa Theologica*. Two semesters of metaphysics are required. These are devoted to the study of several selected problems in which the viewpoints and methods of the major schools of contemporary philosophy are compared. The Senior Seminar is under the direction of the division of philosophy and theology and its purpose is to consider the subject matter of each student's special field of study in relation to her philosophic and theological studies.

Once again we encounter a general program that does not include history as a discrete subject matter among its requirements. This may seem surprising in view of the great importance which Saint Xavier attaches to an awareness of our cultural heritage as a part of a liberal education. The college holds, however, that the true significance of cultural heritage is something that cannot be achieved through a history course or any other single kind of course. On the other hand it is not a mere aggregation of materials. It is "an ordered whole but one whose order is implicit and undifferentiated." As such it can only be achieved through the proper ordering of materials at all levels of education which must be unified ultimately in a philosophy of history and nature.[37] The college is, however, presently considering a revision of its social requirements which would include required work in history.

[37] *Ibid.*, chap. III, pp. 47–54.

SAN FRANCISCO STATE COLLEGE

The California State College System is an outgrowth of the state's system of teachers' colleges. At present there are fifteen state colleges located in strategic population centers of the state. San Francisco State College traces its origins to San Francisco State Normal School, founded in 1899. Like most institutions of its kind which were established in the latter years of the nineteenth century its initial purpose was the training of elementary school teachers. It did not grant the Bachelor of Arts degree until 1923, and its expanded teacher-training curriculums were not uniformly extended to four-year progams until 1930, although the name of the institution was changed to San Francisco State Teachers' College in 1921. Its present name, San Francisco State College, was adopted by legislative action in 1935; and the change reflects a recent trend in the character of teachers' colleges in almost every state in the nation. As the curricular offerings of the teachers' colleges have expanded they have inevitably acquired most of the characteristics of liberal arts colleges. With steadily increasing enrollments which included large numbers of students who were not interested in teaching as a profession, the colleges have ceased to be exclusively teacher-training centers. The prospective teachers are often a minority of the student body. San Francisco State College is a notable example of the extreme character of the evolution which has taken place in the teachers' colleges during the last twenty years.

In 1958–1959 San Francisco State College enrolled nearly 12,000 students. Of these 6,652 were full-time undergraduate students, 4,226 were part-time undergraduates, and 1,032 were graduate students. The college now offers the master's degree in most of its divisional fields, though not in all subject matters. The majority of graduate students in recent years have been registered in the division of education, but this is not true of its undergraduate enrollment. For all practical purposes San Francisco State College is a liberal arts college supported by the state of California and operated under the regulation of a State Board of Trustees. This fact in no way diminishes the importance of the college as a training center for teachers, nor does

251

this fact signify that the origins of the college do not continue to affect its traditions in some degree. It is, however, as a liberal arts college that San Francisco State has a place in this study. It is essentially a nonresidential college. The great majority of its students live in San Francisco and the Bay area. Admission policies are standard for all state colleges in California. High school graduates are admitted who rank in the top third of their class.

The faculty and the curriculum of San Francisco State are organized by divisions subdivided by departments. The divisions are:

> Division of air science
> Division of business
> Division of creative arts
> Division of education
> Division of health, physical education, and recreation
> Division of humanities
> Division of language arts
> Division of natural science
> Division of social science
> Institute of rehabilitation counselor training

The variety of divisions indicates how greatly vocational interests other than education have attended the growth of the institution. The divisions are not the equivalents of autonomous schools such at those which exist in most state universities, but each division defines an area of related subject matters in which students may concentrate their studies for a degree. Each division is under the direction of a chairman, and in the larger divisions he is assisted by a vice chairman. Students are regularly classified with respect to their academic status in terms of semester units earned. Students in the first and second years, who have completed less than 60 units, are in the Lower Division and those who have completed between 60 and 124 are in the Upper Division. The primary work of the first two years is the completion of the program of general education, although students may begin work in their special fields in their first year, and some of the general requirements are normally taken in the third year. The requirements for the bachelor's degree are distributed between general education requirements, concentration, and free electives. Interdivisional degree programs are permitted where the student in consultation with divisional chairmen can plan a satisfactory program.

The state board of education requires that all baccalaureate degree programs shall include 45 semester units or hours which shall be designated as "general education." General education requirements amount to one-third of the total required of a baccalaureate degree. The regulation further prescribes a distribution of these units as follows:

Social sciences	9 units
Natural sciences	9 units
Literature, philosophy, or the arts	6 units
Health and physical education	2 units
Written and oral expression	3 units
Psychology	2 units
Balance to be distributed among any of the above areas	14 units

The planning of courses to satisfy these requirements is left to the experience and wisdom of the several colleges. Since this is the only instance in this study in which a state regulatory body has intervened to impose, not only a gross requirement, but a standard formula for the distribution of courses, the fact is of more than passing interest. It invites speculation as to whether such bodies in other states may adopt similar procedures. In addition to the requirements imposed by the state board, the state Legislature has enacted a law which requires that, to qualify for graduation, each student in a state college must demonstrate "competence in the Constitution of the United States and in American history, including the study of American institutions and ideals, and the principles of state and local government established under the State." [38]

The beginnings of the present program of general education at San Francisco date from 1947. Its planning was a cooperative enterprise which engaged the entire faculty. By 1949 the curriculum had achieved the major elements of its present outline. It was adopted by the faculty, including the distribution of subject matters, before the state board set the uniform standards previously described. A series of annual faculty conferences reviewed the progress of the plan and introduced recommendations for minor revisions. The 14 undistributed units in the state board's plan were absorbed in the distributional scheme adopted by the faculty; in 1959 the general program was composed of the following courses:

[38] San Francisco State College, *Bulletin of Information*, 1958–1959, p. 69.

Psychology (personal, social, and occupational development)	6 units
Basic language skills	6 units
Social science (socio-civic competence)	12 units
Natural science (including health education)	10 units
Humanities (literature, philosophy, world cultures)	6 units
Creative arts	3 units
Physical education	2 units

With the exception of physical education, where a few optional courses are offered, each of these requirements is satisfied by completing a course or courses uniformly required of all students entering as freshmen.

The objectives which guided the faculty in the development of the general education program were formulated during a three-year planning period. They help to explain a curriculum which contains characteristics of an instrumentalist philosophy of education combined with a conception based on formal disciplines. In the 1958–1959 catalogue the objectives were described in some detail under five topics. These can be summarized briefly: (1) recognition and satisfaction of basic individual needs of the student as a person; (2) development of the student as a citizen aware of his responsibilities to his college, his community, his state, his nation, and the world; (3) development of the student's ability to adjust to the problems of home and family life; (4) recognition of the need to offer the student guidance in the choice of a vocation through the exploration of many fields of learning; (5) recognition of the student's need to equip himself with the basic skills required for success in any field of human endeavor.

The formulation of objectives was based upon a careful gathering of statistical data and the long experience of the kinds of students who attended the college. The student body has been described as an urban, commuting group, a working group who came from families in the lower income brackets, and in general a group of average ability.[39] Most of the students were obliged to work full or part time

[39] This account is taken from a survey of student needs made in 1946–1947 which is included in the handbook for the Eighth Annual Faculty Conference, December, 1953. The conference was devoted entirely to the general education program. The handbook contains a detailed account of the objectives of the entire program as well as outlines of the several courses and their particular objectives.

to remain in college. On the whole the students' views about their vocational goals were ill formed or unrealistic, but the majority were primarily concerned with their career needs. These factors and others derived from evidence of problems of personal adjustment have influenced curricular planning in no small degree.

The combination of formal and instrumentalist approaches is evident in the organization of certain courses. The two-semester course in psychology (Personal, Social, and Occupational Development) as given in 1953 began by placing psychology in the context of science and the scientific method; then it proceeded to a study of the psychological development of the individual, dealing with the nature of heredity and environment, growth and development, motivation, emotions, perception, and the differentiation of individual development with a study of personality theories. This was followed by a study of intelligence and the learning process. As the first semester drew to a close the work concluded with problems of personal adjustment; and the second semester dealt with the large problems of vocational planning and social relationships in the family, the community, and other group patterns.

One of the three required semesters in the natural sciences, as given in 1958–1959, was a course in mathematics subtitled "Mathematics in Human Affairs." A brief introduction dealt with mathematics as a means of communication, as an instrument in problem solving, and as a way of thinking. The course then turned to the examination of statistical methods, with reference to the gathering and presentation of data and their analysis and interpretation. This was followed by a study of number systems, their origins, and uses. The concluding topics of the course concerned problems of budgeting, consumer finance, and credit, and problems in mathematical probability.[40]

The two-semester course in humanities in broad outline resembles many courses which study the major literary, philosophical, and religious works of the Western tradition from antiquity to the present day. Prior to 1959 the subtitle of the course, A Study of Life Values, hinted at instrumentalist objectives, which were confirmed by the statement of course objectives. These made clear that the course was

---

[40] This description is taken from a 1953 course outline. It is hardly necessary to comment on the differences between this approach to mathematics and that at St. John's. The extremes, however, indicate the extent of conceptual differences concerning the place of mathematics in a general education.

not considered merely a history of culture or a study of the formal characteristics of literary works. The primary importance which attaches to the masterpieces of world literature lies in the record which they afford of "significant statements and views about major human values." Through the study of the best of human achievement in this field the student, it was hoped, would secure a "better understanding of one's own personal value pattern and that of one's culture, in comparison with those of other individuals and other cultures." In 1959 the instrumentalist approach was eliminated. The course was renamed "An Introduction to the Humanities," and references to "life values" were removed from the description of the course.

The division of creative arts includes the visual arts, drama, music, radio and television, and the industrial arts. The single course which was originally to fulfill the arts requirement of the general education curriculum is still given and is entitled "Creative Arts Exploration." It is described as a practical application of the basic elements of art, music, dance, and drama. It was agreed at a fairly early period in the history of the program that this one course was not adequate to the practical needs of students; consequently, introductory courses in particular arts were admitted as options for the satisfaction of this requirement. In 1959, however, the options were eliminated, and one course was uniformly required.

The four 1-semester courses which constitute the general social science requirement are (1) Culture and Society, (2) The Development of American Institutions and Ideals, (3) Contemporary Economic Society, and (4) International and Intercultural Relations. These courses seem, on the basis of outlines, most nearly to resemble general courses in other colleges in this field.

The administration and faculty have taken the commitment to the program very seriously. Aware of the fact that many students do not understand the reasons for so extensive a group of required courses, the administration has prepared a pamphlet for students which anticipates and answers most of the questions that they might be expected to raise about the nature and purposes of general education. In addition to the annual conferences of the faculty, divisional conferences have been held which have studied the progress of the general course or courses in the respective areas. The college has created the office of curriculum coordinator. The job of the coordinator is to serve as a liaison agent between the several divisions of the program, and his office is a kind of clearinghouse in which problems that are common to all staffs are reviewed. The problem of maintaining staff stability has been greater in some courses than in others. The coordinator's office brings this to common attention and invites discussion of the serious consequences that result from frequent changes in teaching personnel. Instructors have always been responsible for the final grades of their own students. This has raised questions about different criteria for determining grades and considerations of acceptable standards of measurement. The office has been a means of assessing faculty opinion about testing devices, of students' evaluation of courses, and of methods of orienting new staff members to the instructional problems of the courses.

The college does not assume that the program of courses can complete the general education of the students. The coordinator of curriculum has stated the basic problem of evaluation very simply and very practically: "How can we give more of a general education than we are now doing in the maximum number of course hours our institution can allot for this purpose?"

STANFORD UNIVERSITY

Leland Stanford Junior University admitted its first classes in 1891 after six years devoted to planning and building. It is one of the few privately endowed universities which did not evolve from an established liberal arts college.[41] The influence of university ideals and functions have always affected strongly the character of the undergraduate division of universities which evolved in this way. The force of these ideals is unmistakably clear in the educational principles of Stanford's first President, David Starr Jordan, who, before coming to Stanford, had attacked the standard college curriculum of the late nineteenth century as a "patchwork" devoid of thoroughness. He rejected the conception that the principal function of the college is to give "a broad and well rounded culture," since it usually leads to "a slight knowledge of many things accompanied by thoroughness in nothing." He defended the idea of concentration against the charge of "undue specialization" and his defense of the elective principle was scarcely less eloquent than President Eliot's.[42] The influence of the university ideal is also evident in the fact that undergraduate studies have never been administered through a separate and legally constituted unit known as the "college." Instead all programs of study are defined and all degrees are awarded by the several schools which are the basic administrative divisions of the university.

In the first printed announcement of the university the elective principle which was to be the guiding spirit of curricular planning for a quarter of a century was set forth. There would be no requirement of "certain studies deemed essential to all cultures," and there would be "no general curriculum of any sort." The unit of administration of the curricular organization was the professorship, and

---

[41] Stanford, like the University of Chicago which opened just one year later, embraced from the beginning the functions of a university within the precise meaning of the term.

[42] David Starr Jordan, *The Care and Culture of Men*, Whitaker and Ray, San Francisco, 1896. See particularly "The Evaluation of the College Curriculum," pp. 24–56.

each professor was expected to arrange studies in his department as seemed to him best. The courses so arranged would constitute a major, and each freshman student upon matriculation would choose freely his major. For four years thereafter the professor would be his adviser and the final judge of his fitness for graduation. Courses in departments other than the students' majors were freely elective and would count toward a minor. The faculty even exceeded President Jordan's initial idea of the scope of freedom. President Jordan had proposed that students who lacked training in algebra, geometry, trigonometry, English, and foreign language at matriculation be required to complete courses in these fields at some time before graduation. The faculty eliminated all requirements except English.[43]

The extreme freedom of the "major system" was severely criticized by the trustees in 1905. The faculty defended the system, however; and there was no significant change of policy until 1920 when the faculty approved recommendations for the first formidable revisions. The first two years of the undergraduate program were henceforth designated the "Lower Division"; in each of three areas or groups of studies students were required to complete 9 credits in each of the two years. An optional-course plan was adopted, but certain specific course requirements were imposed which limited the freedom of choice in some degree. The three areas were (1) language, literature, and art, (2) natural sciences and mathematics, (3) social sciences, including history, political science, economics, philosophy, and education. Unit requirements in each area might be reduced upon evidence of comparable study in high school; however, the specific requirements often operated to limit the scope of a student's experience in an area. For example, a student who was deficient in writing skills and who had no high school work in a foreign language might be unable to take any courses in literature or philosophy unless his program of studies allowed him some elective time. The reforms of 1920 did not alter the admission policies which imposed no specific distribution of high school studies.

Some of the specific course requirements adopted in the reforms of 1920 might be waived by comparable work in high school. Twenty-

[43] Orrin Leslie Elliott, *Stanford University: the First Twenty-Five Years,* Stanford University Press, Stanford, Calif., 1937, pp. 509–517. See also J. Pearce Mitchell, *Stanford University: 1916–1941,* Stanford University Press, Stanford, Calif., 1958, for an account of major reforms introduced in 1920.

two units of work in one foreign language were required for graduation, but three years of high school study in one language might anticipate this requirement. Nine units each in biology and the physical sciences were required, but one or the other of these might be met by one high school unit in either science area. There appears to have been no mathematics requirement imposed in 1920. At a later date, however, students were granted an option of completing a foreign language requirement or a mathematics requirement for graduation, but no prerequisite of high school preparation in either field was imposed as a uniform requirement for admission. Thus students might enter with no language study and, by electing mathematics rather than foreign language, complete their degree requirements with no experience in a foreign language. In principle, if not in practice, the same conditions applied to mathematics.

One of the specific requirements imposed on all students was a course entitled "Problems of Citizenship" which some years later was replaced by History of Western Civilization. This and English composition were the only uniformly required courses in the curriculum. In the natural sciences general courses in both the biological and physical sciences were developed, primarily in the interest of non-science majors, although they were included among the options in this area.[44]

The general principles which had determined the curriculum adopted in 1920 survived for thirty-five years. With the opening of the autumn quarter in 1956, a new program of undergraduate studies was inaugurated which was based upon principles new in the traditions of Stanford.[45] The adoption of the program followed two years of exacting study by two faculty committees appointed by the president of the university. The record of their work and their recommendations to the faculty have been published in a volume which offers many useful insights into administrative procedures in effecting curricular reforms.[46]

[44] The curricular reforms at Stanford introduced in 1920 are additional evidence of the immense significance of the decade which was then beginning in the reconstruction of concepts of undergraduate education in America.

[45] The new program was introduced just as work began on this study. There has been no time as yet for a fair appraisal by the faculty of the results of the changes which are described here.

[46] Robert Hoopes and Hubert Marshall, *The Undergraduate in the University: a Report to the Faculty by the Executive Committee of the Stanford Study of*

The major changes in the guiding principles of the new program can be summarized briefly:

1. The establishment of specific entrance requirements for all students in English composition and literature (three years); in mathematics (two years of algebra or one of algebra and one of geometry); two years of one foreign language.

2. The abolition of the Lower Division and the substitution of the principle that all general education requirements shall be distributed throughout the four undergraduate years.

3. Redefinition of principles governing specific course requirements and area or group distributional requirements. The principal change here is a provision that area or group distributional requirements shall apply to the two areas in which the student is not majoring.

4. Reorganization of courses offered for satisfaction of area or group requirements to achieve a "terminal" character to the courses without impairing their usefulness as a foundation for continued study.

5. The adoption of additional general requirements for all candidates for the A.B. degree.

6. The adoption of advanced placement tests for the purpose of measuring achievement in certain subjects (notably English, foreign language, and mathematics) at levels normally taught in college but realized by some students while still in high school.

The entrance requirements listed in item 1 above are administered with sufficient flexibility to impose no hardship on exceptional cases where superior students have been unable to fulfill the requirements in high school, but in general the requirements eliminate the possibility that a student may complete his college education with no experience of a foreign language and with merely an elementary knowledge of mathematics. The general requirements of the new program are shown in the following outline.

    I. Requirements for all students:
        English (composition and literature) (one year)
            This requirement increases by one quarter the old requirement and gives greater emphasis to literature than formerly. A one-quarter remedial course which formerly granted credit is retained for those deficient on placement tests but gives no credit. The first quarter of the required course may be satisfied by advanced placement test.

Undergraduate Education, 1954–56, Stanford University Press, Stanford, Calif., 1957.

History of Western civilization (one year)

Foreign language *or* mathematics

The old option is retained, but the entrance requirements make improbable the chance that students will not have some experience in both areas. Students who elect language will either begin at a level beyond the minimum required for entrance or begin a new language. Credit by advanced placement tests for achievement at the level of advanced college courses is granted in both language and mathematics.

II. Area requirements for all students:

All students must satisfy requirements in the two areas in which they do not major.

Humanities (8 units distributed over two groups)

   1. Art, architecture, music, speech, and drama

   2. Philosophy and religion

   3. Literature

Social sciences (2 of the six 5-unit courses listed)

   1. Anthropology   4. Political science

   2. Economics   5. Psychology

   3. Geography   6. Sociology

Natural sciences

  (*a*) For those who have had biology in high school but no physical science, one of the following sequences:

    1. A general physical science course (9 units)

    2. Either of two courses in physics (13 or 15 units)

    3. Introductory chemistry (13 units)

    4. Mineral sciences (10 units)

  (*b*) For those who have had no biology in high school:

    1. General biology (3 quarters) or

    2. Botany and invertebrate zoology (2 quarters)

  (*c*) For those who have had both biology and physical science in high school, any of the above sequences

III. Requirements for all candidates for the Bachelor of Arts degree:

   1. Senior Colloquium

    Two colloquiums (each one quarter and each granted 2 units)

   2. Additional natural science to bring total science courses to 17 units (9 units in area requirements plus 8) to be chosen from:

    (*a*) All science courses listed in the area requirements

    (*b*) Mathematics courses listed in I above

(*c*) Logic
3. A choice of one of the following:
  (*a*) Elementary Mathematical Analysis or an advanced course
  (*b*) Logic
  (*c*) Statistics (a choice of two courses, one for psychology majors)
  (*d*) Four *additional* units of foreign language

Aside from the additional requirements for the A.B. degree, this outline does not reveal the most important elements of change. By reducing area requirements to the two outside the area of concentration, the change implies that in principle there is no distinction to be drawn *within* the area of concentration between the general and specialized aspects of one's education. A more practical consequence is that this provision, when joined with the entrance requirements, does make sure that students will have opportunity for more work in areas other than their special fields. This is important for science majors. Most school requirements for degrees in science demand a reading knowledge of French or German. Science students without adequate prior training in English composition and foreign language previously found almost no opportunity for other work in humanities. Candidates for the A.B. degree are assured additional work in mathematics or natural science beyond the minimal requirements for all students. Altogether, the changes make possible a better balance in the distribution of studies.

In the recommendation of the executive committee covering the two 5-unit requirements in the social sciences (see II, Area requirements, above) the departments were urged to submit courses of a *terminal* character which would serve the needs of educated citizens. The Report pointed to the fact that formerly some students had been able to meet the distributional requirements in the social sciences only by taking two 5-unit courses in a single department and that, for students who elected economics or political science, this was mandatory. Students majoring in engineering or industrial management were usually required or urged to take economics, with the result that they had no experience with other social science areas. Furthermore several of the courses offered were introductory in the sense that they were distinctly preparatory to further study in the department and therefore derived their primary meaning as a consequence of courses which followed. In proposing the creation of *terminal* courses, which the Report said would be "a contribution to general education," the committee said:

> An introductory course in social science ... ought to be an introduction to the subject as a whole, and not solely or primarily a technical foundation for advanced study. An introductory course in political science, for example, should seek to equip all students enrolled, whether or not they proceed to advanced courses in the department, to think more intelligently and independently about the public issues and problems they will be facing as citizens.[47]

A comparison of course offerings as described in the last official Announcement of Courses prior to the inauguration of the new program and those in the Announcements for 1958–1959 shows that considerable effort to achieve the recommendations has been made. In political science, for example, a new course, Major Issues in American Public Policy, has been organized to serve the more comprehensive and terminal functions. In passing, we might observe that, though the course is listed as an offering of the political science department, the description of the course suggests that it is similar in scope and content to some so-called "general" or "interdisciplinary" courses offered in other colleges which are simply listed as "social science." It is well to be mindful of the fact that course titles often do not give adequate signs of either their actual comprehensiveness or their terminal characteristics.

In the humanities area some progress had been made prior to the changes of 1956 in the development of Lower Division courses of general or comprehensive and terminal kinds. This was especially true of courses offered by the music department and the committee for special programs in the humanities. In the latter, which has developed courses of study leading to the bachelor's degree, several lower divisional courses had been developed, among them a three-quarter sequence, World Literature and the History of Ideas, and a one-quarter course, Literature of the Enlightenment and the Modern World. These have been retained, and a new three-quarter sequence, World Personalities, has been added. Similar developments have taken place in speech and drama. There appears to have been less effort to

[47] Hoopes and Marshall, *op. cit.*, p. 99.

develop comprehensive courses of special interest to the nonmajor in art than in other departments of the humanities area.

Something should be said of the course in the History of Western Civilization. Since this course, retained in the new program, has been an all-university requiremeñt for twenty-five years, and is even now the one course which nearly all students take, its popularity ought to be noted. A poll of student opinion taken during the planning period for the new curriculum revealed that it was almost universally held in high regard, since "it provided a common intellectual challenge and interest." The executive committee Report observes that "it spills over into innumerable discussions outside the classroom." The observation touches upon a value often overlooked in certain kinds of courses which are common requirements for large numbers of students. When the courses are well conceived and well taught, they often generate an intellectual excitement that spreads through the greater part of a student body. One of the frequent arguments against the uniform requirement of courses such as the History of Western Civilization and several others is that they produce a rigidity or conformity in thought. The reverse is more likely to be true when instruction is divided among a number of capable instructors who approach a common problem in different ways and, as a result, evoke a variety of answers to problems of value. Students accept the challenge, and there is ample evidence from the experience of a fair number of colleges that intellectual excitement does indeed spill over into discussions outside the classroom.

The Senior Colloquia at Stanford have been conducted somewhat differently from the senior colloquiums and symposiums of other colleges. Instead of one colloquium, usually extending throughout one year, Stanford offers an extensive variety, each of a single quarter's duration. The original intention was to offer as many as a hundred courses. In 1957–1958 thirty-three were offered. In the first few years the program was elective for seniors, but beginning with 1959–1960 all seniors who were candidates for the A.B. degree, except those who were in the first year of the Law or Medical Schools or were candidates for interdepartmental honors, were required to elect two colloquiums. The increase in the number of students is likely to enlarge the number of offerings. The intention from the beginning has been that colloquiums should be offered by members of all departments and that students should choose colloquiums outside their departments of concentration. Each colloquium is limited to fifteen students, and they are conducted as seminars. In 1957–1958 the list offered included the following themes, which afford a fair sampling of the range of subjects:

> Discovery, Invention, and Creation (electrical engineering)
> Critique of Marxist Classics (political science)
> Plato's View of the Ideal Society (philosophy)
> Science, Values, and Intellectualism (geochemistry)
> Crime, Guilt, Responsibility: The Orestes Myth from Aeschylus to Sartre (classics)
> Nationalism and Internationalism (Hoover Institute)
> The Existentialism of Alfred Camus (German-Romanic languages)

The department name in parentheses indicates the locus of the instructor of each colloquium.

The Report of the executive committee examines at some length the considerations which led to the inclusion of the Senior Colloquia as a requirement.[48] One was a desire to counteract the heavy emphasis upon the lecture system in the upper years. Another was the importance of bringing the results of four years of academic studies to bear upon problems of contemporary significance that demanded the exploration of knowledge outside a field of concentration. The Report says:

> Participation in small group discussions and the preparation of essays dealing with the significant problems under consideration are among the most important ways of providing intellectual stimulation. By putting these colloquia in the senior year, the student is not only encouraged to think of his general education as a continuing part in his university experience, but he is given the opportunity to bring to bear on contemporary problems the full fruit of that experience.

One additional all-university requirement must be included to complete the record—one which is interesting because it is not customarily included in the general education requirements of college programs. This is participation "in an organized activity to the total value of six non-credit units, no more than two such units to be allowed in any one quarter." In addition to organized physical activ-

[48] *Ibid.*, pp. 54–57 and 108–110.

ities, students may include chorus, choir, orchestra, band, dramatic performances, and "such other organized group activities as the Committee on General Studies may approve." Physical education is included in the general education requirements of many colleges but it is exceptional to find other so-called "extracurricular activities" so regarded.

It was evident to the various committees that collaborated in the preparations of recommendations for the new program of undergraduate education that the administration of the program would be a vital factor in its success. Two recommendations related directly to the problems. The first of these concerned undergraduate advising services, and the second, the creation of a permanent or continuing committee on general studies. Both recommendations were adopted. As a result the advisory services were reorganized in ways to improve student-faculty relations. One of the achievements has been the issuing of a comprehensive handbook for advisers, outlining procedures and requirements in all parts of the undergraduate program. The second recommendation led to the creation of the committee on general studies, which is the administrative body charged with supervising the General Studies Program, the official title of that part of the undergraduate program which I have thus far described. The committee is expected to keep the program in continuous review. It is within the jurisdiction of the committee to decide upon the validity of any course offered by a department for the fulfillment of general studies requirements. Says the Report of the executive committee: "The principle underlying such a committee is that general education is a primary responsibility of the University at large and not of any department." The committee is empowered to interpret the records of transfer students, deciding upon the extent to which they conform to the spirit of the new requirements. It is also expected to study the educational consequences of the course content of the program and to maintain some observation of innovations and practices in general programs of other institutions. This is a substantial charge to the committee and one that will repay close attention on the part of other colleges.

With regard to the distribution of the courses in the General Studies Program, the faculty approved of the committee recommendation that no fixed sequence for the pursuit of the requirements be established. In fact the recommendation that courses be distributed throughout the four years has been observed. Only the recommendation that the English requirement be met in the first year if possible and that either language or mathematics be begun in that year has been proposed. Thus Stanford belongs to that group of institutions which have sought to reduce the emphasis upon the preparatory value of general education and to strengthen the idea of general education as a continuing and correlative part of the liberal education.

The growth of Stanford University in the sixty-nine years of its history is comparable to that of a few other private universities which have not sought to achieve huge enrollments as a sign of success. In 1958–1959 its total enrollment was 8,405, of which 5,263 were undergraduates. The School of Humanities and Sciences, the largest of the undergraduate schools, enrolled 2,104 undergraduates and 933 graduates. In the concluding chapter of *The Undergraduate in the University* the authors refer to a recent report by President A. Whitney Griswold of Yale University, who called attention to the many ways in which over the years Yale College had fostered the development of the university. He then posed as the pertinent present question: "What can the University now do for the College?" Mr. Hoopes and Mr. Marshall go on to say that, although Stanford has no legally constituted college, it is faced with the same question and that the answer is to attend to undergraduate education and to work at it with the same vigor that we have lavished upon the university's advanced graduate programs and professional schools. Conceding that this is a deceptively simple answer, they call attention to an assumption, too often unexamined, that undergraduate education is bound to be superior when it is surrounded by "the emblems and trophies of high powered graduate research programs." This of course ought to be true, but they add, the goals of graduate research and undergraduate instruction are not the same, and to assume that the excellences of the former will trickle down and "invest the undergraduate program with the kind of strength it needs" may lead to a dangerous complacency.

Views such as these are a far cry from those expressed by President Jordan as he took office in the new university in Palo Alto. The differences and the circumstances which have led to the later views are an epitome of the revolution in the philosophy of collegiate education in the last three-quarters of a century.

WASHINGTON STATE UNIVERSITY

In 1890 the Legislature of the state of Washington passed the enabling acts which established the state's land-grant college. When the college opened for instruction in 1892 (with twenty-one students) it bore the cumbersome title of the Agricultural College, Experimental Station, and School of Science of the State of Washington. The title was changed in 1905 to the State College of Washington, and this name it bore until 1959. Following a trend to designate land-grant colleges as universities, the Legislature once more changed the name to Washington State University. The latest change signifies, as it has among other land-grant colleges, the growing importance of graduate and continuing education in the several schools and colleges. In 1960–1961 the enrollment was slightly over 7,000 students, of which 6,422 were undergraduates. As in all state-supported institutions of higher education, the education of undergraduates continues to be the major instructional task of the university regardless of the official title.

The diversity of instructional services at Washington State University has kept pace with that of other institutions of its kind. Today the university consists of ten colleges and schools including a graduate school. The College of Agriculture, like those in other land-grant colleges, is no longer the largest division. The College of Sciences and Arts is the liberal arts branch of the institution, and its departments provide instruction not only for its own majors but for all undergraduate divisions in the basic courses which are required of all students for the baccalaureate degree. In some of the colleges, notably the professional schools, such as the Schools of Education and Pharmacy, students are not admitted until they have completed at least the first year of undergraduate work.

Admission requirements are similar to those of most state institutions. All legal residents of the state of Washington are admitted upon application if they have graduated from an accredited high school with a grade-point average of C or better. Graduates who do not meet the grade requirement may be admitted after passing an entrance examination, and graduates of nonaccredited high schools must

269

give evidence of having completed 16 units of high school studies and must pass entrance examinations in English, mathematics, social science, and natural science. Nonresident applicants are expected to meet the entrance requirements of comparable institutions in their home states and nonresident freshmen must submit College Entrance Examination Board aptitude test scores. No specific distribution of high school studies is imposed as a general admission requirement, but it is typical that the College of Engineering and Mineral Technology requires that its applicants shall have completed 1½ units of algebra and 1 unit of plane geometry, and recommends an additional ½ unit of algebra and ½ unit of solid geometry or trigonometry. Again we encounter evidence that certain specific kinds of preparation in high school are deemed essential for successful work in technical fields but are not so regarded for a satisfactory liberal education. New admissions policies, to become effective in 1964–1965, have been approved by the faculty; the new policies set somewhat higher standards and make specific and strong recommendations for the distribution of high school courses in natural science, social science, foreign language, and particularly English and mathematics.

The general education of the students in Washington State University is achieved through an optional-course distributional plan. There are general university requirements which all candidates for the bachelor's degree must meet; and in addition to these there are additional general requirements which must be met by all students in the College of Sciences and Arts, in certain programs of the School of Education, and in the department of economics in the School of Business and Economics.

The general all-university requirements are:

1. English composition   6 credit hours
2. Physical education   4 semesters
3. Humanities and social science   12 credit hours
   (a minimum of 3 credit hours
   each in humanities and
   social science)
4. Natural sciences   12 credit hours
   (a minimum of 3 credit hours
   each in biology and in physical
   science, and at least 2 credit
   hours representing 6 class
   hours in laboratory in one science)

The requirement in English is normally met by a course in English composition extending through two semesters. In some instances substitutions are granted which permit students to fulfill all or part of the English requirement by taking one-semester courses in the following: English for Foreign Students, Business English, Advanced Writing, Technical Writing.

In the area of the humanities, students may satisfy the minimal 3 credit hours by electing one course from a list of forty-eight which are distributed among twelve departments including three foreign languages. In the social sciences, the 3 credits may be obtained by electing one course from a total of twenty-six offered by eight departments. In both English and history (which is classified as a social science discipline) students may choose from a list of ten courses. It is interesting to notice that one course in anthropology is offered as acceptable in meeting humanities requirements, a course called "Arts of Pre-literate Peoples"; another course in anthropology (Introduction to Anthropology) will meet minimal social science requirements. A course offered by the department of architectural engineering, Architectural History, is also acceptable in meeting general humanities requirements. The minimal requirement in either the humanities or the social sciences and the highly specialized subject matter of several of the courses indicate that it is possible for a student to meet the general requirements with an extremely limited experience in at least one of these two major fields.

The additional requirements imposed on students in the College of Sciences and Arts, the department of economics, and the School of Education mean that probably the majority of undergraduates do in fact achieve a broader experience of both areas. For these students the combined credit hours in humanities and social science are increased to 21, of which 6 must be in each area. The number of hours in the natural sciences is not increased for these students, but the 12 credit hours must be distributed over four courses. An additional requirement is one year of a foreign language unless the student offers two years of high school credit in a single language.

Among the options in both groups are four general or integrated courses. In biology, physical science, and social science one-semester courses have been developed, and in humanities the course extends over two semesters. Students may elect either or both semesters. In addition to this course two other one-semester humanities courses are offered as a part of the integrated course program, one in mythology and one in Greek and Roman drama. It is not clear why the latter two are regarded as integrated courses. The science courses are non-laboratory courses but employ lecture demonstrations.

The first experiments with integrated courses began in 1945. Since 1950 intensive efforts have been made to strengthen them. An important contributing factor has been the creation of the office of co-ordinator of general education and the curriculum advisory program. Since the integrated courses are all optional courses in their respective subject-matter fields, enrollment in any single semester is not large. This has retarded their growth and it also limits the number of faculty members who may be engaged in the course in any one year. In some instances this has worked hardships, since the withdrawal of one or two teachers from the course has sometimes placed instruction in the charge of new faculty members who have found it difficult to maintain continuity in the structure of the course. On the whole, however, there has been remarkable continuity in faculty personnel over a period of several years.

The principle of integration in the two-semester humanities course is located in the study of the "great books" of the Western tradition. In the first semester the works read, in whole or in part, include selections from the Greek and Roman era. The selections embrace historical, philosophical, dramatic, and poetic works. The second semester includes a representative selection of works from the Middle Ages, the Renaissance, and the early sevententh century. In the other courses integration is achieved through the exercise of related disciplines in the solution of different aspects of one or more problems. Thus in the one-semester course in physical science the central theme (at the time this study began) was the problem of heat energy in the physical world as manifested in a selection of physical phenomena. A manual of exercises prepared by the faculty is supplemented by an extensive reading list of articles related to the central theme. The faculty has recently proposed to increase the time allotted to the general biology course with the addition of one hour of laboratory work per week.

Instructors have considerable freedom in organizing the materials of the courses. All instructors are responsible for determining final grades of their own students, and no system of comprehensive examinations taken by all students in the courses has been developed. Each of the courses grants 3 credit hours.

Exclusive of physical education the general requirements vary from one-fourth to about one-third of a student's program depending upon the college or department in which he is majoring. It is expected that not less than three-fourths of the general requirements will be completed within the first two years. One-half of the freshman year must be devoted to general studies requirements. All students must declare their major field by the end of the sophomore year, and they may declare it at the time of entering.

The principal safeguard to an unbalanced distribution of courses forming a general program lies in the office of coordinator of the curriculum advisory program which supervises curricular planning for all students in their first year. Opportunity for free electives varies considerably among the different degree programs arranged by the schools and departments.

In addition to the core program represented in the general requirements for the baccalaureate degree, the university offers degree programs in general studies. These programs, under the direction of a committee consisting of three members representing humanities, social science, and the natural sciences, are planned for students who are interested in a broader course of study than is usually possible for a major in one department. Three types of programs are offered:

1. A departmental major in general studies
2. An interdepartmental major in general studies
3. Teacher training in general studies

In the program for departmental majors, students must take a minimum of twenty-four hours of work in one department and sixteen hours in another. One-half of the total must be taken in courses at the third- and fourth-year levels. Three of the four integrated courses previously described are required of these students. In other words they are not options among the distributional requirements in the humanities–social science group or the natural science group. Those who select the Interdepartmental Major Program in General Studies must concentrate in one of four areas: humanities, social science, biological science, and physical science. The minimal forty hours required of them in fulfilling the major requirement must be distributed between two closely related departments in a plan approved by the student's adviser. The third program has been developed jointly by the committee on general studies and the School of Education. In certain of the teacher-training programs, students are required to take their degree in general studies with course distributions planned by the committee and the School of Education.

The university also offers three programs of area studies each leading to a degree. The areas are Latin American Studies, Western European Studies, and Eastern European Studies. Course requirements in each area are distributed among several fields: anthropology, economics, geography, history, political science, and sociology. A minimum of four semesters of an appropriate foreign language is required, and in choosing courses to meet the general core requirements students are urged to take certain courses in the social sciences and at least six hours in literature or philosophy, including the general humanities course. The Program of General Studies and the area programs are additional evidence of the transition in conceptions of undergraduate education—transitions which I believe owe much to reflections upon the nature and functions of general education.

The most recent curricular development which bears significantly on the idea of general education is the introduction in 1960 of a four-year Honors Program. In many respects it resembles the Honors College of the University of Oregon. Certainly it is another important sign of the interest in planning more carefully integrated programs and more intensive courses for superior students. Freshmen who rank in the upper 10 per cent of their high school classes will be encouraged to enter the program. Applicants will be selected, however, not only upon the basis of their high school rank but on their grade-point average and upon all admissions and qualifying tests given by the university prior to or at the time of admission. Unlike the Oregon program, the Washington State program establishes no specific prerequisites in high school studies. Students who are not admitted as freshmen to the program may petition for admission at the end of their first semester and thereafter until the end of the sophomore year and will be accepted on the basis of their academic record achieved in residence. All departments, schools, and colleges of the university participate in the program. The program is under the direction of a faculty body called the "honors council."

The curriculum for the Honors Program consists of courses which are required of all students, courses which a student takes as a part of his program of concentration, and those he may take as free electives. All honors students are required to take two semesters of English

Honors, the first of which is an honors course in composition and the second a combination of composition and literature. They are required to take a minimum of one semester of Mathematics Honors, for which three honors courses have been prepared and from which they may choose in accordance with prior experience or with the demands of their field of concentration. From a list of six honors courses in the division of social sciences all students must select two. The content of these courses conforms to conventional departmental subject matters. One honors course each in physical science and biological science is also a uniform requirement. Honors courses in French, German, Russian, and Spanish are offered, but these are not uniformly required. Some departments may require one or two languages, however, in various programs of concentration; others may require none. In addition to the honors courses which are a common requirement and those prepared by the several departments and schools as a part of programs of concentration, the program offers several newly created interdepartmental courses called "university honors courses." These are elective. A few of them are:

> Man and His Physical Environment
> Development of Western Civilization
> Development of Eastern Civilization
> Domain of the Arts

One feature, formally entitled "University Lectures and Readings," consists of a series of approximately twenty-five lectures on the various fields of study available in the university. Small-group colloquiums are arranged following each lecture. All honors students are required to take this sequence which covers two semesters. It is intended for first-year students. Honors students are also expected to do profitable summer reading within their major fields; to give direction to this reading, the various departments and professional schools in cooperation with the honors council provide reading lists for summer reading. Students are examined either orally or by written examination on their competence in their summer reading programs.

Students must maintain a B average in their work to remain in the program. In addition to successful work in all courses, the students are required to pass two comprehensive examinations, the first at the end of the sophomore year and the second in the final semester of the senior year. The sophomore comprehensive covers matters of concern to the student's major department and such general knowledge outside the major field as the honors council deems suitable for examination. The questions set by the council are publicly announced in advance of the examination and are intended to test the student's powers of comprehension and ability to synthesize and relate materials studied in various subject-matter fields. The senior comprehensive is administered by the student's major department and may consist of both oral and written examinations. Departments or schools may, at their option, also require a senior thesis.

Chapter 7

A Retrospective View

1

One can scarcely fail to notice the many connotations in the use of the term "general education" in the foregoing pages. When it is used to distinguish a broad and comprehensive view of knowledge from a thorough command of a limited area of learning it may signify either an educational goal or an educational process. Conceptually the goal assumes an area of common responsibilities and common pleasures which are ours by virtue of our common manhood; and the goal aimed at is an education which qualifies us for the better exercise of our responsibilities and the richer sharing of our pleasures, both of which are a duty and a privilege. It is a goal which unites a man with his fellow men; and it differs from that other goal which aims at the command of some limited field of knowledge because the latter divides men according to their individual competences. Such an idea of general education as a goal is implied by Saint Xavier when that college speaks of "the generally educated" man or woman.

The term "general education" is used to signify the process or means by which the goal of the generally educated citizen is achieved when the University of Minnesota says to its students: "Although your general education began long before you entered college and should continue throughout your life time, it is a particularly important part of your 4-year undergraduate program." President Conant used the term in this sense in the Introduction of *General Education in a Free Society:*

> Unless the educational process includes *at each level of maturity* some continuing contact with those fields in which value judgments are of prime importance, it must fall short of the ideal. The

277

student in high school, in college, and in graduate school must be concerned, in part at least, with the words "right" and "wrong" in both the ethical and mathematical sense. Unless he feels the import of these general ideas and aspirations which have been a deep moving force in the lives of men, he runs the risk of partial blindness.

In this idea of general education as a process, forces both within and without the educational system exercise important functions.

When, however, the University of Minnesota refers to its "curriculum for general education" and San Francisco State College informs its students that they must include 45 units of general education in their baccalaureate degree programs, the connotation is significantly altered by imposing the idea of a formal structure—even one that is quantitatively measurable—upon the concept of means. The identification of the idea of general education with formal means is often carried to an extreme when colleges refer to certain courses as "courses in general education." There is something of this connotation in the usage of Saint Xavier in classifying only the Introduction to Natural Sciences and the Introduction to the Science of Human Action as general education courses. Berea College names three required courses in physical science, humanities, and social science as General Studies 106, 201, and 203, respectively. Strangely enough it does not list a required course in biology under this general classification. The only apparent reason for the distinction at Berea and elsewhere seems to be that most teachers have ceased to think of biology as an "integrated" course.

Our inquiry has necessarily been concerned with ideas of both ends and means—of general education both as a goal and as a process. The historical record shows that since about 1920 colleges have been seriously concerned with means in the formal sense. Yet granting the necessity of the concern, I am inclined to think that the preoccupation has led to carelessness and confusion in the use of terms. I doubt whether any course can properly be called "a course *in* general education." I can see no legitimate reason for designating only "integrated" or "interdepartmental" courses "general education courses." A course in English composition is just as much a part of a student's general education as is a course in humanities. To make such distinctions is to confuse the relationship of means to ends.

Another functional concept has been explicitly attached to the idea of general education by several of the colleges. This is the idea of general education as preparatory to the choice and work of specialized or vocational education. There is nothing necessarily contradictory between this idea and the concept of general education as a continuing process at all levels of maturity. Yet there are good reasons for believing that the preparatory idea, in its practical application, has often inhibited if not smothered the other. The idea of the preparatory function is very old. The classical liberal education was always regarded as preparatory to professional education. When it yielded to the dual curriculums—classical and scientific—the common element of both programs was generally distributed throughout the four years. But as distinctions between "college work" and "university work" increased, the tendency to regard college work in its initial stages as a continuation of high school work grew. This came to be regarded as the sphere of general education. Administrative and curricular distinctions between junior and senior colleges and lower and upper divisions reflected a separation of functions and strengthened the belief that the principal function of the lower division was preparation for the upper.

As a consequence an idea of general education as *terminal* as well as preparatory arose. General education was something to be completed, in so far as possible, before the more mature work of specialization began. As a further consequence the stamp of superficiality was attached to the idea of general education. All this obscured the idea of general education as a continuing process demanding as high a degree of mature thought as does any kind of specialization.

The colleges which we have reviewed would, I think, agree that in the broadest sense of the term general education neither begins nor ends in college and that its function is not solely preparatory to specialization. In practical procedures, however, there is considerable difference in the emphasis which they place upon the two functions. The majority of the colleges have concentrated the content of what they regard as their formal contribution to general education in the first two years. The new curriculums at Antioch and Stanford, on the other hand, require a distribution of their formal general requirements over the four undergraduate years.[1]

[1] In 1945 a committee at Harvard University gave considerable support to the conception of general education as a continuing process throughout the undergraduate years through the publication of *General Education in a Free*

Indeed there is much evidence which justifies the conclusion that there is a trend toward the idea of general education as a continuing part of the college program, complementing studies in concentration. I have referred earlier to the required senior symposiums as one sign. Several of the colleges point to the opportunity to extend one's general education through the exercise of elective privileges; but the regulation of elective time varies. In some colleges the student may use his electives in any way he chooses; in others he is required to distribute some part of his elective time in areas outside the division of concentration, for example, Amherst, Louisville, and Michigan State (in the College of Science and Arts). The opportunity to secure a degree in general studies is another indication of a broader conception of the function of general education. I have frequently stated my opinion that the broader conception of fields of concentration is indicative of a larger view of the nature of general education.

I can find no reason to believe that the American college will surrender its present commitment to the general and the special functions of education. St. John's will, I imagine, travel a lonely, albeit a courageous, road. The principal issues in the future will probably concern the balance and relationships of these functions. There are sound reasons why the emphasis on the general should be greater in the early years. Many students are unprepared to make a wise choice of a field of concentration when they enter college; for these the preparatory function of the general program is legitimate and necessary. But this fact alone does not warrant the confinement of the general program to the first two years. Only those colleges faced with the loss of a large percentage of the student body by the end of the second year are justified in developing two-year terminal programs. The experience of those colleges which strive through a controlled plan to engage students in their more mature years in problems and disciplines outside their fields of specialization will deserve considered attention.

Society. Colgate University distributes its core program, which it calls "University Studies," throughout four years. This program culminates in the junior and senior years with four semester courses required of all students. For the first of these the students may choose one of eight *area* courses which include the Far East, the Mediterranean area, Russia, India and Southeast Asia, and Latin America. Two semesters are devoted to American Ideals and Institutions. The final course, in the senior year, is called "America and the World Community."

Because there are clear distinctions between the ends of general education and those of specialized education, some colleges have assumed that there must be a similar categorical distinction between the courses which serve the ends. They suppose that if a course is listed as a "general education course," it cannot be a part of one's specialization. The assumption needs critical examination. The idea that courses which serve general requirements are outside the sphere of concentration is contradicted by actual practice in many optional-course distributional programs. An introductory course in sociology which will serve general requirements may also be a necessary first step in specialization for sociology majors. The distinction has been made more frequently with respect to interdepartmental courses, but in my opinion it is wrongly made. A well-planned humanities course which trains students to read a selection of great literary works with discrimination is, I think, legitimately a part of the concentration of the student who will specialize in literature. I am not suggesting that certain courses may not serve one end better than another. Just as there is need for courses in every area which will serve the interests of the specialist, there is need for courses especially planned for the non-specialist, but there can be no absolute line drawn between courses which separates them into the general and the special. Rigid categorical distinctions give false impressions of the ratio of general studies to specialized studies.

2

The idea of general education as a continuing process with which all levels of the educational system are concerned raises questions about the part which each level ought to play and how the work of each may best be articulated with what precedes and what follows. For the college this means consideration of its work in relation to the high school at one end and with the graduate and professional school at the other. Although there has been some discussion of the place of general education in graduate and professional studies in recent years, I have made no attempt to investigate this aspect of the problem. The problem of articulation of general studies with the high school, however, could not be avoided for the simple reason that practically all college students have a secondary school foundation for their college studies. The importance of the problems of continuity in the area of general education between the high school and the college has seemed to me to be so great that I have given particular attention to the expectations of the colleges concerning the nature of the educational experience of students prior to admission to college. The standard requirement is graduation from (preferably) an accredited high school with 15 or 16 units of high school studies. Other than this the expectations differ considerably. A summary of the admission policies as they relate to academic preparation is given in Table I of the Appendix.

An issue which concerns the continuity of general education from high school to college is whether the colleges should impose certain specific distributional requirements among high school studies or should merely recommend courses, leaving the choice and emphasis of subjects to the students. On this issue the colleges differ considerably. Two colleges (Brooklyn and Notre Dame) make specific and extensive distributional requirements. One (Stanford) requires specified levels of preparation in English, mathematics, and foreign language; and one (Goucher) requires four years of English. One (Michigan State) requires three years of English. The others are content to be more or less firm regarding the distribution of high school courses. The firm suggest patterns of distribution even while they avow that they are more concerned with promise of performance than with any quantitative accounting of high school courses. The less firm list "academic courses" from which students may choose the majority of their 15 or 16 units—usually 11 or 12—and accept the remainder from any courses which the high school accepts for graduation.

The high school subjects which are either required, recommended, or listed as acceptable are fairly uniform: English, mathematics, foreign language, history, social studies, natural science, and occasionally art and music appreciation. A casual glance at the subject matters which make up the formal requirements of the general education programs of every one of the eighteen colleges is sufficient to show that, under various classifying terms, they are nearly identical with those which are recommended for study in high school. The only significant additions are philosophy and/or religion. It seems paradoxical that none of the colleges hesitates to impose specific distributional requirements in its own program, yet most of them refrain from making more than a recommendation for the distribution of high school subjects. I have commented previously on the effect of this policy in inviting early specialization and the consequent unevenness in preparation for college courses. The policy of the liberal arts colleges is contrary to that of the engineering schools which do not hesitate to require 3 units of mathematics and 1 or 2 units of laboratory science as a prerequisite for admission. As a matter of fact the professional requirements for a B.S. degree in the physical sciences are so standardized and so widely known that few prospective science majors will enter a liberal arts college without this preparation. A clear and interesting issue is presented, namely, whether a planned continuity in subject matters forming the foundation of a general education is any less desirable than a planned continuity in subjects forming the foundation of a technological or scientific education. Despite an approximate agreement about the subject matters that ought to be a part of a general education, there is no clear agreement about the level of knowledge that ought to be aimed at in each subject. Consequently it is impossible for the colleges and the high schools to reach a common understanding about the particular responsibilities of each in a common task.

Only three of the eighteen colleges specifically require mathematics for entrance: Brooklyn, Notre Dame, and Stanford. Tradition makes it probable that most students will enter college with one or two years of work, usually algebra and geometry. Five of the colleges, however, regard mathematics of sufficient importance to include some additional study in their general requirements. Eight offer mathematics as options in their distributional requirements. Five make no optional provision for mathematics in their general requirements. Since most accredited high schools offer three or four years of mathematics and have shown their capacity to prepare students for the requirements of scientific programs, there is little reason to doubt that the high schools are competent to give the kind of instruction appropriate to a general education—if there were any agreement about what that instruction should be. Table II in the Appendix is a summary of practices in English and mathematics.

The place of foreign languages as a continuing part of general education is no clearer than that of mathematics. In one respect the problem of continuity between school and college is the reverse of that in mathematics. The college can reasonably expect that most students will have one or two years of mathematics; but the majority of them make no explicit requirement for the continuation of mathematical studies. In contrast to this the colleges are aware that many students will have studied no foreign language in high school; yet one-half of the eighteen colleges in this study require all students to demonstrate some level of proficiency in one language as a condition for graduation. For most of this group the level is the equivalent of that attained by two years of collegiate study or three or four years of high school study. Three of the colleges require two or more years of foreign language study in high school as a prerequisite for admission, and two of these require some amount of continuation in college or the beginning of a new language. Stanford, which requires two years of a language and two years of mathematics as a minimum for admission, also requires students to continue one or the other in college. Three of the colleges require a specified proficiency of all candidates for the B.A. degree but not uniformly of candidates for the B.S. degree. In four of the colleges the language requirement is solely within the jurisdiction of departments and varies from none at all to the minimal requirements for a major. Table III in the Appendix summarizes these practices in the foreign languages.

Obviously the majority of the colleges believe that some familiarity with a foreign language is essential to the general education of their students. Why they think so is not always clear. Arguments on the ground of vocational utility and the needs of research appeal to professional rather than general needs. St. John's undertakes ambitiously to relate the study of foreign languages to English in order that the student may secure a better understanding of the nature of language as the principal means of human discourse and reason. The other colleges appear to stress the importance of a minimal acquaintance with *a language* rather than an understanding of language as such. The ability to read and speak at least one foreign language in a polylingual world might seem to be a desirable goal for the liberally educated, particularly in an age in which space is no longer a barrier which separates Americans from the rest of mankind. This, however, is a goal which is attained from habitual use of a foreign language and rarely from the minimal college requirements which are now the rule.

So we return to the problem of continuity between school and college. The decline of foreign language instruction in the schools is evidence that the American public does not regard it as a general need. The colleges have not been sufficiently convinced of its value to insist that the schools share the responsibilities of instruction or to agree that students must make its study a part of their preparation for a continuing general education. There have been within the last few years some signs of a changing attitude. The introduction of French, Spanish, and German in elementary school programs is at least a recognition of the importance of an early foundation in language study; but the practice is isolated, and as yet there is not much evidence of a sustained effort to achieve continuity through elementary school and high school. There has been some increase in the number of foreign languages taught in high school, though the quality of instruction at the secondary school level, particularly oral-aural instruction, has been subject to severe criticism. It is a matter of record that a startlingly high percentage of high school teachers of a modern language cannot speak even with a minimal degree of confidence the language which they teach. If high school students choose to study a language for only one or two years, there would be good reason for advising those who will continue a liberal arts program in college to postpone the study until their junior and senior years in high school, but such advice is seldom given. All too often the consequence is a waste of the student's time in the earlier study as well as a waste of instructional time at the collegiate level. Meanwhile instruction survives in the schools because some students enjoy languages, some anticipate professional needs, and perhaps because the tradition of an education which once gave high place to the knowledge of languages is not quite dead.

As for the colleges and universities, there is little doubt that the lingering tradition of the importance of languages in the liberal arts is more strongly supported by the private institutions than by the public ones. In our sample of twenty college programs, we find that, to an overwhelming degree, those which require all students to meet some standard of proficiency in one or more languages are private. The ratio is 9 to 2. Of those which impose no entrance requirement and leave all requirements to the decisions of departments, three are state-supported and one is private.

With respect to English, continuity of a kind between school and college is more assured. Three or four years of English are generally required for high school graduation, and all the colleges make some provision for continued training in writing. Only two (Antioch and

Reed) do not include a course in composition or communication skills in their formal requirements, preferring to treat the disciplines of writing functionally in association with the demands of "content courses." "English" is an ambiguous term, and it is difficult for colleges to know, merely from the fact of 3 or 4 units of high school English, precisely what measure of competence in writing and reading those units represent. Colleges expect what they do not always get, a substantial foundation in these arts. Not infrequently students declare that they have completed high school with very little sustained training in writing. Many colleges give qualifying tests in composition which release the most able from the formal requirement. For students who have serious deficiencies, they offer some form of remedial training, though as a rule not bearing that pejorative name. The major problems of continuity in instruction in writing are less concerned with the amount of available time than with the efficient use of the time.

The study of history has been so widely regarded as an essential part of a liberal education that we might expect a much more carefully planned continuity in this subject matter than the evidence seems to indicate. It is not easy to make an accurate estimate of the scope of historical study represented in the total high school and college programs because of the present practice of "integrating" history in a variety of social science and humanities courses in both high school and college. State laws generally require that all high school graduates shall receive some instruction in American history, but there is no consistent rule governing its location in the curriculum. In some schools it is given in the freshman year; in others in the senior year. Many students enter college with no more history than the minimum prescribed by their respective states. Most colleges recommend that students include history among their high school studies; some, however, submerge history in the broader recommendation that preparation should include work in social studies.

In Chapter 4 I referred to several proposals for curricular reform made near the beginning of the century in which history was accorded a prominent place in a required common core of studies, and to one or two which held history to be the one indispensable discipline (e.g., a proposal by Woodrow Wilson). Perhaps the majority of the humanities "survey courses" introduced after 1920 were organized within a historical framework which dealt with the political and cultural history of the Western world illuminated by a selection of great works in literature, philosophy, and fine arts. The type is still very popular. Yet despite the reverence with which educators often speak of the importance of history in a general education there is still great difference of opinion about the substantive character of the subject matter or the quantitative measure which it should have in the curriculum. Table IV in the Appendix gives a summary of the general requirements in historical courses among the colleges in this study. If it is a reliable index of the place of history in the general education programs of American colleges, then attitudes about the function and value of history as a discrete discipline differ more widely than even the most optimistic may have anticipated. In quantitative terms it is accorded so little as no place at all to as much as two years in the general requirements. At Stanford the History of Western Civilization is a required one-year course, and besides the English course, it is the only common course requirement in all degree programs. At Reed the history of the Western world from ancient times to the end of the eighteenth century is the core of the freshman humanities course, which is the only common course requirement in the curriculum. At Amherst and Notre Dame (in the Regular Program) one year each of European and American history is required; but at Amherst this is the sum of the general requirement in social science, and at Notre Dame the requirement is in addition to required courses in social science and literature. Brooklyn and Louisville require one year of Western civilization in addition to the general requirement in social science and humanities. At Michigan State the one-year general humanities course is a survey of the development of the Western cultural tradition. Berea requires a one-semester course in Western civilization, and San Francisco requires a one-semester course in American history (The Development of American Institutions and Ideals). A course similar in design at Mills (Values of American Life) is accorded one year, and for some time has been the only course required of all students except the course in composition and literature. For most of the other colleges, history is optional and is grouped with either the social sciences, the humanities, or both. All these colleges are well aware of the wide range of differences in the amount and kind of historical knowledge among their students at the time that they enter college. The diversity in their practices with regard to history in the general curriculum suggests that the colleges are far from entertaining a common opinion about the importance of history as a part of a general education.

In other subject matters which are common to the high school and college curriculums and their programs of general studies there are usually opportunities for continuity. The chief problems concern the uses of those opportunities. Colleges generally agree that the intellectual experiences which students encounter upon entering college should be fresh, stimulating, and more demanding than their high school experiences. But with uncertain knowledge of the preparation which one may expect of students in any given subject matter, it is difficult to plan courses which will be equally fresh and stimulating to all. The Advanced Placement Program, developed cooperatively by schools and colleges, has done much to secure better preparation for the more able or more ambitious high school students. It does not solve the problem of students who have successfully avoided work in some areas which they will need to study later in college. For these the colleges must either resort to courses of precollegiate standards or risk the danger that the students will be lost in courses beyond their competence.

3

We have reviewed twenty undergraduate programs in eighteen colleges. Attention has been directed chiefly to that part of the program which consists of certain formal course requirements imposed on all students and which is variously named "the program of general studies," "all-university requirements," "a curriculum in liberal education," "the program for general education," or simply "general requirements." Precise control of the students' general education is limited to these requirements, and any extension beyond them largely depends upon the students' exercise of elective privileges of various kinds. With the exception of St. John's and the General Program of Liberal Education at Notre Dame, the sum of the general requirements ranges from one-fourth to about two-thirds of the whole of the undergraduate requirements. In the majority, the amount is one-half or less.

Students complete these requirements in two ways: by taking courses which are uniformly prescribed for all and by choosing courses from lists of options in each of several broadly defined subject-matter fields.[2] Fifteen of the twenty programs employ some combination of the common course requirement and the optional-course distributional plan. Table V in the Appendix is a summary of the general requirements classified in terms of uniformly required courses and areas which permit options. From it one can form an idea of the differences among the colleges in the uses they make of, and presumably the values they attach to, the two methods of meeting general requirements. A conspicuous difference is the balance between the areas in which all students are required to take one or more courses and the areas in which options are granted. Although the range is from no options to all options, by a slight majority the number of courses uniformly required equals or exceeds the number of areas in which options are available. It should be understood that courses which are uniformly required are not necessarily general or interdisciplinary. Both departmental courses (English, history, philosophy, mathematics) and general courses (humanities, social science, physical science) appear among both required lists and optional lists.

Differences seem to have little correlation with the size or type of institution. One signficant difference concerns the substantive character of the courses deemed suitable as a uniform requirement. In a few colleges English or English and a foreign language only are regarded as suitable. It is interesting that they have chosen not to offer a common course in those subject matters which many colleges have found to provide "a common intellectual interest and challenge," to quote from an observation in the Stanford Report about its History of Western Civilization.

It is difficult to appraise all the factors which have influenced the judgments of faculties on this issue. Local conditions within an institution or the desires of a particular segment of the faculty are

---

[2] Although formal requirements are stated in terms of courses, whether optional or uniformly required, we must not overlook the fact that in several colleges the requirements may be satisfied by passing exemption or placement examinations. The exemption examination is usually regarded as an opportunity to "accelerate" which is often interpreted as a means of beginning specialization early and of gaining more time for specialization. This attitude strengthens the idea of general education as both terminal and preparatory. In fairness, however, it must be remembered that some colleges stress the exemption examination as a means of extending one's general education through a gain in free elective time. In the new program at Antioch, the results of the achievement examinations may determine whether a student is excused from a general requirement or is required to take an advanced course in the general program.

strong factors. From discussions with faculties and from occasional published statements I have found several opinions which account for a positive distrust of the uniform course requirement.

1. Whether the course is a departmental course or a general course, if it is required of several hundred students simultaneously, it must be either a lecture course or a staff-taught course. The staff-taught course demands a cooperative spirit among instructors and cooperative labor in the planning and administration of the courses that is time-consuming and occasionally resented by instructors. In subject matters other than the so-called "skills courses," conflicting opinions concerning content and methods of instruction have sometimes been disastrous.

2. Closely related to this is the fear of a strong personality or of an influential member of the faculty who may impose an intellectual strait jacket on his colleagues.

3. A considerable number of uniformly required courses are general or interdepartmental. These are viewed suspiciously by many teachers. Even when they are willing to admit such courses as options they do not have sufficient confidence in the courses to impose them as uniform requirements.

4. General courses are distasteful to some teachers either because they do not like to teach subject matters outside the fields which are in their special competence or because they resent the invasion of instructors not specialists in their own domain.

5. One of the arguments frequently heard is that the uniformly required course, whether departmental or general, tends to induce an intellectual conformity.

6. The positive form of this argument holds that independence of mind is best cultivated when students have some freedom in the choice of courses which they may take.

7. It is claimed that a uniformly required course may work well in some subject matters but not in others. There is no agreement on what these subjects matters are. One college may find that a social science course uniformly required is very successful; another may regard this an improper area for a uniform course requirement.

8. Finally there is a conviction that no single course can effectively accommodate the variety of aptitudes and experiences found in a group of students that numbers into the hundreds or thousands.

The validity of some of these arguments cannot be ignored. On the other hand there are colleges both within this group and without that have found ways of overcoming the most serious of these objections. There are many courses required of large student bodies that have survived changes in administration, changes in faculty personnel, and changes in other areas of the curriculum to which they belong, and have retained all the while the respect of the student body as a whole. These courses have not remained static over the years, but basic concepts have not altered materially. The arguments offered in their defense deserve equal consideration.

In the first place, it is acknowledged that continued success of the uniformly required course is possible only under certain conditions. It cannot succeed if imposed by administrative fiat. It cannot succeed when it is dominated entirely by one person who resists all constructive criticism from other instructors. It cannot succeed if it is not intellectually stimulating. If instructors do not respect the course, the students will not. It cannot succeed if the instructional staff is not granted the necessary time for the many cooperative labors required. It *can* succeed only where there is a spirit of mutual respect and trust among participating instructors. A course which is uniformly required of all students is necessarily more in the public view than any other. Good or bad, because all students are at some time involved in it, everyone hears about it. The confidence of the faculty, at the very least of those instructors engaged in teaching it, is essential to success.

1. Under the ideal conditions implied in the foregoing paragraph, the most important achievement of a course which is uniformly required is the creation of a community of learning. In defense of the common course requirement it is argued that a college ought to be more than a social community; a college should be an intellectual community. The demands of specialization tend to create small intellectual communities. Ideally, the common course offers an intellectual experience which is shared by an entire student body. The evidence of several of the colleges we have reviewed supports the conclusion that when the whole student body has been engaged in a well-planned and well-taught course, a general student interest does extend outside the classroom. Learning continues informally on a large scale long after classes are dismissed, because there is a common basis for discourse.

2. The dangers of intellectual conformity are not implicit in the uniformly required course but are within the control of the faculty. No course need be doctrinaire. Normally such courses engage the services of several instructors. In the experience of a number of colleges, this is a safeguard against imposing doctrinaire views on students. Instructors do not approach problems in the same ways; they differ on points of textual

interpretation; they emphasize different aspects of issues. These differences have been found to enliven the staff and, as they are communicated to the students, to stimulate interest and encourage further inquiry as the complexities of ideas are realized.

3. The views of instructors who disapprove of required general courses on the ground that instruction is in the hands of teachers who have no special competence in some aspects of the course invite questions about their concept of liberal education. The theory that the liberally educated person should be able to understand the relationships between closely associated disciplines is mocked by the specialist in political science who considers himself unqualified to discuss the economic aspects of matters of public policy or by the specialist in economics who distrusts the competence of the sociologist to deal with economic problems. These attitudes betray a confusion of the means of instruction for specialized and professional ends with those designed for more general and liberal ends. Moreover, they are a contradiction of the fundamental principle of the optional-course distributional plan of general education. One assumption of the optional-course plan has always been that an introduction to the basic principles and methods of one discipline will provide the student with the knowledge of methods which he can apply independently to problems in related fields. How can the student be expected to gain such wisdom if the instructor whose professional life is devoted to a particular science or an art feels insecure when called upon to discuss the nature of relationships among the disciplines that are within his general domain?

Defense of the values of the general course taught by a staff drawn from several departments does not imply indifference to the importance of a special competence on the part of each staff member. It is manifestly necessary, and no greater disservice is done to general courses or to students than to assign instruction very largely to the least experienced members of a department. The cooperation of experienced teachers, each bringing his special knowledge to bear on problems that transcend the artificial boundaries of departments, can go far to demonstrate to students the true nature of the relationships that exist among the several branches of learning.

4. The argument that no single course, whether departmental or general, can be adjusted successfully to the variety of aptitudes and experiences which characterize a large and heterogeneous student body cannot be dismissed casually. From a practical viewpoint it becomes more serious with the constant expansion of the size of student bodies. Two methods which are useful in coping with this problem have been disclosed in the practices of some of the colleges.

One of these I have called the "variant course principle." It may be used in several ways. The practice of the University of Minnesota in placing students in any one of several English composition courses on the basis of aptitudes shown in a qualifying test is one example. Materials and methods of instruction may vary, but the general goal is common. A somewhat similar use of the principle is made by Brooklyn College in offering several courses in mathematics from which students may choose the one best adapted to their previous experience. The principle is used in a different way by Reed College in the required humanities course and in the optional courses in mathematics and biology. Two variants of each of these courses are offered. In the mathematics and biology courses one is slightly abridged and planned for nonspecialists. In the humanities course the abridged version has been limited to science majors whose special degree programs compel some reduction of the time required for the "parent" version of the course. There are other uses of the variant principle which have been tried elsewhere and which permit adaptations of instructional procedures and materials to personal interests without the sacrifice of precise common objectives.[3] Imaginative use of the variant course principle permits the adaptation of a subject matter to individual interests as well as to abilities. But the limited and controlled use of options in such cases differs greatly from the open option between two or more different subject matters.

Another method of adjusting the formal requirements for general education to the variety of aptitudes and interests of large student bodies is exemplified by the Sophomore Honors Program of the University of Ore-

---

[3] The University of Chicago has used the variant principle successfully for several years in two ways. Students enrolled in certain general courses have been permitted after the first quarter to apply for admission to "preceptorial" sections if their grades show more than average ability. From one to three preceptorial variants may be offered in these courses. A single theme or topic relevant to the subject matter of the parent course is the subject of the preceptorial. Only twelve to fifteen students are admitted to a preceptorial, and the class is conducted as a seminar. In the final quarter of the year, most of the student's time is devoted to the independent preparation of an essay on a theme chosen by him with the approval of his preceptor. The essay is a part of his final examination. Other parts of the final comprehensive examination are common to all sections of the course.

In a general humanities course concerned with principles and practice in the criticism of the arts, the materials of the parent course are selected from works in English and English translation. Variants are offered in modern languages, open to students with adequate reading ability. Variants in art and music are also offered. In the latter variants, the students take the parent course in the opening quarter and continue in the variant in either art or music in the second and third quarters. Some readings and some portion of all final examinations are common to all variants of the course.

gon and the General Program for Liberal Education at Notre Dame. Both of these are optional to the regular programs offered in their liberal arts colleges, although both are under the jurisdiction of their liberal arts division. Both are selective and are planned for students above the average in aptitude. I have spoken of their similarity to programs which have been offered for many years at Yale and Wisconsin. The prospect of increasing enrollments gives reason to think that large colleges and universities will do well to study plans for developing more than one program of general studies and possibly more than one program of liberal education through the device of dividing unwieldy liberal arts colleges into several smaller colleges.[4]

The summary of data in Table V in the Appendix shows that several colleges prefer the optional-course plan as a means of satisfying the major part of the general requirements. I have commented on the differences in the use of the optional principle previously, particularly in a comparison of its uses by Reed College and the College of Science, Letters, and the Arts of the University of Minnesota (pp. 225–227). In general these colleges agree that students must distribute their general requirements in ways that will include some experience with all major fields of learning. Aside from this very general point of agreement there is little consistency in the uses of the distributional principle.

1. The classification of subjects by groups or divisions which is in greatest favor is the threefold division into the natural sciences, the social sciences, and the humanities. This classification is not used by all the colleges.

2. The allocation of subject matters or departments among these major divisions is more or less uniform, but there are some significant differences. There is considerable difference of opinion about the allocation of

---

[4] Wayne State University in Detroit has recently undertaken an ambitious experiment with the opening of a new undergraduate unit, Monteith College. Monteith is an autonomous college with its own faculty and administrative officers. It will offer a four-year undergraduate program of liberal education but one that differs from the programs of the College of Liberal Arts. It is based on an integrated curriculum of general studies that complements studies in special fields throughout the four years. Students are admitted to the college on a voluntary basis, but they are selected from applicants in a way to secure a more or less even distribution of each entering class into six groups: those who plan to transfer to any of five professional schools and those who wish to complete a liberal arts program in Monteith. In 1959–1960 it limited the size of its entering class to about 320 students.

history, religion, philosophy, and psychology. In a few instances colleges acknowledge that the line of distinction between groups is vague; they meet the issue by listing certain courses as satisfying *either* a social science or a humanities requirement, or *either* a natural science or a social science requirement. In one college a course in mathematics may satisfy either part of a natural science requirement or part of a humanities requirement. The theory that one or two subject matters in a group are a satisfactory introduction to the disciplines common to the group is somewhat weakened by these uncertainties about the relationships among disciplines.

3. The range of options in any division and in any department within a division is very great. Policies with respect to control of options differ considerably. In some colleges freedom of option is restricted not only by a limited number of options in each division but by a watchful guidance program. In others there is great freedom of choice and little guidance. One justification of the optional plan is the argument that it is better to study one subject well than to spread time and energies among several subjects. The multiplication of options tends to defeat this goal. A principal defense of the *general course* as an alternative to the optional-course plan is that it offers a coherent view of the functions of related disciplines. The optional plan which permits widely scattered distribution of courses within a division is open to the charge of superficiality quite as much as the *general course*, but it lacks the defense that the results form a coherent or systematic view of the broad subject-matter field.

4

The functional dualism in American undergraduate education presents certain administrative problems which are not perfectly understood or are conveniently ignored. The formulation of programs of concentration is necessarily the business of the departments, divisions, and schools. The formulation of programs for general education is the business of the entire faculty. Departments may recommend, but the faculty in its collective capacity must decide what subjects shall be included in the general program, how much time shall be allotted to it, and whether it shall be organized on an optional-course plan or on the basis of courses which are common requirements or on a combination of both. Where the curriculum is organized by divisional fields the faculty is responsible for the classification of subject matters. Evidence cited in this study drawn from committee reports and self-study projects reveals the total engagement of faculties in these problems. In most institutions a committee, representative of the whole faculty, is appointed to study and recommend action, but final approval rests with the faculty or its elected council.

Once a program has been approved, however, there remains the task of its effective direction. We have seen how widely practices vary in this matter. The faculty may, as it has at Michigan State University, create an autonomous college or division—complete with dean, faculty, and budget—to discharge all duties in planning and instruction. It may, as the faculties at Antioch, Mills, and Stanford have done, authorize the appointment of a permanent administrative committee to supervise the operation of the program. It may grant the committee power to recommend changes in courses, to approve or reject proposed optional courses, and to assign certain types of instructional duties. Some committees are granted operating budgets and even limited power to make faculty appointments. Finally the faculty may, as the majority of the institutions in this study have done, place administrative responsibilities in the hands of the several staffs, departments, or divisions which are concerned with the program. There are numerous modifications of these basic plans; but whatever the nature of administrative control, there are direct relationships between it and the way a program functions. The acknowledged difference in objectives between general and specialized programs is not always supported by a firm acceptance of the difference between the collective responsibilities of the faculty and its divisional or departmental responsibilities. A program of general education is not general simply in the scope of its content. It is general because the whole of the program has been planned with a view to problems which are of continuing concern to all students. It is therefore within the general interest of the faculty that the whole of the program shall be under the same continuous review that a department gives to a program of concentration. Such supervision is necessary both for the protection of the program and for its improvement.

There is no single mode of supervision which is suitable to all kinds of institutions. The plan of University College of Michigan State University cannot be used in small liberal arts colleges. In some large institutions it may be the most effective means of securing a whole-hearted devotion by one part of the faculty for achieving the ends of general education. The objection most frequently voiced to the plan is that it restricts too narrowly the instructional activities of the general studies faculty. An objection equally persuasive, though seldom heard, is that it frees the largest part of the faculty from any direct participation in the problems of planning and instruction in the general program. Thus, though the prevailing theory of modern undergraduate education in America assumes that general education is an integral part of liberal education, the principle underlying University College tends to divide the entire university faculty in the performance of a task in which it ought to be united.

These objections would be more convincing if all the members of liberal arts faculties were fully committed to their collective responsibilities and equally cooperative in discharging them. The evidence indicates that the commitment of many faculty members is less than wholehearted. I do not suggest that one can divide colleges into those which are wholeheartedly committed and those which are not. Rather, I would say that in most colleges there are faculty members who are deeply concerned about the welfare of the entire general program and others who are indifferent. Where the faculty supervision of the general program is decentralized, with each department discharging its assigned duties independently, there is a real danger that each department or division will lose sight of the program as a whole. The inclination of departments to place a priority on the interests of their "majors" is often excessive—to such a degree that they fail to consider the best interests of the nonmajors with respect to the kinds of courses most useful to them and to the kind and quality of instruction. Responsibility does not end with planning a course; it includes effective teaching.

The general or interdepartmental course often presents difficult problems. When the cooperating departments are enthusiastic about a general course they usually take pride in contributing the ablest of their members to serve on the general staff. When they are not enthusiastic, they have been known to make only grudging concessions to requests for assistance from the chairman of the course. No chairman of a general course should be obliged to beg for his staff, nor should he be deprived of the right to pass judgment on the qualifications of intructors who may be offered him. No instructor should be made to feel that participation in a general course contributes little to his professional advancement. If the faculty has authorized the development of interdepartmental courses, the departments concerned are morally obligated to give their best efforts to making the courses effective. The ethical principles of a department are questionable if it first fails to give full support to the undertaking and subsequently condemns the results as a failure.

In some colleges committed to the optional-course principle, departments have sole jurisdiction in determining the number and kinds of courses which shall be included in the general program. This presents a sensitive issue, since to question this jurisdiction seems to question the competence of the departments in their own fields. However, whether an undergraduate curriculum should be greatly fragmented or relatively limited in scope is a matter of policy which concerns the entire faculty. Within the area of formal general requirements, the decision is even more important than within areas of concentration, for it concerns a fundamental issue: whether the community of understanding which is a goal of general education is best served by adapting options to a wide variety of individual interests of students or by limiting options to a few courses concerned with basic disciplines in the sciences and the arts. The college faculty which leaves the answer to this issue entirely to departments either approves in principle of unlimited freedom or has not studied all aspects of the issue critically. When one reviews the variety of options offered by some departments and contemplates the likely content of some courses, one is inclined to think that courses find their way into the list of options more from the special interests of an instructor than from a concern for the most urgent needs of the students. This tendency alone is adequate justification for an administrative committee representing the whole faculty which is authorized to review all proposed courses in an optional program.

The colleges which have created permanent committees for the administration of their programs of general studies, those within this group and others as well, imply that it is in the general interest of the college to balance departmental authority with an authority that acts for the entire faculty. The duties of such committees are not merely those of a watchdog. The account of the duties charged to the committee on general studies at Stanford records several continuing tasks of a constructive nature. The existence of such a committee impinges in no way upon the responsibilities or authority of deans and presidents. It is, however, a reminder that the ultimate responsibility for the whole curriculum belongs to all the faculty.

Although the faculties of the eighteen colleges we have reviewed have not, *in their collective capacities,* approached the many problems of general education with equal ardor, patience, and humility, there is none in which some members of the faculty have not worked zealously toward the improvement of the program of their own institution. These faculty members have made valuable contributions to the sum of ideas and practices that form the current record of general education in American colleges. Often they have worked under great difficulty, without adequate release of time or proper compensation for performing assigned tasks. Staff loads vary greatly from institution to institution, but a heavy load has not prevented teachers from cooperating fully in the discharge of every obligation imposed by the program.

The extreme differences in the formal requirements and procedural methods represented by these programs are without doubt a fair image of the differences to be found among all the colleges of the nation. The differences make it abundantly clear that there is no single curricular formula and no administrative or instructional procedure that satisfactorily defines general education. All the colleges agree that some part of the student's program of studies lies outside any field of concentration and that the college is responsible for providing some kind of formal structure for this part of the student's work. At least one of the colleges denies that concentration in the conventional sense of the term is a necessary part of a liberal education, and two or three others make provisions for granting a Bachelor of Arts degree in programs which do not require a departmental concentration. Hence not only is the term "general education" ambiguous but also the term "liberal education." Most of the colleges maintain that there is a clear and firm distinction between general education and liberal education; but those colleges which grant a baccalaureate degree upon the completion of a four-year program in "general studies" imply that the distinction is not absolute. The title of the program at Notre Dame called "The General Program of Liberal Education" reflects the belief that a college education can be liberal even without the customary modes of specialization. The tendency may be a sign of a change from the basic assumption that a general education, because it is comprehensive in its content, must perforce be shallow. The defense of concentration, when it has not been based upon purely vocational objectives, has been that the liberally educated man is one who respects thoroughness and has formed habits of thoroughness. No sensible person will dispute the point. But it is well worth considering the possibility that in the course of four years the proper respect and habits may be formed in programs of a more comprehensive nature than the usual departmental "major." Not only does it seem possible, but there is reason to think that for many students the results will be more useful. The slogan that the student "should know one thing well" is acceptable in principle but its application has been too greatly influenced by standards determined by graduate and professional studies. There are many ways of defining the *thing* which the student should know well, and by no means do all of them conform to the standard departmental classifications of knowledge.

5

There have been signs in recent years which might be construed as a disenchantment with the whole business of general education. More than one of the colleges reviewed in this study have within the past five years abandoned or deemphasized the use of the term "general education" in descriptions of their academic programs. The trend, if it is a trend, seems to me to be a reaction to a name rather than to a basic educational idea. The fundamental principle for which the term has traditionally stood does not appear to have been rejected, since the same colleges continue to speak of the "broad foundation of learning" or "the common body of knowledge" or "the introduction to all major fields of knowledge" which they assert should be a part of every student's experience. Yet the substitution of one cliché for another solves no problem and illuminates nothing that was formerly obscure. The *substance* of the "broad foundation" is likely to remain as uncertain and as much a matter of dispute as is the substance of "general education."

So long as the American liberal arts colleges remain committed to the discharge of the dual educational functions they now profess—giving an intensive view of some limited field of knowledge (with professional or preprofessional ends in view) and imparting a general or comprehensive view of all major fields—there will of necessity be some term which differentiates these functions. The two functions are concerned with different ends; they are also concerned with content that differs in its scope. So long as the colleges believe that the liberally educated graduate has achieved some success in realizing the goals sought by both these functions, the term "liberal education" is no satisfactory substitute for that part of the intellectual experience which seeks to produce an understanding of the interrelationships and interdependence of all human inquiry. The idea of liberal education was once consonant with the idea now commonly expressed in the term "general education." Except in rare instances this is no longer true. Historically the term "general education" has stood for the idea of a common learning, a knowledge of man's achievements and of the processes by which he has achieved greatness in intellectual inquiry, in social institutions, and in the products of the arts. The belief in the necessity of this common learning—this general education—rests upon the belief that no man realizes himself as an *individual* man except as he comes to understand through the breadth of his knowledge his identity with all men. Historically "general education" has proved itself a useful term to denote this goal. It ought to be freed from some of the misconceptions and abuses it has suffered from both friend and foe.

1. The idea of general education should be disassociated from the notion that it is merely preparatory to the more serious business of specialization.

2. The idea should be permanently dispelled that general education, because it aims at breadth of knowledge, must necessarily be shallow or superficial. Breadth of learning, properly ordered, is productive of its own kind of depth, of insights which no limited form of concentration can achieve.

3. We must give over the idea that general education and specialized education are categorically distinct. Though their goals are ultimately distinct, they share much in their content. All disciplines that are instruments of expression and communication are basic to general education, but no one can deny that they have their special utilities also. Every form of human activity has its own history, but the products of all forms materially affect the history of all mankind and are therefore a matter of common concern. The content of general education—if it be truly general—must touch at some point upon the domain of every student's special interests.

4. The idea that general education can be defined simply and solely by reference to certain kinds of courses—whether called "general," "interdepartmental," "interdisciplinary," or otherwise—must

be rejected. They are means to an end, and at their best they are excellent means; but they do not signify in themselves or collectively all that is embraced in the substance of general education.

5. As a corollary to the last statement, I would add that the friends of general education ought to abandon all reference to "courses in general education." There are no such courses.

6. Certain misconceptions and certain abuses of the principle of the general or interdisciplinary course should be corrected. Charges of superficiality are valid only in so far as they apply to particular examples. They are invalid as a generalization. The best of such courses have proved themselves beyond question and need no apology. The abuses, such as attempts to do too much in too short a time, to *integrate* what is not capable of integration, are subject to correction by patient endeavor.

7. The supposition that general education necessarily impedes the development of individual initiative and the expression of the individual personality is false. It is not even necessarily true of programs in which all courses are uniformly required, of which there are very few. Breadth of intellectual experience has much to do with developing initiative and self-confidence. Next to this, methods of instruction are most important.

8. The development of each individual's unique talents through intensive study within that area in which his special competence lies has long been honored as an obligation of a free society to its citizens. But a free society preserves its freedom to the extent that its citizens understand and accept the responsibilities of freedom. Liberal education is something more than the development of individual talents, and it is with that *something more* that general education is vitally concerned and with which American colleges must continue to be concerned.

Appendix

TABLE I

REQUIREMENTS FOR ADMISSION TO
COLLEGE WITH FRESHMAN STANDING
(1958–1959)

Amherst	High school graduate; *recommended:* English, 4 years; mathematics, 3 years; foreign language, 2–3 years; history, 1 year; laboratory science, 1 year; C.E.E.B. aptitude and achievement tests.
Antioch	High school graduate; *recommended:* ability to read and write; good foundation in mathematics; general knowledge of history; elementary science; 1 or more years of foreign language; C.E.E.B. aptitude test.
Berea	High school graduate; *recommended:* usual background of high school subjects (English, mathematics, science, social science, and foreign language).
Brooklyn	16 units high school; *required* (11½ units): English, 4 years; American history, 1 year; foreign language, 3 years; mathematics, 2½ years; science, 1 year.
Goucher	16 units high school; *required:* English, 4 years; *recommended:* 12 units distributed among foreign language, mathematics, science, and social science; C.E.E.B. aptitude and achievement tests.
Louisville	15 units high school; *recommended:* 12 units of academic subjects; English (as much as possible), foreign language, history, social science, mathematics, science, music, and art appreciation.
Macalester	High school graduate; *recommended:* English, 3 years; foreign language, 2 years; mathematics, 2 years; history, 1 year; science, 1 year.

TABLE I (*Continued*)

Michigan State	15 units high school; meet the "college-recommending mark" of local high school; *required:* English, 3 or 4 years; *recommended:* 7 or 6 units distributed among mathematics, foreign language, science, social science; 3 units from any of above or agriculture, home economics, commercial, industrial arts, art, and music; 2 units in any course accepted by high school for graduation.
Mills	16 units high school; *required:* 12 units in academic subjects; *recommended:* English, 4 years; history, 2 years; foreign language, 2–4 years; mathematics, 3 years; science, 2 years; C.E.E.B. aptitude and achievement tests.
Minnesota S.L.A.	12 units high school, completed in grades 10–12; 9 units distributed among English, social science and history, mathematics, science, foreign language; *recommended:* 3 units English, 2 units mathematics.
General College	High school graduate; no specific recommendation of courses. Students are admitted who might not meet recommended distribution for S.L.A.
Notre Dame	15 units high school; *required:* English, 3 years; mathematics, 2 years; foreign language, 2 years; history, 1 year; science, 1 year. C.E.E.B. aptitude and achievement tests.
Oregon	High school graduate; 60th percentile on standard aptitude test or C average on all subjects taken for high school graduation. No recommended distribution of high school courses given, except for students applying to the Honors College. For the latter, specific course requirements are stated.
Reed	High school graduate; *recommended:* English, foreign language, mathematics, science, history, social science; C.E.E.B aptitude and achievement tests.
St. John's	High school graduate; *recommended:* foreign language, 2 years; mathematics, 2½ years.
Saint Xavier	High school graduate; *recommended:* English, 3 years; foreign language, 2 years; mathematics, 2 years; science and social science, 4 years (total); C.E.E.B. aptitude test.
San Francisco State	High school graduate; no recommended distribution; must rank in the top third of graduating class.

TABLE I (*Continued*)

Stanford
High school graduate; *required:* English composition and literature, 3 years; mathematics, 2 years; foreign language, 2 years; other courses from regular high school academic subjects; C.E.E.B. aptitude and achievement tests.

Washington
State
16 units high school; average of C in high school courses for residents of state; *recommended:* "a high level of competence in the areas of natural science, social science, foreign language, and particularly in English and mathematics."

Notes: Several colleges admit a small number of students of exceptional promise prior to high school graduation.
I have not listed transcript of high school record since this is a standard requirement in all institutions.
Private colleges urge personal interview with applicants.
In most states, 15 or 16 units of high school courses are the normal requirement for graduation. State-supported institutions tend to be slightly more generous in accepting nonacademic courses.

TABLE II

GENERAL REQUIREMENTS
IN ENGLISH AND MATHEMATICS
(1958–1959)

	ENGLISH	MATHEMATICS
Amherst	English composition, 1 year.	Mathematics is part of the required physical science course.
Antioch	No required course. All students must pass qualifying test based on samples of writing in courses as condition for graduation.	Mathematics courses include as options in physical science requirement.
Berea	English composition, ½ year.	No mathematics required.

TABLE II (*Continued*)

Brooklyn	English literature and writing, 1 year.	Any one of six courses required.
Goucher	English composition, 2 terms.	Mathematics courses optional in natural science requirement.
Louisville	English composition, 1 year.	No mathematics required.
Macalester	English composition, 1 year.	Mathematics courses optional in physical science requirement.
Michigan State	English composition, 1 year.	No mathematics required.
Mills	English literature and writing, 1 year.	No mathematics required.
Minnesota S.L.A.	English composition, 1 year.	Mathematics courses optional in natural science requirement; also certain courses accepted in humanities requirement.
General College	English writing met by comprehensive examination. Courses in writing optional.	Mathematics optional in natural science requirement.
Notre Dame Regular	English composition (rhetoric), 1 year.	Mathematics, 1 year.
General Program of Liberal Education	Logic and language (senior year), 1 semester in addition to rhetoric requirement in first year of regular program.	Mathematics, 1 year, in addition to requirement of regular program.
Oregon	English composition, 1 year.	Mathematics optional in natural science requirement.
Reed	No required course. Instruction responsibility of all departments.	Mathematics optional in natural science requirement.
St. John's	Language tutorial in first 2 years stresses English writing.	Mathematics tutorial required in each of 4 years.
Saint Xavier	English composition, 1 year.	Mathematics, 1 year.

TABLE II (*Continued*)

San Francisco	English composition, 1 year.	Mathematics, 1 year.
Stanford	English composition and literature, 1 year.	Mathematics, 1 year, optional with foreign language.
Washington State	English composition, 1 year.	Mathematics optional in natural science requirement.

Notes: I have used the term "English composition" to designate a specific course requirement, although the term is misleading. In three colleges a combined literature and writing course is given. In several others the one required course which gives instruction in writing is called "Communication Skills," "Basic Language Skills," or some similar term which may embrace reading, speech, and other related exercises.

The notation "No mathematics required" does not imply that a physical science course may not make use of students' mathematical knowledge. It merely signifies that no specific mathematics course is required at a level beyond elementary algebra and geometry.

TABLE III

GENERAL REQUIREMENTS
IN FOREIGN LANGUAGE
(1958–1959)

Amherst	Equivalent of two years of one language at college level.
Antioch	No general requirement. Required in some areas of concentration.
Berea	Equivalent of two years at college level required of all A.B. candidates except elementary education. Not required in B.S. programs (agriculture, business administration, home economics, and nursing).
Brooklyn	Three years of one language required for entrance. Minimal requirement for continuation: one semester. Further requirement determined by qualifying test. Minimal requirement for

TABLE III (*Continued*)

	students beginning a new language in college: three semesters. Requirement applicable to all A.B. programs and all B.S. except home economics, physical education, and health education, which require no language beyond entrance requirement.
Goucher	Equivalent of two years of one language at college level.
Louisville	Equivalent of two years of one language at college level required of all A.B. candidates. No general requirement for B.S.
Macalester	Equivalent of two years at college level required of all A.B. candidates. An option of one year of language or a course in English or world literature permitted to B.S. candidates.
Michigan State	No general requirement.
Mills	Equivalent of two years at college level required of all A.B. candidates.
Minnesota S.L.A.	If no language in high school, one year is required. If one year in high school, two terms are required. If two years in high school, one term is required.
General College	No requirement.
Notre Dame Regular	Two years of one language required for entrance. One year of continuing study or one year in a new language.
General Program of Liberal Education	Same entrance requirement. Two years of continuing study required, including the first-year requirement of the regular program.
Oregon	No general requirement. The Honors College requires two years for admission and passing a proficiency test equal to the standard for a second-year college course.
Reed	Equivalent of two years at college level.
St. John's	Two years of Greek and two years of French.
Saint Xavier	Equivalent of one year at college level.
San Francisco	No general requirement.
Stanford	Two years of one language required for entrance. All students granted an option between

TABLE III (*Continued*)

Washington State
College of Sciences
and Arts

an additional year of language or mathematics.
One year at college level or two years in high
school.

TABLE IV

GENERAL REQUIREMENTS IN HISTORY
(1958–1959)

Amherst	Two years	European Civilization, first year, American civilization, second year (courses meet the social science requirement).
Antioch	Optional in both Levels I and II	In Level I, Group A (history and philosophy), four of six courses are history.
Berea	One semester	Western Civilization (this course is independent of the requirements in social science and humanities).
Brooklyn	One year	Western Civilization (this requirement is independent of the one-year requirements in social science and humanities).
Goucher	No requirement	Optional in social science at first level.
Louisville	One year	Western Civilization (this requirement is independent of the one-year requirements in social science and humanities).
Macalester	Optional in social science group	Two of the seven options are history courses.
Michigan State	One year	Humanities course, oriented to the cultural and political history of the Western world.
Mills	One year	Values of American Life (a historically oriented course which is the basic requirement in the humanities–social science area).

TABLE IV (*Continued*)

Minnesota S.L.A.	Optional	A variety of courses acceptable in both the humanities and the social sciences.
General College	Optional	A variety of courses in the Socio-Civic orientation area.
Notre Dame Regular	Two years	European history, first year, American history, second year. Requirement is independent of one-year requirement in both social science and literature.
General Program of Liberal Education	No requirement	
Oregon	Optional	In the social science group. Note: Candidates for Sophomore Honors must pass examination in the history of Western civilization.
Reed	One year	Humanities course, historically oriented to Western culture.
St. John's	No requirement	
Saint Xavier	No formal course	A one-semester course called "Historiography" is one of the options in the social science requirement.
San Francisco State	One semester	American Institutions and Ideals (historically oriented).
Stanford	One year	History of Western Civilization.
Washington State	Optional	In humanities–social science group.

TABLE V

COMPARISON OF UNIFORMLY REQUIRED
COURSES AND AREAS IN WHICH
OPTIONAL COURSES ARE OFFERED
(1958–1959)

	REQUIRED COURSES	OPTIONAL AREAS
Amherst	English composition, physical science and mathematics,	Natural science, second year, human-

TABLE V (*Continued*)

	humanities (first year), history–social science (first and second years), public speaking, foreign language.	ities, second year.
Antioch	No required courses.	Courses classified by divisions and by levels. Approximately 2 years' work in each of 3 areas required.
Berea	All courses required; some modification of requirements for students in B.S. programs.	
Brooklyn	English literature and writing, classics in translation, foreign language, history of Western civilization, philosophy, speech.	Art or music, mathematics, natural science, social science.
Goucher	English composition, religion, foreign language.	Courses classified by divisions. Options in each division.
Louisville	English composition, history of Western civilization, foreign language, natural science, social science, humanities.	Option between art or music, second semester of humanities. Limited options in natural science and social science in some preprofessional programs.
Macalester	English composition, philosophy, religion, foreign language.	Natural science, social science, fine arts, humanities.
Michigan State	All courses in University College required.	
Mills	English literature and writing, humanities, foreign language (Note: no distinction is made between humanities and social science).	Natural science, fine arts.
Minnesota S.L.A.	English composition, foreign language.	Courses classified by divisions. Numerous

TABLE V (*Continued*)

		options in each division.
General College	No courses required.	Achievement is measured by comprehensive examinations, and students must pass in 5 of 7 areas. Numerous options in each area.
Notre Dame Regular	English composition, foreign language, mathematics, philosophy and religion, social science, Junior Seminar.	Literature, limited option; natural science.
General Program of Liberal Education	All courses required.	Provision for one elective in junior and senior years.
Oregon	English composition.	Courses classified in 3 divisions. Options in each division.
Reed	Humanities (first year), foreign language.	Courses classified in 3 groups.
St. John's	All courses required.	
Saint Xavier	All courses required except	limited option in social science.
San Francisco	All courses required.	
Stanford	English composition, history of Western civilization.	Courses classified in 3 divisions. Options in each division. All students must continue either mathematics or foreign language. Two Senior Colloquia required of all A.B. (with minor exceptions) but options among colloquiums permitted.

TABLE V (*Continued*)

| Washington State | English composition, foreign language if not taken in high school. | Courses classified in 3 divisions. Numerous options in each division. |

Note: Several colleges employ placement or exemptions examinations which may reduce the number of formal course requirements, either in the area of options or among the uniform course requirements.

TABLE VI

SELF-STUDY REPORTS

The following list of self-study reports is reproduced here by permission of the Association of American Colleges, 1818 R Street, N.W., Washington 9, D.C. Most of these reports were made possible by grants from various educational foundations. They all are not directly concerned with the liberal arts curriculum or specifically with the problem of general education, but the majority are so concerned, and in many of them the subject is a matter of primary attention. These reports are available *on loan* from the association. Some of them have been published as books or monographs by their respective institutions. Those which are marked with an asterisk (*) are among the colleges included in this study. To this list there should be added the *Report on a Project of Self-Study* by the Faculty of St. John's College, to which I have referred in the text, but which does not appear in the association's list. The St. John's self-study was published in 1955 by the college as vol. VII, no. 2, of *Bulletin of St. John's College*. Titles of other published reports by colleges in this study are *Education at Amherst*, Gail Kennedy (ed.), Harper & Brothers, New York, 1955; *The Undergraduate in the University* (Stanford University), Robert Hoopes and Hubert Marshall, Stanford University Press, Stanford, Calif., 1957; and *The Saint Xavier College Self-Study: the Liberal Education of the Christian Person*, Saint Xavier College Bookstore, Chicago, 1953.

TABLE VI (*Continued*)

List No. 1
(Revised April, 1958)

	TYPE	CONTROLLED BY
Adrian College, Michigan	coed	Methodist
Allegheny College, Pennsylvania	coed	Methodist
*Amherst College, Massachusetts	men	private
Beloit College, Wisconsin	coed	Congregational
Bowdoin College, Maine	men	private
*Brooklyn College, New York	coed	city
Buffalo, University of, New York	coed	private
City College of the City of New York	coed	city
Colby College, Maine	coed	private
Cornell College, Iowa	coed	Methodist
Cornell University, New York	coed	state and private
DePauw University, Indiana	coed	Methodist
Drake University, Iowa	coed	Disciples of Christ
Findlay College, Ohio	coed	Church of God
Florida State University	coed	state
Georgia Institute of Technology	coed	state
*Goucher College, Maryland	women	private
Hampton Institute, Virginia	coed	private
Heidelberg College, Ohio	coed	Evangelical Reform
Iowa, State University of	coed	state
Jamestown College, North Dakota	coed	Presbyterian
Lafayette College, Pennsylvania	men	Presbyterian
Lawrence College, Wisconsin	coed	private
Marycrest College, Iowa	women	Roman Catholic
Milton College, Wisconsin	coed	private
New York University	coed	private
Ohio Wesleyan University	coed	Methodist
Olivet Nazarene College, Illinois	coed	Nazarene Church
Pittsburgh, University of, Pennsylvania	coed	private
Queens College of the City of New York	coed	city
*Reed College, Oregon	coed	private
Rutgers University, New Jersey	coed	state and private
St. Olaf College, Minnesota	coed	Evangelical Lutheran
*Saint Xavier College, Illinois	women	Roman Catholic

TABLE VI *(Continued)*

Scripps College, California	women	private
Southern Methodist University, Texas	coed	Methodist
Southwestern at Memphis, Tennessee	coed	Presbyterian
*Stanford University, California	coed	private

    (1) "Study of Undergraduate Education," February, 1956

    (2) "The Undergraduate in the University," February, 1957

Texas Technological College	coed	state
Wesleyan University, Connecticut	men	private
Wisconsin, University of	coed	state

List No. 2
(May 24, 1961)

	TYPE	CONTROLLED BY
Abilene Christian College, Texas	coed	private
*Antioch College, Ohio	coed	private
Arkansas, University of	coed	state
Birmingham–Southern College, Alabama	coed	Methodist
Chatham College, Pennsylvania	women	private
Coe College, Iowa	coed	private
Defiance College, Ohio	coed	Congregational Christian
Franklin & Marshall College, Pennsylvania	men	private
Hawaii, University of	coed	state
Harding College, Arkansas	coed	Church of Christ
Hendrix College, Arkansas	coed	Methodist
Hope College, Michigan	coed	Reformed Church
Hunter College of the City of New York (3 parts)		city
Kansas Wesleyan University, Kansas		Methodist
King College, Tennessee	coed	Presbyterian
Lewis and Clark College, Oregon	coed	Presbyterian
Miami University, Ohio	coed	state
Miami, University of, Florida	coed	private

TABLE VI (*Continued*)

Morgan State College, Maryland	coed	state
Nevada, University of: Self-evaluation Reports 1 and 2; also Report of College of Business	coed	state
*Notre Dame, University of, Indiana	men	Roman Catholic
Ohio Northern University, Ohio	coed	Methodist
Saint Mary's College, Minnesota	men	Roman Catholic
Seattle Pacific College, Washington	coed	Free Methodist
Sweet Briar College, Virginia	women	private
Tift College, Georgia (an article on the usefulness of making a self-study)	women	Baptist
Union College (of Union University), New York	men	private
Virginia Polytechnic Institute, Virginia	coed	state
Wabash College, Indiana	men	private
Westminster College, Utah	coed	Interdenominational
Wheaton College, Illinois	coed	private
William Penn College, Iowa	coed	Society of Friends
Winthrop College, South Carolina, "Winthrop Faces the 1960's"	women	state
Wyoming, University of, "Higher Education in Wyoming"	coed	state

INSTITUTIONS WHICH RECEIVED GRANTS FROM
THE FUND FOR THE ADVANCEMENT OF
EDUCATION FOR SELF-STUDIES

Allegheny College	Colby College
Beloit College	Cornell College
Bowdoin College	DePauw University
*Brooklyn College	Dillard University
Brown University	Drake University
University of Buffalo	Earlham College
Carleton College	University of Florida
City College of New York	*Goucher College

Hampton Institute
Heidelberg College
Hope College
State University of Iowa
Jamestown College
Lafayette College
Lincoln University
*University of Notre Dame
Ohio Wesleyan University
Parsons School of Design
University of Pittsburgh

*Reed College
Rutgers University
*St. John's College
*Saint Xavier College
St. Olaf College
Scripps College
Southern Methodist University
Southwestern at Memphis
*Stanford University
Wellesley College
Wesleyan University (Connecticut)

* Institutions included in this study.

Index

Numbers in *italic* type indicate descriptive sections

319